DATE DUE			

ON BEAR'S HEAD

Books by Philip Whalen

POETRY

The Calendar

Three Satires

Like I Say

Memoirs of an Interglacial Age

Monday in the Evening

Every Day

T/O

Vanilla

The Winter

PROSE

You Didn't Even Try

DOODLES & TEXTS

Highgrade

News from the Vegetable Kingdom

The Invention of the Letter

ON
BEAR'S
HEAD

———

PHILIP
WHALEN

Harcourt, Brace & World, Inc. and *Coyote* / *New York*

Author's Note

I don't like the idea of a volume of collected poems; I'm still writing more and I'm not really satisfied with the ones which appear here. Nevertheless, here are most of the ones I've written "*ad interim.*"

It's necessary to acknowledge here the love and patience and help which my family and friends have put into the production of this work. I must also thank several institutions: Reed College, San Francisco State College, and the University of California: at different times they paid me money to read my poems to them and made it possible for people to hear me. Quite unexpectedly the Poets Foundation gave me a prize one year, and the American Academy of Arts and Letters gave me a grant-in-aid which made it possible for me to travel to Japan, where friends had set up a part-time job for me. And last, or first, I must mention my great debts to the "underground" press: the little magazines where most of this material first appeared, and the individual publishers and printers who had to scrimp and borrow and blarney their way into money enough to print my first books: LeRoi Jones's Totem Press, Dave Haselwood's Auerhahn Press, Bill Thomas's Toad Press, and the Coyote Books firm's Bill and Zoe Brown and James Koller. (I must add here the fact that one magazine, *Northwest Review*, and its editor, Mr. Edward Van Aelstyn, were suppressed, censured, fired, and investigated by the authorities of the University of Oregon, the Oregon Board of Higher Education, and the Oregon State Legislature because some of my work was published there. It was this trouble and bother that resulted in the founding of *Coyote's Journal*, and, later, of Coyote Books.) Without the continued interest and encouragement of the private publisher and the little magazine it would have been much harder for me to find out how my writing looked in print and, incidentally, whether anybody could get any good out of it. I'm always flattered when somebody tells me that they did.

FURTHER ACKNOWLEDGMENTS

LeRoi Jones, Elias Wilentz, and Theodore Wilentz, of Totem Press and
Corinth Books, New York, for permission to reprint *Like I Say*, first published
by them in 1960.

David Haselwood and Jay McIlroy, of the Auerhahn Press, San Francisco,
for permission to reprint *Memoirs of an Interglacial Age*, first published by
them in 1960.

"Monday in the Evening" first appeared in *The Northwest Review*, published at the University of Oregon, Eugene, Oregon. It subsequently appeared
as a separate book, printed by serigraphy on handmade Italian papers in Milan
by Serigrafia Pezzoli Milano, as number 3 in the series "Autori scelti da
Fernanda Pivano." Many thanks are due to the director and editor of the
series, Fernanda Pivano Sottsass, and to her husband, Ettore Sottsass, whose
photographs of the author embellish the book.

Charles Plymell, brilliant young painter, poet, and revolutionary, was responsible for the first publication of several poems and doodles and prose
pieces of mine, either as broadsides or as contributions to his various magazines: *Now*; *Now, Now*; and *Now, Now, Now*. All of these were printed in
San Francisco.

Bill Thomas, of Toad Press, Eugene, Oregon, first published the poem
"The Education Continues Along" as part of an issue of his magazine, *In-
transit*, which was devoted to my work.

I must acknowledge Diane di Prima's immense good will and hard work
and worry, expended on behalf of trying to get my poems before the public.

The original crew of *Coyote's Journal*, the Messrs. Edward Van Aelstyn,
James Koller, and William Wroth, produced the first printing of the book
Every Day in Eugene, Oregon, in 1964. The present management of Coyote
Books, William D. Brown and James Koller, produced the second printing
in 1967. They have also projected independent editions of several other books
of mine, and produced my first novel, *You Didn't Even Try*, in 1967.

Three of the poems from *Vanilla*: "T/O," "Love, Love, Love Again," and
"Priapic Hymn," have been printed in a special small edition from hand-set
type on handmade English paper by Dave Haselwood in 1967 at San Francisco.

The poem called "Three Mornings," from *Braincandy*, was first printed as
a broadside for sale at a reading given by Gary Snyder, Lewis Welch, and
myself in San Francisco. The broadside was published for the occasion by the
Four Seasons Foundation under the direction of Mr. Donald M. Allen. Mr.
Allen and the same Foundation also published a broadside version of "Hymnus
ad Patrem Sinensis," as a contribution to a portfolio of poems made for sale
at the San Francisco Art Festival in 1963. I must also thank Mr. Allen for
his continuous interest in my writing and for his endless efforts toward getting it published—first in *Evergreen Review*, of which he was editor; then in
his anthology, *The New American Poetry*, and most recently in a Penguin
book of contemporary American writing.

Professor Thomas Parkinson's anthology, *A Casebook on the Beat*, has introduced my work to many college students. He has also made it possible for me to appear on the University of California campus as a reader of my own work and as a fleeting consultant to young writers who may be passing through through or around the Berkeley campus.

Thanks to the Library of Congress, Washington, D.C., for the honor of inviting me to record my poems for their tape-recorded collection. Also thanks to Mr. John Sweeney, curator of the poetry room in the Lamont Library at Harvard, for the same favor.

Thanks to Mr. Donald R. Carpenter and the committee who awarded me the first V. K. Ratliff Award in 1964, and who arranged for the printing of the poem "Goddess," from *Every Day*, as a broadside. The broadside was produced from hand-set type, with a decorative capital letter designed by the author, on handmade Tovil paper, by Dave Haselwood at the Auerhahn Press.

As I type this page, a number of projects are under way; I suppose they will be realized before this book appears. Consequently, I will add here my thanks to Miss Harriet Rohmer of the Brownstone Press in New York, who will produce a broadside version of the poem "Imagination of the Taj Mahal"; to Thomas Clark, Esq., and *The Paris Review*, for poems they are about to print; and to Mr. Lewis Warsh of *Angel Hair* magazine.

I owe much gratitude to the people who have translated poems of mine into Swedish, German, Italian, Czech, and Hungarian: Mr. Reidar Ekner, of Stockholm; Prof. Walter Hollerer, of Hamburg; Mr. Karl O. Paetel, of New York; the Messrs. Stanislav Mares and Jan Zabrana, of Prague; the unknown Hungarian editor who is presently at work; Mr. Hugh Fox, of Los Angeles; and to an unknown (to me, at least) Brazilian or Paraguayan or whoever it was who pirated some things of mine into a Spanish anthology.

And to the editors and publishers of the following magazines I wish to express my thanks for their first publication of so much of my work and for their permission to reprint: *Ark II Moby I*, San Francisco, and *Ark III*, San Francisco, the first edited by Mike McClure and James Harmon, the second by James Harmon alone; *Beatitude*, San Francisco, edited by several hands; *C*, New York, edited by Ted Berrigan and crew; *Desert Review*, somewhere in New Mexico; *Evergreen Review*, New York, edited by Don Allen and later by Barney Rosset and others; *Fuck You / The Magazine of Art*, edited by Ed Sanders, New York; *Fux Magascene*, edited by the painter Robert Ronnie Brannaman, San Francisco; *Coyote's Journal*, edited by Edward Van Aelstyn, James Koller, and William Wroth, Eugene, Oregon, and later by James Koller and Bill Brown in San Francisco; *Floating Bear*, edited first by LeRoi Jones and later by Diane di Prima in New York; *Nomad*, Los Angeles; *Open Space*, edited by Stanley Persky in San Francisco; *Poetry*, edited by Henry Rago in Chicago; *Foot*, edited by Richard Duerden in San Francisco, who also published *Rivoli Review*; Richard Brautigan and Ron Loewinsohn, who were editors of *Change*, San Francisco; *New Student Review* at the University of New York, Buffalo; *Intrepid*, New York; *Upriver*, Philadelphia; *Tri-quarterly Review*, Northwestern University; *Things*, New York; *Wild Dog*, edited by Gino Clays and several other hands in several different cities and villages in the West; *Poetry Review,* Tampa; *Between Worlds,* Interamerican University, Puerto Rico; *Northwest Review,* Eugene, Oregon; *Grande Ronde Review,* published by Ron Bayes and his students at Eastern Oregon College in La Grande, Oregon; *Ferret,* California College of Arts and Crafts student publication, Oakland, California; *Outburst,* London; *Mithrander,* San Francisco; *Genesis West,* Menlo Park, California; *The Beat Scene,* Corinth Books, New York, edited by Elias Wilentz; *Variegation* and *Recurrence,* both published by Grover Jacoby of Los Angeles; *Origin,* published by Cid Corman in Kyoto, Japan; *Yugen,* published by LeRoi Jones; *Paris Review,* New York and Paris; *Boss,* edited by Reginald Gay, New York; *Lines,* edited by Aram Saroyan, New York; *Or,* edited by David Sandberg, Berkeley; Neil Barret of Cambridge, Massachusetts, editor of *Drainage.*

I fear that many of the more fugitive publications have been forgotten; I hope not, but if so, I apologize and offer belated thanks and rose petals and beer.

Philip Whalen

Bolinas
Christmas 1967

Contents

BRAINCANDY

E V E R Y   D A Y

THE DAYS

LIKE I SAY
1950-1958

To Stanworth Russell Beckler

NEWPORT, OREGON 1958

"Plus Ça Change . . ."

What are you doing?

    I am coldly calculating.

I didn't ask for a characterization.
Tell me what we're going to do.

    That's what I'm coldly calculating.

You had better say "plotting" or "scheming"
You never could calculate without a machine.

    Then I'm brooding. Presently
    A plot will hatch.

Who are you trying to kid?

    Be nice.

        (SILENCE)

Listen. Whatever we do from here on out
Let's for God's sake not look at each other
Keep our eyes shut and the lights turned off—
We won't mind touching if we don't have to see.

    I'll ignore those preposterous feathers.

Say what you please, we brought it all on ourselves
But nobody's going out of his way to look.

    Who'd recognize us now?

We'll just pretend we're used to it.
(Watch out with that goddamned tail!)
Pull the shades down. Turn off the lights.
Shut your eyes.

        (SILENCE)

3

There is no satisfactory explanation.
You can talk until you're blue

Just how much bluer can I get?

Well, save breath you need to cool

Will you please shove the cuttlebone a little closer?

All right, until the perfumes of Arabia

Grow cold. Ah! Sunflower seeds!

Will you listen, please? I'm trying to make
A rational suggestion. Do you mind?

Certainly not. Just what *shall* we tell the children?

28:ix:53
1:ii:55

The Road-Runner

FOR L. J. REYNOLDS

Thin long bird
        with a taste for snakes' eyes
Frayed tail, wildcat claws
His pinions are bludgeons.

Few brains, topped
By a crown
And a flair for swift in-fighting—
Try to take it from him.

23:iii:50

If You're So Smart, Why Ain't You Rich?

I need everything else
Anything else
    Desperately
But I have nothing
Shall have nothing
    but this
Immediate, inescapable
    and invaluable
No one can afford
    THIS
Being made here and now

      (Seattle, Washington
       17 May, 1955)

MARIGOLDS

Concise (wooden)
    Orange.
Behind them, the garage door
    Pink
(Paint sold under a fatuous name:
"Old Rose"
    which brings a war to mind)

And the mind slides over the fence again
Orange against pink and green
Uncontrollable!

Returned of its own accord
It can explain nothing
Give no account

What good? What worth?

Dying!

You have less than a second
      To live
To try to explain:
Say that light
      in particular wave-lengths
      or bundles wobbling at a given speed
Produces the experience
Orange against pink

Better than a sirloin steak?
A screen by Korin?

The effect of this, taken internally
The effect
            of beauty
                        on the mind

There is no equivalent, least of all
These objects
Which ought to manifest
A surface disorientation, pitting
Or striae
Admitting *some* plausible interpretation

But the cost
Can't be expressed in numbers
Dodging between
            a vagrancy rap
            and the newest electrical brain-curette
Eating what the rich are bullied into giving
Or the poor willingly share
Depriving themselves

More expensive than ambergris
      Although the stink
            isn't as loud. (A few

Wise men have said,
    "Produced the same way . . .
    Vomited out by sick whales.")
Valuable for the same qualities
    Staying-power and penetration
I've squandered every crying dime.

Seattle 17–18:v:55

The Slop Barrel:

Slices of the Paideuma for All Sentient Beings

N O T E : "Slices" was suggested as a title by Mike McClure. The anecdote of the bicycle's demise is the original property of Mr. Grover Grauman Sales, Jr., of Louisville and San Francisco & used with his kind permission.

I

We must see, we must know
What's the name of that star?
How that ship got inside the bottle
Is it true your father was a swan?
What do you look like without any clothes?

    My daddy was a steamboat man
    His name was Lohengrin, his ship
    The Swan, a stern-wheeler—
    Cargoes of oil and wheat between Umatilla
    And The Dalles before the dam was built

I want to look at you all over
I want to feel every part of you

So we compare our moles and hair

    You have as many scars as my brother, Polydeuces
    That's the only mole I've got
    Don't look at it. I worry sometimes it will
    Turn into cancer. Is that the mark of Asia
    On your body? It is different from my husband's.

It was done when I was born
A minor sacrifice to Astarte (the priests
Lose everything)
A barbarous practice, I suppose.

Gods demand a great deal. This coming war
Nothing will be saved; they claim
It will rid the earth of human wickedness . . .

Nevertheless when we are vaporized
To descend as rain across strange countries
That we will never see
The roses will grow human ears for petals
To hear the savoy cabbages philosophize.

II

You say you're all right
Everything's all right
Am I supposed to be content with that?

If I told you everything
You'd have nothing to say
If I fell to pieces you'd walk away flat
(A weather-vane)

Suppose we were the first to begin
Living forever. Let's start
Right now.

Do you want this peach?
It's immortal.

Both my watches are busted.

Meanwhile, back at the ranch
Pao Pu-tzu ("in the latter years
Of a long lifetime")
Is making those pills . . . ("the size of a hemp-seed")

8

(I would prefer the hemp, myself
Since *Sa majesté impériale*
"took a red pill . . . and was not."
None of them artificial kicks for me.)

to show up later
Riding a Bengal tiger
Both man and beast gassed out of their minds
Laughing and scratching
Pockets and saddlebags full of those pills:
"Come on, man, have a jellybean!"

The business of this world
Is to deceive but *it*
Is never deceived. *Maya Desnudata*
And the *Duchess*: the same woman. Admire her.
Nevertheless she is somebody else's
Wife. I don't mean unavailable
I mean preoccupied.

You and me
We make out, the question is
How to avoid future hangups, and/or
Is this one of them now?
We could take a decent time
Figuring out how to avoid repeating
Ourselves

I know where I'm going
I been there before
I know when I get there
I'll travel no more

Do you?
Are you still all right?
I don't want you to freeze.

I guess my troubles are pride
And doubt. You *are*
All right.

Have a jellybean . . .
Here comes a tiger.

III

By standing on the rim of the slop barrel
We could look right into the birds' nest.
Thelma, too little, insisted on seeing
We boosted her up
                              and over the edge
Head first among the slops in her best Sunday dress
Now let's regret things for a while
That you can't read music
That I never learned Classical languages
That we never grew up, never learned to behave
But devoted ourselves to magic:

> Creature, you are a cow
> Come when I call you and be milked.
> Creature, you are a lion. Be so kind
> As to eat something other than my cow or me.
> Object, you are a tree, to go or stay
> At my bidding . . .

> Or more simply still, tree, you are lumber
> Top-grade Douglas fir
> At so many bucks per thousand board-feet
> A given amount of credit in the bank
> So that beyond a certain number of trees
> Or volume of credit you don't have to know or see
> Nothing

Nevertheless we look
And seeing, love.
From loving we learn
And knowingly choose:
Greasy wisdom is better than clothes.

I mean I love those trees
And the printing that goes on them

A forest of words and music
You do the translations, I can sing.

IV

Between water and ice
(Fluid and crystal)
A single chance

Helen, Blodeuwedd manufactured
Entirely of flowers
or flames
A trilium for every step
White trifolium, purple-veined
(Later completely purple)

> The heavy folds of your brocade
> Black waves of your hair
> Spilled across the *tatami*
> Black water smashed white at Suma
> "No permanent home"

I just don't understand you, I'm really stumped

Petal from the prune tree
Spins on a spider web
Slung between leaves
A flash in the sun

Baby scrooches around on the rug trying
To pick up the design

PAY NO ATTENTION TO ME

The pen forms the letters
Their shape is in the muscles
Of my hand and arm

Bells in the air!

At this distance the overtone
Fourth above the fundamental
Carries louder
Distorting the melody just enough
To make it unrecognizable

YOU DON'T LOVE ME LIKE YOU USED TO
YOU DON'T LOVE ME ANY MORE.

The sun has failed entirely
Mountains no longer convince
The technician asks me every morning
"Whattaya know?" and I am
Froze.
Unless I ask I am not alive
Until I find out who is asking
I am only half alive and there is only

WU!

(An ingrown toenail?)

WU!

(A harvest of bats??)

WU!

A row of pink potted geraniums///???)

smashed flat!!!
The tonga-walla swerved, the cyclist leapt and
The bicycle folded under the wheels before they stopped
The tonga-walla cursing in Bengali while the outraged
Cyclist sullenly repeats:
You *knows* you got to *pay* for the motherfucker
You knows you *got* to pay for the motherfucker

The bells have stopped
Flash in the wind
Dog in the pond.

Berkeley 5:iii:56
11:viii:56

Homage to Robert Creeley

What I thought
    was a fly on the window was
A knot on the branch outside

Near it a real fly sat
Quiet in the sun

Wind rocked all the branches the fly
    sat still

25:v:56

Scholiast

Regards the chrysanthemums
Stalks flat on the ground
Flowers twisting the tips
Past the roof shadow

A honeycomb
A hornet's nest
Significant once, as a pattern—
But a theory of progress?

A constant explosion produces all shapes
Quiet fringed yellow
Burning—and the bush
Utterly consumed!

Venice 4:xi:51
San Francisco 4:ii:53

The Same Old Jazz

OK, it's imperishable or a world as Will
& Idea, a Hindu illusion that our habits continuously
Create. Whatever I think, it
Keeps changing from bright to dark, from clear
To colored: Thus before I began to think and
So after I've stopped, as if it were real & I
Were its illusion

But as Jaime de Angulo said, "What's wrong with two?"

So Sunday morning I'm in bed with Cleo
She wants to sleep & I get up naked at the table
Writing
And it all snaps into focus
The world inside my head & the cat outside the window
A one-to-one relationship
While I imagine whatever I imagine

Weed
dry stalks of yarrow,
repeated Y-branching V's, a multiplication

Of antelope, deer-horns? Umbels
Hairy brown stars at the tip of brown wires
A *menorah*, or more learnedly, "hand" written in Great Seal Script

Almost against the window, horns again
Reindeer colored (in the sun) branching
Bare young loquat tree

Next door on the right the neighbors are building
Something in the garage, sawing & whirly-grinding
On wood. Models of the NIÑA, the PINTA & the SANTA MARIA
Life-size with television sails

Bright sky & airplanes & bugs mixed with
Flying paper ashes, the lid's off somebody's incinerator

There all that is & the reflection of *tatami*-color
In the silver bowl of my hanging lamp.

What if I never told any of this?

White cat
Spooked in the grass, alert against the satyrs
That pursue, she's full of kittens already
          . . . gone under the steps, under the porch

Cleo rises to bathe
& closes the bathroom door
My own bathtub becomes a mystery

Now that cat's on the window-ledge
Propped against the green sash, whiter
In the creamy light reflected off the kitchen door

What if I never said?

Singing & splashing in the bathtub
A mystery, a transformation, a different woman
Will emerge

          The birds have been pleased to show up
Bugs in the air won't last

And the chief satyr cat arrives
Ignores the birds, ascends the back stairs to spray the newel-post
A Message To The White Queen:
          "Sweet Papa is here."

He disappears and immediately
There she is, delicate pink nose reading:
          "Sweet Papa! The same old jazz."

Water glugs in the drain
A strange girl scours herself with my tired old towels
I think of her body & stop writing
To admire my own, some of her beauty rubbed off on me

Now some of my ugliness, some of my age
Whirls down the bathroom drain.

She'll go away. I'll go away. The world will go away.
      ("The idea of emptiness engenders compassion
        Compassion does away with the distinction
                    between Self & Other . . .")
But through her everything else is real to me & I have
No other self.
"What's wrong with two?"

                                        Berkeley 27:i:57–6:ii:57

from *Three Variations, All About Love*

I

So much to tell you
Not just that I love
There is so much more
You must hear and see

If I came to explain
It would do no good
Wordlessly nibbling your ear
Burying my face in your belly

> All I would tell is you
> And love; I must tell
> Me, that I am a world
> Containing more than love
>
> Holding you and all your other
> Lovers wherein you
> And I are free from each other
> A world that anyone can walk alone
> Music, coathangers, the sea
> Mountains, ink, trashy novels

Trees, pancakes, *The Tokaido Road*
The desert—it is yours

Refuse to see me!
Don't answer the door or the telephone
Fly off in a dragon-chariot
Forget you ever knew me

But wherever you are
Is a corner of me, San Juan Letrán
Or Montreal, Brooklyn
Or the Lion Gate

Under my skin at the Potala
Behind my eyes at Benares
Far in my shoulder at Port-au-Prince
Lifted in my palm among stars

Anywhere you must be you
Drugged, drunk or mad
As old, as young, whatever you are
Living or dying the place will be me

And I alone the car that carries you away.

III

(Big High Song for Somebody)

F
Train
Absolutely stoned
Rocking bug-eyed billboards WAFF!
No more bridge than Adam's
 off ox
  Pouring over 16⅔ds MPH sodium-

Vapor light yellow light

LOVE YOU!

Got *you* on
    like a coat of paint
Steamy girder tile

      LOVE YOU!

Cutting-out blues
        (Tlaxcala) left me
  like stoned on the F-train
whole week's load ready
    for that long stretch ahead
      Prisoners jailed
          SHBAM
Train chained to this train
    boring through diamonds
        SQUALL

      LOVE YOU!

Barreling zero up Balcony Street
    Leaning from ladders
      Same angle of lean; different cars
The Route of the PHOEBE SNOW

      LOVE YOU!

Blue-black baby
    16-foot gold buddha in your arms
  Taking you with me!
      Straight up Shattuck Avenue
Hay-burning train, bull-chariot
  With bliss bestowing hands

      LOVE YOU!

And I'm the laughing man
  with a load of goodies for all

Bridge still stands, bulls may safely graze,
    Bee-birds in the frangipani
            clock

        LOVE YOU!

Berkeley 28–31:x:55
17:xi:55

Invocation to the Muse

Green eyes, you always change
A rose-bed complete with briars
Making liars of angels
Cats-meat of gods
Boxers into queens.

Let down that golden ladder
        one more time
I'll shinny up and make a song or two
Before the withered hand
        clips those locks
And tumbles me among the thorns.

Portland xi?:50

Small Tantric Sermon

The release itself—
The comfort of your body—

Our freedom together and more, a
Revelation
Of myself as father, as a landscape as a universe
Being. . . .

This breaks down,
Here, on paper, although I am free
To spread these words, putting them
Where I want them (something of a release
In itself)
All they can say is
      Your foot
      Braced against the table-leg beside the bed
      Springing your hips to admit
      My gross weight, the other foot
      Stroking the small of my back:
A salacious picture of a man and a woman
Making out together
Or ingenuous autobiography—
"Memoirs of a Fat & Silly Poet"—
It might as well show them gathering tulips
Or playing cards

To say concisely
That the man in the picture
Really made it out through the roof
Or clear through the floor, the ground itself
Into free space beyond direction—

Impossible gibberish no one
Can understand, let alone believe;
Still, I try, I insist I can
Say it and persuade you
That the knowledge is there that the revelation
Is yours.

Berkeley 17:ix:56

Invocation & Dark Sayings, in the Tibetan Style

1.

The biggest problem in the world:

> "Where are you?"

And the second:

> To persuade you that I truly
> Want you here. I mean goddamit
That since you removed that celestial
> SNATCH
From these now desolated regions

> Nothing.
> Blank.

Vaseline,
Soap,
Hand-lotion,
Cold-cream,
Baby-oil,
Raw eggs,
Butter,
One pound of raw liver (delicately oven warmed),
One canteloupe   (″   ″   ″   ),
Several chickens,
One heifer,
Half a dozen assorted trulls,
A versatile but rather confused young man: : : :

> Double-blank equalling
> Half-nothing
With which I'm supposed to be content while you
Retain the only delectable sparkling furry magical

> WHEN ARE YOU COMING HOME?

2.

MESSAGE: To the Reader
         ½ of me is asleep
When it wakes up
              EVERYTHING
Will be destroyed
Or transmogrified.

              (Have you got a hard-on?
               I've got a hard-on.)

You will never know what I think
Because I'm not saying.

              "This is a picture of a man.
                The man is hiding something.
                Try to guess what it is.
                If you guess wrong . . ."

Look at that old thing stand up there!

A midge crosses the page
Slowly
Then feels his way (wings balancing)
Along the edge and falls
On his head.
When he wakes up,
Watch out!
I mean like

      "Look where it comes again!"

              (You dirty bastard, where did you ever get
               Such a filthy mind?

               My daddy lay on a sunny stone
               Fiddling with his cock
               The sun shone hot, the sun yelled
                        "Sam!"
               My daddy went home
               But here I am.)

"Knowledge cannot be transmitted.
You can recount your own experiences
And a person who has had similar experiences
MIGHT know what you meant. Perhaps
That is communication. However . . ."

You will never know what I think.
What you see
Is a dead idea.
Now I'm thinking of
Something else:

I can't tell it fast enough.

9–10:*viii*:56

Takeout, 15:*iv*:57

To have something fall is bad
To fall and break   worse.

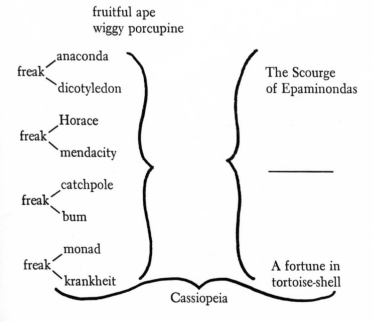

fruitful ape
wiggy porcupine

freak ⟨ anaconda / dicotyledon

freak ⟨ Horace / mendacity

freak ⟨ catchpole / bum

freak ⟨ monad / krankheit

Cassiopeia

The Scourge
of Epaminondas

———

A fortune in
tortoise-shell

We must learn to make mistakes gracefully;
However, all the fun resides in trying to be right
every time

Suppose it had floated in mid-air
That heavy solid porcelain teacup?

                    TERROR

The contravention of seemliness, abrogation
                    of all that is, &c.

   ("&c." equaling "if p, then q; if not p,
   then x, solve for x," a simple quadratic) let it

Go.

Harangue from Newport,
to John Wieners, 21 : ix : 57

What if I never told you
What if I never said what I'm trying
To say now?

A long time ago I thought it would be better
If I hadn't been born
But since I had been it might save trouble
To minimize the whole thing:
Play it not only cool but invisible

That doesn't work any more, everybody
Asks: "What's the matter"   "Are you mad about something?"
              "What's worrying you now?"

Well, what . . .
    I just saw my landlord go by
        the great carbuncle on his nose
        a sea anemone at low tide, petals retracted
        center full of sand, the circulation
        in his legs is bad so his feet hurt & he has
        dizzy spells because he won't stop eating
        fried fish
            (athero- or arteriosclerosis,
            anyway, too much cholesterol)
        being some sort of Swede
Now what?
    My hernia has skidded again
   More:
    I found a couple chunks of jasper-agate on the beach
    and one entire family (7 or 8 of them) jumping about
    in the surf with all their clothes on
    being some sort of Dukhobors-in-reverse?
   More?
    I should burn the garbage and wash the frying pan
    I should write you something that would
    Scare you, make you laugh
    Or generally turn you on
   WHAT
    I'm doing now: Trying hard to be visible, to be
    Totally conscious of this time and place,
            of you
    And every sentient being

    I'm stacking bb's day & night
    Working miracles left & right

   (Log-truck poops by in the street while I'm writing—I
changed it into gold: perfect wisdom, perfect compassion,
perfect freedom. . . . Texas-boot red shirt sideburns bodhisattva
                                 driver
instantly swung out of the cab to render his bows and performs
his circumambulations)

NOTICE,
> That the landlord still has his carbuncle
> That the family who frolicked in the waves have wet sandy
>> clothes which chafe them
> That the frying pan remains unwashed
> That the log truck must go live at Ft. Knox
> And that nobody can see me, I've closed all the blinds
>> it being night outside
> But everybody knows I'm here
>> the light's turned on

Notice also that you not only see me clearly

(A MIRACLE!)

You understand everything I say.

4:2:59 *Take I*

What I need is lots of money
No
What I need is somebody to love with unparalleled energy
> and devotion for 24 hours and then goodbye

I can escape too easily from this time & this place
That isn't the reason I'm here

What I need is where am I

Sometimes a bed of nails is really necessary to any man
Or a wall (Olson, in conversation, "That wall, it *has* to be there!")

Where are my hands.
Where are my lungs.
All the lights are on in here I don't see nothing.

I don't admit that this is personality disintegration
My personality has a half-life of 10^∞ years; besides

I can put my toe in my mouth
If (CENSORED), then (CENSORED), something like
Plato his vision of the archetypal human being

Or the Gnostic Worm.

People see me; they like that . . .
I try to warn them that it's really me

They don't listen; afterwards they complain
About how I had no right to be really just that:
Invisible & in complete control of everything.

LETTER, to Mme. E.T.S., 2:i:58

so T. comes on with the usual
"Come, tell me how you live" routine & I:
"Like a pope, on indulgences; like the king
on benevolences."

Poor little fly ain't got no home

Nor the seagulls outside, dining—
an abundance of Pacific decapods
(copepods?)

T: "But what can you *do* there? Noplace to go,
you don't see anybody . . ."
I: "I have a part-time job;
I read and write."

& everyone marvels at my Devotion to Literature
Or figures I'm coming on too innocent, I must be
Up to Something
(T. imagines, "Some chick is on the scene"
& L., "Or an infallible connection . . . ?")

All day Christmas the sea whirled this tangle—
Spruce logs, redwood stumps, fishboxes and lightglobes—
A big eddy at the creek mouth
Carting several tons of debris back & forth across a hundred feet
                                                    of beach

In water maybe a foot & ½ in depth

As the tide went out a gull rode a heavy smooth-swimming log
Perfectly flat-footed, no trouble balancing
Nothing to hang on to
Nothing to hang on with, raining like hell
      Poor little seagull got no home
Riding just now for the fun of it
In a generally Japanese direction

                  I think of children in a department store
                  Playing on the escalators, kings and queens
                  In magic palaces where the stairs walk up & down
                  Whether you move your feet or not
                  Hop to the stationary (moving) floor
                  Then sink through it & soar out of the ceiling
                  An angel in lights and music floating down
                  Just above Mama's head among the yard-goods
                      & costume jewelry

Poor little fly ain't got no clothes

Even to me this looks fishy, all
I get out of it is these idiot routines about seagulls—
The astrologers and palm-readers insist I have
Great Executive Ability a head for business
            & organization
(You can imagine the opinion
Of "eminent medical authorities,"
Not to mention the police)

L. (at the end of a letter) "What are *you*
            doing?"

28

& most of the time I'm not even writing this
Wishing I'd get started
& having started . . . .

THE DISCOVERY,

That it's sheerest self-indulgence
Just like the Pope building bridges to heaven
   (I presume that's the point of the *Pontifex Maximus* jazz)
Whether you move your feet or not

Laid end for end this poem is exactly
   a foot & ½ in depth
      Try to buy it

         BOOK DEPT. . . . . 6th Floor
   Children Not Allowed On Escalators Unaccompanied By Adults

For C.

I wanted to bring you this Jap iris
Orchid-white with yellow blazons
But I couldn't face carrying it down the street
Afraid everyone would laugh
And now they're dying of my cowardice.

Abstract beauty in the garden
In my hand, in the street it is a sign
A whole procession of ithyphallic satyrs
Through a town whose people like to believe:
"I was made like Jesus, out of Love; my daddy was a spook."

The upright flower would scare them. "What's shot,"
They think, "from the big flesh cannon will decay."
Not being there I can't say that being born is a chance
To learn, to love and to save each other from ourselves:
Live ignorance rots us worse than any grave.

29

And lacking the courage to tell you, "I'm here,
Such as I am; I need you and you need me"
Planning to give you this flower instead—
Intending it to mean "This is really I, tall, slender,
Perfectly formed"—is uglier than their holy fantasies,

Worse to look at than my own gross shape.
After all this fuss about flowers I walked out
Just to walk, not going to see you (I had nothing to bring—
This poem wasn't finished, didn't say
What was on my mind; I'd given up)

I saw bushes of crimson rhododendron, sparkling wet
Beside the hospital walk—I had to see you.
If you were out, I'd leave these flowers.
Even if I couldn't write or speak
At least I broke and stole that branch with love.

Berkeley 16:iv:57

Soufflé

TAKE I Carol said, "I looked at all my cells today
      Blood & smear samples from all over me.
      They were all individuals, all different shapes
      Doing whatever they were supposed to
      And all seeming so far away, some other world
      Being I."

TAKE II How do you feel?
      Me? Oh, I feel all right but sometimes
      I feel like a motherless child.
      I feel like walking out of here & spending
        vast sums of money. How do you
      Feel? I feel with my.

TAKE III   The wind increases as the sun goes down
The weight of that star pulling air after it
Naturally the prune trees blossom now
And some kind of bush with pink trumpet flowers
All the other trees except acacias have quit

TAKE IV   High strato-cumulus clouds and a
Light north-easterly wind (possibly
Two m. p. h. on the Beaufort Scale)
     "What ever became of old Whatch-callum,
     Old what's his name,
     Old . . . you know, the old fellow
     Who had that little ranch out by Mt. Pisgah,
     Out by the Pisgah Home? Had that
     Eight-finger Chinese cook & everything
         tasted like kerosene,
     We went out there once & put up blackberries."

    "Why, Dell, I don't remember . . .
He was a friend of yours."

TAKE V   How do I feel? I'm under it
Way under but I'm
Coming out, working out
The weight, the pressure
Piles of detritus already removed
The weight of half the earth, slowly
You can hear me underneath it all
Breathing, a faint
Scraping, a sifting rattle
Falling away below
Back towards the hollow center.
A little more
And I peer out

TAKE VI   Intolerable
You don't accept or reject it
You see it and know.
There is a difference.

> "*You got to wash them dishes*
>   (pronounced "deeshes")
> *And hesh that clattering tongue!*
> *Lolly-too dum, too-dum, &c.*"
No particular reply because the question
Isn't a question at all, it's the presence
Or absence of light
                              among those trees.

TAKE VII   Nowhere, this is getting us no-
                                                  where
And we need a place to do it.

TAKE VIII   I drank myself into a crying jag face down
On Ginsberg's woolly green rug
Roaring, "Gone, everything gone,
Cold, cold, cold, cold, cold!"

A nearly perfect vacuum at minus 278 degrees
           Absolute
HORREUR DU VIDE

The Messrs. Ginsberg & Kerouac, also juiced,
Wrapped me in blankets while I froze & squalled

TAKE IX   "I want you to go out & amount to something;
I don't want you to be an old ditch-digger all your
                                                              life
Work with your head if you can, let other people
           use their hands"

TAKE X   Can you look at a bug without squashing it?
Can you look into a glass without hate, without
Love, without murder?

We have nothing but thoughts of murder, i.e.
Complete ignorance of the world's own nature; or
Where there's no sense there's no feeling.

As for myself, I'm a genuine thug, I believe
in Kali the Black, the horrific aspect
the total power of Siva
absolute destruction
BUT it don't mean
What it looks like
          and the description misleads.

TAKE XI   Bud-clusters hang straight down from the sharply-
                                  crooked
Geranium stem like strawberries, the wild mountain
                                  kind
These flowers almost as wild right here
Barbarous thick-jointed tangle, waist-high
Escaped once for all from the green-houses of the
                                  north
A weed, its heavy stalks jointing upwards & winding
                                  out
In all directions, too heavy to stand straight
The neighbors clipped some out of their yard
The stalks lay in the gutter & grew for days
In the rain water, flowering red
Ignorant of their disconnection

TAKE XII   I shall be in LA
            La Puebla de Nuestra Señora La Reina de los
                                Angeles
On Palm Sunday
                 a necklace of skulls & fingers,
                 her belt dangling human arms,
                        legs & heads
                 her several hands brandishing
                   the noose
                   the sword
                   the axe
                   the skull-cup of blood
                   the *dorje* (double lightning-
                                  bolt)

                    Fire
                    Drum
                    Rosary
        Having (DV) arrived by streamline train
                "Coast Daylight"
        "in a throng of happy apprehensions"

TAKE XIII   Don't you ever get tired
             of your own sunny disposition?

TAKE XIV   I know perfectly well what became of old Mr.
                                                Daigler
             Greatly advanced in years he removed from Mt.
                                                Pisgah
             To the Odd-Fellows Home in Portland where he
                                                died
             Of malnutrition and the radio.

TAKE XV   The whole point of it is,
             When I saw that her necklace was made of my own
             Severed fingers, that I'd only just combed the hair
                     on that skull
                 (now containing lots of my blood
                     & her wasting it, slopping it
                     All down one of her arms)
             She was mine & we made it together
             The Island Of Jewels
             On a tiger-skin rug

             The Sun & Moon shining together.

TAKE XVI   It was so noisy in my head a rush of lights & motion
             And music & now the type lies on the page
             Perfectly silent, perfectly static, perfect
             The same temperature as the space between

                Minus 278 ABSOLUTE

radio frequencies in the ten-meter band
from the direction of the constellation
Herakles

Light

Hard radiation (cosmic particles, beta
& gamma rays)

A few vagrant atoms of hydrogen, scat-
terings
of metallic &/or mineral dust shoved along
by the pressure of the

Light

Absolute

o

Berkeley, The Anchor Inn, 23:ii:57
8:iv:57

10:x:57, 45 Years Since the Fall of the Ch'ing Dynasty

The Summer Palace burnt, the Winter Palace, wherever it was
"*Ordre, ordre, Je suis une maniaque pour l'ordre!*"
(Meaning that all those sheets are promptly sent to the wooden
Laundries of the Seine,
That all the shoes and sox are lined up in rows
That the words follow each other in ecstatic parentheses, NOT
That you and me are lined up against the innocent wall, torn
By the bullets of righteousness)

I am hid, as William Blake puts it, where nobody can see me not
Even those sad angels who busted the slippery membrane across
My stifled face so I could breathe the incense coming in
From the pavilion under Coal Hill my brocade sleeves raveling
Among the chips of jade and the withered peony blossoms and
The night of the boat-light Dragonboat orgies on the River
In pious memory of whosis that first made the water scene
With an ingenious system of *canali* and Nationally Federated
                                                                    Dams

    Where nobody can see me
        I read all about Jimmy Dean with 16 photographs
        and more than a hundred pages of vulgar prose

Nobody can find me I came here with that purpose of being alone
    (R. . . . says we have all these self-destructive impulses and it
    BUGS him, like he went to the neighborhood soda-fountain
For a coca-cola and everybody/all these monster teen-age
                                                                    hoods/

Jumped on him at once)

Not unlike the United States Marines building teakwood camp-
                                                                    fires
Out of the Empress's bedroom furniture on the Phoenix-Viewing
Terrace roasting their wienies.

Letter to Charles Olson

This surface (which grows increasingly Riemannian)

    how's your topology now? When you turn this over
    do you have a right- or a left-hand glove?

                (A WALL)

Right now is just fine, don't monkey with the postoffice
It's shut for the night:

I won't be able to buy a stamp for this until after 9 A.M.
No matter what I do, no matter how hard I try.

(A WALL)

So here we are, sweet Indolence and I and middling Luxury

(NO WALL)

And at last I can hear the radio say:
    "It is 29 minutes past 3 A.M."
Without flipping into a spin about being on time in the "morning"
Because I shall . . .

                          No strain
But—can I turn off Brahms' *Tragic Overture*
    now? Put out my pipe and go to bed?
Not until
    (ouch! a pain in the skull!)
I've said this
    (and in the left eye, the frontal sinus
    breaking down.)

(A WALL)

I guess it's tragic if he said so, incidental music
For some Shakespearian or Goethean tragedy, I forget
    although I read about it ONCE

No, I'll get up . . .

Well, go on, let Brahms take over with plenty of tremolo,
e.g.:
    I will collapse time, it is 4 A.M.
    And this is the Berkeley cottage, I've been drinking
    Wine with Allen & Jack, I must be at my sink at 8
    ON TIME, as I was the morning before, after a similar
    4 A.M. wine & goof-balls

(AN ARTIFICIAL PARTITION)

TIME IS RELATIVE/ or irrelevant; it is space, the surface
Which makes the distinction?

   (& of course Rexroth has the last word,
     it is the PERSON)
Or more nearly canonical, Epictetus: "Not events
But the judgment of men . . ."

   ("all that learning so gratuitously hurled at us—
     why don't he (i.e., PW) get a job in a college?")
Dryden sang, ". . . Jealousy, that Tyrant of the mind"
As if the mind weren't tyrannical enough
          on its own hook

   (Very beautiful lady on a visit to apartment inhabited
   by Snyder & me, years ago . . . she views a hunk of my
   library:
   "Did you take English 1109 at Cal.?"
   "No."
   "But you have all the *books!*"

(A WALL . . . OF BOOKS)

Lacking either space or time
Here we sit between Planck's Constant & the Speed of Light (c)
Theoretically discontinuous & haunted by an antique radio voice
(Mr. Jack Pearl in the character of "Baron Munchausen":
   "Was you there, Charlie?")
The whole world looking at its hand,
Betelgeuse at or near the eighteenth turning of whose particular
Small intestine? (Cf. a cartoon by Mr. George Gamow)
   (our editor writes me,
    "You are *not* interested in geometry!")
  "the judgment of men"
  the postoffice: Closed
  the time: Well, my watch is wrong
  but now is more or less six days since the first line.
  The library is in storage. Leave it there.

(A WALL . . . OF BOOKS)

People is a door, particularly for me, ladies I have loved
And the mind a Moebius-strip, a single surface
Turned through itself—or better, a sphere inside a sphere
That can be a torus (like the body) without losing anything
No wasted material.

Wall certainly is here, ⅗ths Philippine mahogany
Peachy-painted plaster for the rest.
There is a top and a bottom and two ends—
And another side! which is yellow, a DISCONTINUITY
Like radiation (Planck again)
        "each radiator emitting energy in equal amounts
        termed *quanta*, the value of which depend on a universal
        constant (A WALL) and the frequency of the vibration
        of the radiators"

I said LEAVE IT THERE!
The song tells it best:
        So high you can't get over it;
        So low you can't get under it;
        So wide you can't get around it—
        Got to come in by the door.
   which is what don't exist, although the wall does
(Notice the absence of "Therefore, etc.")

               FOR REFERENCE ONLY

Wm. Shakespeare: A *Midsummer Night's Dream*,
                      Act V, Sc I, ll. 161–162:
  Wall. "This loam, this roughcast, and this stone doth show
            That I am that same wall. The truth is so."

TORUS: looks like a smooth & perfect doughnut. It will bear
      only 7 contiguous areas of differently colored paints
      without the repetition of a color. Turning itself through
      itself it becomes a sphere with a sphere inside itself.
Which way is up? Charles is in Gloucester. I am here.

                      Newport 23:iv:58

Newport North-Window View

FOR BRUCE MC GAW

Graveled vacant lot
Left corner breaks into blackberry gulch

Straight ahead, spruce and jackpine grove
A set-up for Sesshu, the jackpines good as his
Sitka spruce behind them, stiff ragged feather wall

(Marred, I thought at first, by these trashy little shacks:

> Left-hand cabin partly dropped in the gully, its base
>   battered a little outward, a single row of windows
>   under the roof-line, not badly proportioned,
>   a jackpine leans toward its left back corner and up
>   then my direction; hazelbush hides front corner

> A pile of stovewood
> High square end of a blue bus (truck? trailer?)
> Half-round-top cabin, government colored, up on blocks
>   portable office for a construction boss
> Square gray house, white trim, its corner facing me, its
>   back against two pines)

Yesterday early evening fog dissolved the shacks into the scene
An occasional plane edge or corner, two or three steady lights
While up above, black tree earth air water transmutations

> Cloud becomes mountain
> Tree becomes beast
> Beast into cloud

Now in full sunlight
Trunks and branches carve black space out of walls and roofs
Which become flat irregular plane surfaces of light
    floating among the trees;
jumbled apricot pyramid woodpile blazes on the tawny ground.

27:vii:58

Take #4, 15:viii:57

FOR N.

You say, "I want you to kiss me" and you being
Beautiful I comply becoming right then
Beautiful and universally loved, like I don't know what
Year it is or come away with me into the lush life

Which is this,
Sitting in the dark by the radio jazz writing in the light
From the bathroom, one cat already stone out on the floor
The tradition of this place
You never saw such a pad all the wine all the ones
Who made it here the poems proliferating from this point

THE MUSES HELICON

I know what I want I want you and all this
Which is impossible . . . what can I

    Not just the most the best I want the superb
    With hot and cold running water unimaginable nothing
    Else will do, in the center of an impenetrable wilderness
    Square miles of it you couldn't guess that . . . or that I've
    Had it and it's not enough . . . what can I

        With my last paycheck buy a new suit & a pair of sox
        And a good paying job to keep you?

We are nowhere and nothing ever started

I guess you wanted a point of reference, right then
To locate yourself, OK? But I've been further than you
And back again, it's the same at both ends: You're looking
At two sides, your own and one that's different and scary

    (I have an argument with X . . . who keeps talking about
    "Low Life," "I keep wanting to do a novel about Low Life,

Like I knew a lady boxer, I was crazy about her, she had
A beautiful body, I used to strap her into her iron brassiere
She was a gorgeous woman . . . and absolutely queer.")

It's an imaginary choice between two imaginary worlds
Here I am high as a kite writing or trying to spell properly
The Tearful Tragedy of the Minotaur in Love or, *The Bull-Headed
Monster* (as Picasso draws him, although I don't have as good a
build) . . . the body of a man
but alien
Non-human from the neck up
Most Notable Monster

Our children would have the heads of angels
And the bodies of cows

*

*

All that's the honest picture of a cheating mind
I mean hogwash—I didn't have or want anything—
I needed you and didn't know it
I hung the monster mask on you and ran away
Imagining scenes of you asleep at nine and I
Standing by the bed at two A.M. trying to waken you

"Come outside, the stars are falling,
I've found a caterpillar that glows in the dark!"

For all I know, I'm the biggest prize there is
Certainly you are
& maybe you would like to starve with me
& if I had you what would I care about food or the telephone bill?

But I never asked you
Supposing that I knew all the answers. . . .

What else is there to find out?
It's all very simple, it's all like this,
We are 750 miles apart.

I stand here in my underwear wondering what to do
What was I going to do. . . .
                              clean these pipes,
Illuminate all these worlds. . . .
                              I'll eat breakfast
Attentively as possible
Thinking of you.

Denunciation, or, Unfrock'd Again

The trouble with you is
That sitting on a bench in the back yard
You see an old plank in the fence become
A jeweled honeycomb of golden wires
Discoursing music, etc.

The trouble is aggravated by the grass
Flashing alternately green and invisible
Green and non-existent
While the piano in the house plays
The Stars & Stripes Forever

The landlady's son has a tin ear

"The trouble with you is you keep acting
Like a genius: Now you're not a genius
You're nothing but a prick . . . in fact you're
Not even that, you're nothing but a son-of-a-bitch

GET OUT OF MY HOUSE!"

"There you are, sitting in the sun too . . .
Have you noticed all the flowers? There
Is an iris; there are hyacinths; these
Are tulip buds. I thought that was
A peach tree in the neighbor's yard; the
Landlady says it is an almond,
But the almond is always the first to flower."

The trouble with you is
You neither take it nor leave it alone.

What plant puts out those
Tall thin stiff green leaves? Lines
Drawn from the tip of each one
Would describe the surface of what
Regular solid polyhedron?

You don't dare invent a name;
Nameless, it threatens you with destruction.
To hell with it. It's a subtropical lily.

The trouble with you is that you're backed up
Against a wall
Convinced that any instant
You will fall right through it.
The real trouble with you really is
That you don't think,
You simply worry.

I sat down in my house and ate a carrot.

11:iii:56

Unfinished, 3:xii:55

We have so much
That contemplating it
We never learn the use—

Poisoning ourselves with food, with books
      with sleep

Ignorance quicker than cyanide
Cuts us down

No lack of opportunity to learn;
Flat-footed refusal! Call it
Perversion, abuse, bullheadedness
It is rejection of all we know

A single waking moment destroys us
And we cannot live without
Ourselves

You come to me for an answer? I
Invented it all, I
Am your tormentor, there is no
Escape, no redress

You are powerless against me: You
Must suffer agonies until you know
You are suffering;

Work on that.

Further Notice

I can't live in this world
And I refuse to kill myself
Or let you kill me

The dill plant lives, the airplane
My alarm clock, this ink
I won't go away

I shall be myself—
Free, a genius, an embarrassment
Like the Indian, the buffalo

Like Yellowstone National Park.

22:ix:56

Sourdough Mountain Lookout

Tsung Ping (375–443): "Now I am old and infirm. I fear I shall no more be able to roam among the beautiful mountains. Clarifying my mind, I meditate on the mountain trails and wander about only in dreams."
                    —in *The Spirit of the Brush*, tr. by Shio Sakanishi, p. 34.

FOR KENNETH REXROTH

I always say I won't go back to the mountains
I am too old and fat there are bugs mean mules
And pancakes every morning of the world

Mr. Edward Wyman (63)
Steams along the trail ahead of us all
Moaning, "My poor old feet ache, my back
Is tired and I've got a stiff prick"
Uprooting alder shoots in the rain

Then I'm alone in a glass house on a ridge
Encircled by chiming mountains
With one sun roaring through the house all day
& the others crashing through the glass all night
Conscious even while sleeping

 Morning fog in the southern gorge
 Gleaming foam restoring the old sea-level
 The lakes in two lights green soap and indigo
 The high cirque-lake black half-open eye

Ptarmigan hunt for bugs in the snow
Bear peers through the wall at noon
Deer crowd up to see the lamp
A mouse nearly drowns in the honey
I see my bootprints mingle with deer-foot
Bear-paw mule-shoe in the dusty path to the privy

Much later I write down:
    "raging. Viking sunrise
    The gorgeous death of summer in the east"
(Influence of a Byronic landscape—
Bent pages exhibiting depravity of style.)

Outside the lookout I lay nude on the granite
Mountain hot September sun but inside my head
Calm dark night with all the other stars

HERACLITUS: "The waking have one common world
But the sleeping turn aside
Each into a world of his own."

I keep telling myself what I really like
Are music, books, certain land and sea-scapes
The way light falls across them, diffusion of
Light through agate, light itself . . . I suppose
I'm still afraid of the dark

                "Remember smart-guy there's something
                Bigger something smarter than you."
                Ireland's fear of unknown holies drives
                My father's voice (a country neither he
                Nor his great-grandfather ever saw)

                A sparkly tomb a plated grave
                A holy thumb beneath a wave

Everything else they hauled across Atlantic
Scattered and lost in the buffalo plains
Among these trees and mountains

From Duns Scotus to this page
A thousand years

> (". . . a dog walking on his hind legs—
> not that he does it well but that he
> does it at all.")

Virtually a blank except for the hypothesis
That there is more to a man
Than the contents of his jock-strap

EMPEDOCLES: "At one time all the limbs
Which are the body's portion are brought together
By Love in blooming life's high season; at another
Severed by cruel Strife, they wander each alone
By the breakers of life's sea."

Fire and pressure from the sun bear down
Bear down centipede shadow of palm-frond
A limestone lithograph—oysters and clams of stone
Half a black rock bomb displaying brilliant crystals
Fire and pressure Love and Strife bear down
Brontosaurus, look away

My sweat runs down the rock

HERACLITUS: "The transformations of fire
are, first of all, sea; and half of the sea
is earth, half whirlwind. . . .
It scatters and it gathers; it advances
and retires."

I move out of a sweaty pool
          (The sea!)
And sit up higher on the rock

Is anything burning?

The sun itself! Dying

Pooping out, exhausted
Having produced brontosaurus, Heraclitus
This rock, me,
To no purpose
I tell you anyway (as a kind of loving) . . .
Flies & other insects come from miles around
To listen
I also address the rock, the heather,
The alpine fir

BUDDHA: "All the constituents of being are
Transitory: Work out your salvation with diligence."

(And everything, as one eminent disciple of that master
Pointed out, has been tediously complex ever since.)

There was a bird
Lived in an egg
And by ingenious chemistry
Wrought molecules of albumen
To beak and eye
Gizzard and craw
Feather and claw

My grandmother said:
"Look at them poor bed-
raggled pigeons!"

And the sign in McAlister Street:

> "IF YOU CAN'T COME IN
> SMILE AS YOU GO BY
> L♡VE
> THE BUTCHER

I destroy myself, the universe (an egg)
And time—to get an answer:
There are a smiler, a sleeper and a dancer

We repeat our conversation in the glittering dark
Floating beside the sleeper.
The child remarks, "You knew it all the time."
I: "I keep forgetting that the smiler is
Sleeping; the sleeper, dancing."

From Sauk Lookout two years before
Some of the view was down the Skagit
To Puget Sound: From above the lower ranges,
Deep in forest—lighthouses on clear nights.

This year's rock is a spur from the main range
Cuts the valley in two and is broken
By the river; Ross Dam repairs the break,
Makes trolley buses run
Through the streets of dim Seattle far away.

I'm surrounded by mountains here
A circle of 108 beads, originally seeds
    of *ficus religiosa*
        Bo-Tree
A circle, continuous, one odd bead
Larger than the rest and bearing
A tassel (hair-tuft) (the man who sat
        under the tree)
In the center of the circle,
A void, an empty figure containing
All that's multiplied;
Each bead a repetition, a world
Of ignorance and sleep.

Today is the day the goose gets cooked
Day of liberation for the crumbling flower
Knobcone pinecone in the flames
Brandy in the sun

Which, as I said, will disappear
Anyway it'll be invisible soon
Exchanging places with stars now in my head
To be growing rice in China through the night.

Magnetic storms across the solar plains
Make Aurora Borealis shimmy bright
Beyond the mountains to the north.

Closing the lookout in the morning
Thick ice on the shutters
Coyote almost whistling on a nearby ridge
The mountain is THERE (between two lakes)
I brought back a piece of its rock
Heavy dark-honey color
With a seam of crystal, some of the quartz
Stained by its matrix
Practically indestructible
A shift from opacity to brilliance
(The Zenbos say, "Lightning-flash & flint-spark")
Like the mountains where it was made

What we see of the world is the mind's
Invention and the mind
Though stained by it, becoming
Rivers, sun, mule-dung, flies—
Can shift instantly
A dirty bird in a square time

Gone
Gone
REALLY gone
Into the cool
O MAMA!

Like they say, "Four times up,
Three times down." I'm still on the mountain.

Sourdough Mountain 15:viii:55
Berkeley 27–28:viii:56

N O T E : The quotes of Empedocles and Heraclitus are from John Burnet's
Early Greek Philosophy, Meridian Books, New York.

MEMOIRS OF AN INTERGLACIAL AGE 1958-1959

Address to the Boobus,

with her Hieratic Formulas in reply

O Great Priestess
O Keeper of the Mystic Shrine
O Holy & Thrice More Holy

Prussian Blue   Dark Blue   Light Blue   French Blue

Blyni & Pirozhki   Sapphire   Aquamarine
To Take Out   Turquoise   Zircon
                      Lapis Lazuli

        Malachite, a sea-color stone

O Hidden!

       (Vestal maenad bacchante)
among the leaves bright & dark

       ". . . a rubber baby . . .
       ". . . a plastic baby . . .
       "cloth baby whose eyes
             close"

O Blessed Damozel
          (flies & lilies)
Rosetti saw you weeping, leaning
    over heaven's gold bar
(Crocodile tears?)
        yellow hair

       "I NEED TO HAVE A PAPER!"
       ". . . a hand for you, a HAND for you
       a hand!"

Power & clemency
                    VEIL
                              a shroud (only a slip-cover) a curtain
Covering
            from dusty eyes, the vapid gaze of

        THE TABERNACLE & blazing lamps the Molten Sea

& the Sybil also, her eyes closed under the cloth
& covered baskets containing that which none but the initiated
may look upon

                    ". . . I have one
                    I have two
                    I have a pencil
            I'm going to get another chair
                              & stand up
                    I need
                    I need to push it

                        THERE!"

                                                    10:vii:59

Boobus Hierophante,

Her Incantations

Heavy
Heavy
Hangs

        over thy head

                    "A HAND!
                    "A HAND!
                    "A HAND!

This gruesome object was employed in unspeakable rites,
   the fingers burning as tapers

WHAT SHALL THE OWNER DO TO REDEEM IT?

                    TAKE 3 STEPS FORWARD

"A TABLE
"A TABLE
"A WHEEL FOR THE TABLE
"ANOTHER WHEEL FOR THE TABLE
               "RED
               "RED
               "RED
               "RED
               "MONKEY
               "A FLEMING POOL
               "A LITTLE TINY MOUSE RIGHT THERE

full terror

              "LOOK AT THAT I MADE!"

                              10:vii:59

Metaphysical Insomnia Jazz. Mumonkan xxix.

                              Of
Course I could go to sleep right here
With all the lights on & the radio going

(April is behind the refrigerator)

              Far from the wicked city
              Far from the virtuous town
              I met my fragile Kitty
              In her greeny silken gown

fairly near the summit of Nanga Parbat & back again, the wind
flapping the prayer-flags

"IT IS THE WIND MOVING."

"IT IS THE FLAG MOVING."

Hypnotized by the windshield swipes, Mr. Harold Wood:
"Back & forth;   back & forth."

> We walked beside the moony lake
> Eating dried apricots
> Lemons bananas & bright wedding cake
> & benefits forgot

"IT IS THE MIND MOVING."

& now I'm in my bed alone
Wide awake as any stone

7:iv:58

20:vii:58, On Which I Renounce the Notion of Social Responsibility

The minute I'm out of town
My friends get sick, go back on the sauce
Engage in unhappy love affairs
They write me letters & I worry

Am I their brains, their better sense?

All of us want something to do.

I am breathing. I am not asleep.

In this context: Fenellosa translated No (Japanese word)
as "accomplishment"

(a pun for the hip?)

Something to do

"I will drag you there by the hair of your head!"
& he began doing just that to his beautiful wife
Until their neighbors (having nothing better to do)
Broke it up

If nothing else we must submit ourselves
To the charitable impulses of our friends
Give them a crack at being bodhisattvas
(although their benevolence is a heavy weight on my head
their good intentions an act of aggression)

Motion of shadows where there's neither light nor eye to see
Mind a revolving door
My head a falling star

7:v–20:vii:58

Unsuccessful Spring Poem

Warm night/morning walking
I'm looking for anything

Beside a white wall: Soft ponderous callas, white against white
Nothing can move them in this heavy moon & streetlight

when no one shall marry

women clean house, bank all fires, a white cone of ashes
the coals deep inside
girls & their marble images bathe in the sea

men & boys keep to the rivers, fish for spring salmon
(Stay away from the ocean!)
after steam-baths & fasting, eat dream-journey medicine
gathering   power

Although completely open, perfectly formed, white
Nothing will move these massive lilies until June

3:v:58

Trying Too Hard to Write a Poem Sitting on the Beach

Planted among driftwood
I watch the tide go out
It pulls the sundown with it
& across this scene & against the wind
Man on a motorbike white crash-helmet
His young son rides the gas tank before him
Slows down for the creek mouth
& not too fast up the beach north

Flat dull whistle buoy heard again
And though the wind is right the bell buoy is inaudible

Fat seagull picks at a new hake skeleton
Choosily—not hungry walks away
Returns a moment later,
Room for a few more bites inside

Here comes a family of five
Man prodding with a stick whatever the children test
                    with their fingers
Mama is bundled up naturally cold & yellow plastic bucket
Complaining a little ". . . kind of a long way from the car . . ."

The children explore ahead the beach goes on forever & they
Will see it all this evening they aren't tired

Motorbike man coming back slows down for them
            & for the creek mouth

Fog joined into fat clouds cover the sun
Move south stretching rivers & islands of blue
Fine moving sheets & shafts of light on the water horizon

I'm not making it, I'm cold, I go into the house.

                                                    12:vii:58

Hymnus Ad Patrem Sinensis

I praise those ancient Chinamen
Who left me a few words,
Usually a pointless joke or a silly question
A line of poetry drunkenly scrawled on the margin of a quick
                    splashed picture—bug, leaf,
                    caricature of Teacher
        on paper held together now by little more than ink
        & their own strength brushed momentarily over it

Their world & several others since
Gone to hell in a handbasket, they knew it—
Cheered as it whizzed by—
& conked out among the busted spring rain cherryblossom winejars
Happy to have saved us all.

31:viii:58

Prose Take-Out, Portland 13:ix:58

I shall know better next time than to drink with any but certified
drunks (or drinker) that is to say like J-L. K. who don't fade away
with the first false showing of dawn through the Doug-fir & hem-
lock now here Cornell Road First of Autumn Festival

    a mosquito-hawk awakened by my borrowed kitchen light
    scrabbles at the cupboard door
& the rain (this is Portland) all over the outdoor scene—let it—
I'm all in favor of whatever the nowhere grey overhead sends—
which used (so much, so thoroughly) to bug me
               Let it (Shakespeare) come down
                 (& thanks to Paul Bowles for
reminding me)
there it rains & here—long after rain has stopped—continues from
the sodden branch needles—to rain, equated, identified with nowhere self indulgence drip off the eaves onto stone drizzle mist
among fern puddles—so in a manner of speaking (Henry James
tells us)   "There we are."
the booze (except for a hidden inch or so of rosé in the kitchen
jug) gone & the cigarets few—I mean where IS everybody & they
are (indisputably) very sensibly abed & asleep—
               one car slops by fast on overhead Cornell Road the
fireplace pops I wouldn't have anything else just now except the
rest of the wine & what am I trying to prove & of course nothing
but the sounds of water & fire & refusing to surrender to uncon-
sciousness as if that were the END of everything—Goodbye, goodbye, at last I'm tired of this & leave you wondering why anybody

has bothered to say "The sun is rising" when there's a solar ephemeris newly printed, it makes no difference—but you will be less than nowhere without this pleasurable & instructive guide.

13:ix:58

From a Letter to Ron Loewinsohn, 19:xi:58

Well, love, sure, love, ok, love if
(As it is) penultimate to action, the ultimate being
                    compassion
                    (a detached interest)
& some sort of understanding in between the letters

> "PRETTY IS AS PRETTY DOES"

> (What are you doing with your hand between my legs?
> (
> (Why don't we just go down to the corner for a choco-
> late malt?
> (
> (& 2 straws & Norman Rockwell to draw it?

Anyway, you've seen these people, the one trying desperately
To Make It & I mean on a strictly H E R E hardup basis

& the other WONT (stand/sit/lay) still for it
Because it might complicate things (or any other REASON)
IT IS PRIDE: A false humility, we put ourselves down
None of us believes
                "I am a prize package"
                that we aren't idly chosen

        (Darwin is all about South American bugs)

        or that our own taste in lovers
                is infallible

19:xi:58

Complaint: To the Muse

You do understand I've waited long enough
There's nobody else that interests me more than a minute
I've got no more ambition to shop around for poems or love
Come back!
             or at least answer your telephone
I'm nowhere without you

    This is the greatest possible drag
    Slower than the speed of light or always
    A little less than critical mass

    The energy the steam the poop is here
    Everything is (by Nature) Energy, I myself
    A natural thing & certainly massive enough

    A block of lead (the end of all radiation)
    I don't even reflect much daylight, not to speak of
                glowing in the dark
    I'll never get it off the ground

This room is full of 1 fly & an alarmclock
It is uninhabitable

If I wasn't drunk & blowing wine-fumes & peanut breath in your
                                  face
Maybe you'd be nice to me.

You do understand
I'd much rather listen, Lady
Than go on babbling this way, O rare gentle
& wise, it isn't enough that your face, your body
Are uniquely beautiful—I must hear you tell me
              about the weather
We might even quarrel if nothing else

64

You know the answer & don't, won't quit kidding me along
Hanging me up like Sir John Suckling
                in a tag of lace or muslin

I can see right through all those veils
But you can run fast & I've got a bum knee

& you been a long time gone

11–12:ix:58

A Reply

You ask, "a flash in the pan?" (i.e. can you
                dismiss us?)
I say, "No.
No torches, no beacons—
            FLASHES OF MEN IN TIME: rare,
            discontinuous, an after-image
Remains, a retinal overcharge (& add:
            persistence of vision)
EFFECT AN AMBIENCE OF LIGHT

4:iv:59

Something Nice About Myself

Lots of people who no longer love each other
Keep on loving me
& I

I make myself rarely available.

19:xii:58

A Distraction Fit

I walk around town with my baby
While I'm sound asleep the middle of a nervous breakdown

Big pieces of the world break off
       Slowly
      sleeping
             she didn't know the right way home, I lead the way
               with my eyes closed

Pieces of myself plaster & stucco walls
          Potemkin facades
       drifting away

Lungs breathe me out
Heart circulates me through pipes & tubing
Brains imagine something walking
        asleep

She holds this man by the arm it stretches
         across the world
Hand in his pocket
Dream of love in 2 houses
        asleep
She breathes me in

                                 4:v:59

With Compliments to E. H.

               a target

        a crooked arrow

                      an asymptote

a balance, an
anomaly

             a dissonance, an intentional
               asymmetry

Sound B & B-flat together (in the bass) & hear
yet another: "beat frequency"

Light through a diffraction-grating projects rings
of darkness (a silence)
"cancellation"

Paradigms, correspondences i.e. inverse proportions

_____

        _____

_____A mutual confusion
or mine alone?

                    _____

_____   _____

        a confutation of Hermes Trismegistus

I think mostly I remember, am remembered
By my own brains muscle skin
                            which never sleep
An imaginary difference of frequency between them
        speaks here?

                    *

(interrupted by a poet:
            "Going to work as an airline purser
            all my friends will forget me
            I'll be up in the air

            . . . .
            I'll see you again before the world blows up."

I: "That's a solipsist view."
He: "What do I know about New York?"

                    *

A TARGET
A CROOKED ARROW
AN ASYMPTOTE
"You hit the nail right on the thumb!"

A false note between "The Real" &
        "The Illusory"

HONK

"I don't think you want to talk to me"
        (this is another, earlier poet)
"Why don't you just tell me to go home?"

The brain
        actually T H E R E 1 minute
                out of any waking hour
        busy between whiles talking & listening
        in cahoots with skin & bones to make a raft
                sentient beings without number

NOT A DECISION OR A CHOICE:

DISCOVERY

---

sidewheel steamboat carried
Grandpa Kelly from San Francisco to Portland
sank on the return trip, all hands lost

                        *

                        *

                ". . . no permanent home . . ."

CHAO-CHOU SAYS "WOOF!"
      "Open Scandal," Mumon Decl
   NORTH-SOUTH ZEN RIFT WIDENS
     Jiriki or *Tariki?*

(PHOTO)

MR. A. C. PILLSBURY

Flour Magnate Says, "Eventually . . . why not now?"

Accused of Southern Sympathy

PALACE SOURCES MUM

> so he says gimmee the coat & I says
> it's yours if you're man enough to pick
> it up so he grunts & strains & say I
> magicked it so he couldn't & wants me to
> teach him how, I told him it wasn't me,
> the boss didn't want it to go no further
> & it wasn't any good to me neither & if
> anybody hexed it it was him the Old Man
> No. 5, I said I'll tell you all I know about
> it but you'll have to figure it out for
> yourself

Intentionally out of whack
The bow-string, the bent bow

DISTORTION

Power, to kink space (distance)
    the target impaled on the arrow!
The bow-string hauling the target
    to where I stand
Snaps back

THWUNK!

               7/8:v:59

HERAKLEITOS OF EPHESOS, Frs. 45 & 66 (John Burnet
                                    translation):

"(45) Men do not know how what is at variance agrees with itself.
It is an attunement of opposite tensions, like that of the bow and
the lyre.

(66) The bow (Βιὸς) is called life (Βίος), but its work is death."

"Love is a law, a discord of such force,
  That 'twixt our sense and reason makes divorce;"
                            —Anon., from *The Thracian Wonder*, 1661

                                        6:v–8:v:59

Poem for a Blonde Lady

Clearly I must not (on any account) stir one muscle
Until it moves
                    a real necessity
                        interior
        to it,
                towards or away from
You

I don't mean "love" or "sanity," I want to answer
            all your crooked questions
                absolutely straight

                            & if away

Only a pausing a thoughtless rearrangement
                to include you
As we really are

                                        8:v:59

"Everywhere I Wander"

Sweet sleep a spider of dreams downy fuzz & thistle blanket
dragdown tourniquet too long & frequently applied
afternoon a soporific sad & flicker dim & horizontal dol-
drum a distant intensity of cloud

                             fern

                shape   shape   shape

a crystal

          my face warped into sleep-wrinkle taste
still asleep

            crystal electrically bent
               a tone

                                          12:V:59

A Reflection on My Own Times

Now's

       the wrong place
       to start an argument (to
       say nothing about being otherwise unready)

WHAT ideas? Not a brain in my head, only
       "Education" & a few *"idées reçus"* (read
                "conditioned reflexes")
But necessary to open my small
          yap
      maybe just to say "ouch"
          as the lobotomy knife slides
          ("painlessly," they say)
                     IN

                                      13:V:59

Haiku for Mike

Bouquet of H U G E
        nasturtium leaves
"HOW can I support myself?"

                    13:v:59

Self-Portrait, from Another Direction

Tuned in on my own frequency
I watch myself looking
Lying abed late in the morning
With music, thinking of Y.
Salal manzanita ferns grasses & grey sky block the window
Mossy ground

I think what is thinking
What is that use or motion of the mind that compares with
A wink, the motion of the belly

        Beside the highway
        Young bullock savages the lower branches
                    of a big cedar tree

A Journey,

        Lownsdale Square
To The City   Huge seagull on rump of bronze elk
        Looking the other way

        Wm Jennyns Baker (getting breakfast for his
           family & me):
        "Count your blessings
        Name them one by one
        You will be surprised
        What the L O R D hath done!"

THOUGHT IS NOT SWIFT!

perhaps the mind is slower than this pencil, its rate of motion
nearer that of the heartbeat—
moving slower than the head which turns
    not as quick as a wink

Pieces broken off a sandstone cliff
Grass & salal bushes still growing on it, roots exposed
I said a new landslide; the Judge: "It fell off two years ago"

POSSIBLE TRUE STATEMENTS ABOUT A REAL PIECE OF SANDSTONE

        Now it is here.
        Now it is falling.
        Now it is there.

                which we agree upon . . .
What comes next?

        The landslide has revealed
        The bones of Adam protruding from the soil
        A bronze door into Magic Land
        Z. really *was* sore at me seven years ago in
        Hollywood, which is the reason Sandra never
        returned my umbrella,—I see it all now . . .
Any of these things?

    "wasn't built in a day"

Considerably faster, the Basilica of St Peter
A momentary flash, a brainstorm, an internal shifting
Nothing to do with time-keeping or spending, the rules of the
                         stonemason's guild
Maybe a headache between the hours of 1 & 10 P.M.
Walking the street alone

    I said leave it the hell alone now or you'll have the whole
                     thing all gee-hawed up
    Quicker than dammit

Rain/wind bulging the window
An Absolute, i.e. what we think of as
        "an Absolute," "Force," "NATURE"
    know nothing of my love, my mind
Looking into a mirror, shaving, is I?
& I told Q., "the toes, knee-caps *et cetera*
All thinking"   or this

                    Lights on or off
                    The kitchen is the same
                    Tuesday or Wednesday

    2 Reedies cross-legged on Taylor Street sidewalk
    Beards   *Another*
    Waiting for the campus bus   *Journey*
                                                    To The
    On Broadway another one gets off a trolley   *Same City*
    Full pack & walking-shoes dangling

    Moral: Not all the younger generation going to hell

                                to bed & all my nerves
woke up to sing & dance I got up & dressed made a pot of tea lit a
                                pipe &
sat patiently watching them hop, flashing red, blue, etc. random
                                motion
through a number of dimensions &/or continua—fascinating but
                                completely
exhausting to watch, to be

                    (*2 lines canceled*)

Climb on & ride—
                progress by explosion
All the elements analyzed out & recombined

                    /with your finger on the throttle
                    & your foot upon the treadle of the clutch

an open eye neither *oculus Dei* nor yet the sun
"*omicron*" the lesser "o"

(2 *lines canceled*)

Any word you see here defies all fear doubt destruction ignorance &
                  hatefulness
All the impossibilities unfavorable chance or luck
It will have overcome all my strength (the total power of a raging
                                                    maniac
          self-hypnotized berserk missing one arm part of the entrails
                                                    exposed
          running with incredible speed)
Superhuman force,   an exorbitance—
                    slingstone hurled at a tangent to the circle
                    in which it lately whirled
                    zipping off in high-speed parabola

Into the mirror (NOW showing many men) all of them "I"

                                                    11:*ii*:59

Delights of Winter at the Shore

A little sauce having unglued me from my book
I take the present (Ernest Bloch on the phonograph)
I salute the fire in the fireplace
The red sectional settee
All the potted plants I moved onto the diningroom table
            so they could get more light
And beyond the window North Pacific Ocean

An editor writes to me, "Takes, takes, all the time takes . . . what
            are you scared of, nobody's trying to cut your throat . . .
            Why don't you just sit down & write a novel?"

& wild with energy & power I'm curled up in the grey reclining chair
Carefully writing one letter at a time

> Check the barometer .... falling
> Check the swiss steak in the oven .....
> .... turn up the heat

It goes like that, all the "talent," the "promise"
My mortgage very nearly foreclosed
My light going out

> X. keeps telling me how sad everything is
> (he cries all the time)
> Maybe he's right, but I don't *see* sad
> & the pursuit of happiness around a square track

How loyal have I been to myself?
How far do I trust .... anything?
I wonder "self-confidence" *vs.* years of self-indulgence
(am I feeling guilty?)
How would anything get done if I quit? Stopped
whatever it is you choose to call it?

Put it as fancy & complicated as possible:
Here I sit drunk beside the biggest ocean in the world
Tosca destroying me on the phonograph
Everybody else in the world dying of starvation, cruelty
lack of my love

No amount of promise or talent about to do anything to fix that.
It was 20 years ago they worried about what I might do
Now everybody can see what I've done, what I'm doing

> Everybody starves
> Everybody is a huge (biological) success
> Everybody's maybe like me: perpetually scared
> & not giving a shit
> > As long as there's beef in the oven
> > Out of jail
> > Drunk

Everybody says Horace was a two-bit snob, writing
        "Odi profanum vulgis"
Maybe he meant he hated himself for being lazy, preferring old wine
Pretty girls & sunshine
To the dignity & usefulness of public office?

Now the Second Act of *Tosca:*
Big party downstairs, the cantata going on
Police interrogation upstairs, Cavaradossi on the rack
(These *palazzi*—a real idea of splendor)
& topping it all off, as if it explained E V E R Y T H I N G

      "Vissi d'arte, vissi d'amore . . ." I've lived for Art,
      I've lived for love . . ."
                (incontinently stabbing the villain)

DIE!   DIE!   DIE!

I eat an olive out of my glass

    TOSCA: ". . . *tutta Roma!"*

                  & 1 is left

Some psychiatrist says "Quotation, a relaxation for, an evasion by
the *id.*"

I eat the second final olive & pretend to hurl my glass
        into the fireplace
I don't actually throw it, the glass isn't mine & there's a screen
        in front of the fireplace

             *

             *

24 hours later, not drunk but dissociated completely from past
        & present (absolute rejection of any future)
3 severed heads are staring at me through the windows above the
                        door

A large patient hungry monster breathes once a minute at the
                                                          keyhole
All violence has returned to sit on my chest, slide into my armpits
The whole works only part of this particular link of a heavy gold
            suspended chain circle
                        the chain is also manifest as music

I try to decide if it's light on dark
Or dark on a light ground . . . intensely occupied with this . . .

& start again: Air is colder than ice
Interstellar space is (a few parsecs from a star)
Colder than air, *et cetera*

The way I'm sitting now is the past, the way my fingers hold this
                                                          pen
The letters themselves
2 minutes from now I'll do something equally characteristic
Something I've lived, survived 35 years in order to accomplish

Viz., Laid aside the pen, took off my glasses & rubbed my eyes
Considering the idea of staying up until daylight

Everything between time
Crazy as a peach-orchard bull . . .
                                    I turn my head
Expecting the ocean to be empty & black;

                        there are tiers of lights
Apparition of downtown office building standing on the waves

GANDHARVA CITY!

A Swede boat bound for China

                                    17, 18, 19:xii:58

Self-Portrait Sad 22:ix:58

At last I realize my true position: hovering face down above the
                                                                world
(At this point the Pacific Coast of The United States)
The lights of the cities & my lives & times there
A second rate well finished nothing too much wrong with it but
                                              not too interesting
Piece of music—think of De Falla's *Nights in the*
                              Gardens of Spain:
Very like that—mildly extravagant, vaguely romantic
Some overtones of a home grown exoticism

Trying to break this all up I meditate a while
Walk on the beach to look at the moon (some sort of festival
                                              moon surely
First full moon after Autumn Equinox)

Sudden seabird exclamations very loud just over my head invisible

Broken tooth. Shrouded typewriter. Noisy clock. Poorly tuned
                                                        radio.
Sick refrigerator in the next apartment.
I know exactly what I'm doing
& after sleeping and waking again the rest of this day will be
                                              wonderful

(DREAM PANTOMIME)

Stacked high around us while we practice unspeakable
                                              vices
Bones of Senacherib his victims
O Babylon, dear Babylon all drowned!

The irresponsible waves & fickle winds
        (Great Atlantis!)
Flying fish & giant cephalopods
Poison floating dumpling Portuguese man o' war
        (O Camoens!)
& immoral Plotinian nautilus high above the temple courts

Alas dainty Belshazar!   Divine Exogamite!
                    Perished!

Folie de grandeur: horror & degradation is my name

Another damned lie, my name is I
Which is a habit of dreaming & carelessness
              no nearer the real truth of any matter
In any direction myself bound & divided by notions

                    ACT!   MOVE!   SPEAK!

Forgetting last night's moon & paying no attention now
To the sunlight in these pines

                    Deer Demon & Yak Demon stir my brains
                    Mouth grows tinier, belly
                    Huge—I'm a *preta*, starving ghost
                         Self-devoured

                    PARALYZED   AGAIN!

                    (*O rage, O désespoire,* &c.)

Swinging in the same eccentric orbit from depression
To mania—imbecility to genius

Unlike Tobit I'm awake but the seagulls mute
              dung as warm as sparrows
                    per usual

& I'm tired of being tired of it
A simple switch from hating to loving
That's not enough, walking from one end of a teeter-board
                    to the other
Go sit under a chestnut tree & contemplate the schoolhouse
You won't believe that its thin tall red brick
Peaked roof & elegant cupola with bell
Narrow high green-trim crumble-sill windows (& this

is the NEW side, the 1910 Union St. facade
the Court St. front is 1897 its great solid doubledoors
Sealed)

& now the tree's cut down
>Oh, well
>I was never good at throwing rocks to knock down
>Pods from it anyway, horsechestnuts
>Cold calsomine smell, solid chunks of brown watered-
>>silk inside
>To contemplate
>>or decorate with a pocket knife

DOTE   DOTE   DOTE

Suppose (unbelievably) you were fat & forty for the last 20 years
With sporadic fits of low-frequency radiation
Lots of side-bands, poor modulation, the oscillator
>Unstable

DOTE   DOTE

(PLEASE REPLACE YOUR OLD TANK WITH A ((PIEZO-
ELECTRIC)) CRYSTAL!   —Yours truly, F.C.C.)

Useless for any practical purpose
i.e. unemployable for clear transmission

So it was the wrong tree; the school remains
>>&

There's a library not far away
Also brick but under vines with slick blueblack poison berries
A mansard roof thanks to Mr. Carnegie

Mama said: "You don't HAVE to believe EVERYTHING they
>tell you in school—think for yourself a little bit!"

The library: A house of correction

81

There is a boardinghouse
Far far away
Where they serve hash & beans
Every Saturday

Intermezzo

O how those boarders yell
When they hear that dinnerbell
O how the boarders yell
Far far away

Teeter-totter   Contemplate the schoolhouse
Bread & water   Look at the library

chestnuts

DOTE

I go home again all the time
It nearly drives me dotty but I go & will go again

. . . Far away

& it's as real as anything else
However changed in many particulars—specifically
The love & hate gone out of it leaving what the Friends call
"A concern"
                    (is it properly "compassion"?)

DOTE

I forget how Tobit saw again
          neither school nor library
          not that kind of ignorance
He had to bring some story
Tell the truth on at least one
Occasion or subject
He had to DO
                    something first & then the Angels
                    The Archangel Raphael, I think?
                    brought him eye-cups

Telling you I'm paralyzed—
Inside a thin cast of seagull lime—
None of that was true for more than a minute (vile
                                    hyperbole!)
You are the ones walking around inside your shells, I soar
Face down high above the shore & sea

                          Ho ho, *skreak*, &c.
                    Come live on salmon & grow wise!

                          22:ix–28:ix:58

I Return to San Francisco

Scared?

M.M. says, I just found out what's wrong with me
            is fear & it scares the shit out of me

Jo B.,   Intellectual comics, they've taken EVERYTHING
          there's nothing left—jokes about Proust, Joyce, Zen
          Buddhism, it's the end of culture, the world . . .

And J.W., What are we going to do?

          I said, I'm going home & start typing
          I'm tired of nothing happening

                          *

          CONTINUATION, IN ANOTHER KEY

E N O U G H , I'm tired of sound & silence, the alternation of
                                          opposites
The weak middle sagging between both
            ALL RHYTHMS
There must be an eruption, a boil, an imposthumation
            Come to a head

Horace Walpole writes to one of his boyfriends, "at least
write & tell me that you have nothing to write me about"

So I take off down the street with my bed on my back
   easy as not

The time element is the least important:
   Strobe-light photograph shows a one-drop milk-splash

   A solid coronet shape, the walls faithfully reflecting the light
      which was faster than the crown-world's history . . .
   How long did it take to build that circular wall of milk
      its pointed towers
            & each of them transforming into a satellite droplet
            heading out to make smaller, briefer crowns?

Our notion of time, of history . . . what's wrong?

Figuring it all out again
            A, B, C . . .
         1, 2, 3 . . .
We don't really GET what it is, looking at it drives it
      someplace else (consider the eye in the act of looking;
      can we see it?)
Only fair-sized lumps make any sense at all—
            (the idea of "critical mass")
Form patterns that suggest a moral, with fright, sleep, the skin
   as LIMIT?

                           *

Too hot this evening, I whistle for a wind
      hilltop bayview bridgewink Golden Gate
& breeze from the South green marble apartmenthouse lobby wall

                           *

CLT,   A lovely day
         Rain has washed the car all beautifully clean
         & the battery is completely dead

                           *

Something on this page about waterlilies
& how these lines are distant mountain ridges seen
From across the desert, the old "*horreur du vide*" routine

                              *

While I wait, a shining beige/brown chevron clothes-moth
                settles on the bedspread
Eyebrow-hair antennae heavy beads under the lens
Moves now to the wall

                    this would happen easier if I got laid oftener
                    stayed away from crowds
                    worked very hard at it

Long hair from my left eyebrow just fell out
                One inch long
I hate putting it in the ashtray

              or maybe I'm trying to tell about it without looking
                                                        at it
                  remembering it all wrong or some doctored cut version

            I saw a butterfly set in clear unbreakable plastic block
            I start out with a rubber balloon & a live bug
            Blow up the balloon & this bug
                        flies around outside . . .
            Something entirely different, a failure, a mistake . . .
            What I want you to see is yet another lovely
                        & inexplicable thing

                              *

something complicated going on in the kitchen
turn off the gas & the stove (cooling)
exchanges heat for noise & motion

                              *

RIGHT NOW
If I had a pet rabbit right now
I'd pinch it & make it squeak
NOBODY pays any attention to me & I really need LOTS
of loving

*

Since you won't come to me
I'll think about mountain cypress trees
Something has taken the bark away the wood weathers orange &
twisty

*

While I'm looking for sleep
Bright shapes of day bedevil my eyes
identification with one's own "good" qualities
and vice-versa—where does that put you?
identification with neither—what you call that?
or with both?
With ANYTHING ELSE . . . shape, form, quality,
mode
what then?
"What was your original face, before you were conceived?"

*

same routine as above, with respect to our *common*
space/time continuum?

*

IDENTIFICATIONS : : : : RESONANCES. . . . ? (*vide* Erwin
Schroedinger)

*

while I'm looking for sleep's bright devils the day of the fly the
morning's blank dissociations cannons & waterclocks sunny towered
fugal castles torrents of malicious corn & fleet shadows of a dear
remembrance falling by

*

Naturally there's no recollection of your low forehead peculiar
Cheekbones & curious nose
　　in the silk-paintings from Tun Huang
　　the rock-sculptures at Ellura

The complications of living with love
& without it—an absolutely even balance?

Spending more hours asleep than awake, happy than unhappy
Talking more than listening

Do we breathe in one more time than we breathe out?

Julian Huxley is worried about the population explosion
If he understood what I'm saying here
He'd come at me personally, a pair of shears held low

　　　　WHAT *IS* (properly) THE QUESTION?

　　a false proposition (?):　All any of us wants is a simple life;
　　　　　　　　　　　A simple mind invents a complicated life.

　　　　　　　　　　　*

BIRD WORLD
　　　　J.M., A bird's head (while it sits on a perch) stays
　　　　　　in one place its body
　　　　　　moves from side to side, up & down, conditioned
　　　　　　(ORIENTED) to operate in 4-dimensional space

CARNELIAN MARABOU EYE

　　　　Something will happen if we let it
　　　　Everything happens no matter what we decide

　　　　　　　　　　*

Now dreams are nearer, brighter, louder & sleep a progression of
paralyses difficult pose/gestures (infinitely long-lasting) with waking
breaks between them recalling summer in lookout as in poem,
"conscious even while sleeping"—& after waking the dream continues somewhere "underneath" my present "consciousness"?

I keep getting takes on the stone face with live glass eyes—from 1) statue at Jo B.'s house, & 2) dream wherein it was a significant figure, 30:III:59

20:iii:59–15:iv:59

All About Art & Life

a compulsion to make
          marks on paper

whatever good or bad

          "& as for meaning
          let them alone to mean
          themselves"

or that I'm ill
out of adjustment
not relating with real situation in living
room I just left below
       i.e. two other people, friends of mine
       reading books

a shock out of the eye-corner
Dome & cornices of Sherith Israel
       blue sky & fog streaks
       (reminiscences of Corot, Piranesi)

          to mean themselves
          Adam & Eve & Pinch-Me

walks out of silence, monotony
many colors dangling & sparkling

       (TINKLE?)

there.   You know.   Uh-huh.
          we kill ourselves making it

PICTURE: a wood-engraving by Bewick
                     GIANT WOOLY COW

PICTURE: children, their faces concealed
                     by their hats which are heads which are
                     flowers

PICTURE: Leonardo: *Madonna & Child, with
                     S. Giovanbattista*

PICTURE: Ladies in marble palace with fountains
                     located high in Canadian Rockies a peacock
                     light the color of burning incense

PICTURE: a room, & through the door a hallway with
                     a small round or octagonal window

PICTURE: 2 Bedouins praying in sand/ocean a camel
                     with square quizzing-glass on head

PICTURE: All of us when we were young before you
                     were born

2 PICTURES: Battle scenes (medieval-type) in high plaster
                     relief curved glass not lens, no sound

LARGE PICTURE: C. S. Price: Indian women who might be
                     mountains picking huckleberries in moun-
                     tains that might be Indian women

PICTURE: 5 Persimmons (Chinese)

52 PICTURES: (Mexican provenance) playing-cards, each
                     one different, repellent & instructive

PICTURE: 360 degrees: the world is outdoors it is both
                     inaccessible & unobtainable
                     we belong to it

. . . most of your problems will disappear if you sit
still (privately, *i.e.* in solitude) 1 hour per day
without going to sleep (do not speak, hum or whistle
the while) . . .

The orders of architecture we are to suppose symbols of the
human intellect & inspiration (in this case, severe Romano-Judaic)

"a symbol doesn't MEAN
anything
it IS
something . . . relationship of that kind doesn't exist
except in the old philosophy whose vocabulary
you insist on using . . ."

MANIFESTS itself
whether I write or not
we call it good, bad, indifferent as
we feel ourselves exalted or brought down
it has its own name but never answers
never at home
& we want a stage for our scene
(wow)
as if Shakespeare
LIED

all of us end up

Zero for Conduct

You bet.

Why bother to say I detest liver
                 & adore magnolia flowers
Liver keeps its flavor the blossoms
            drop off
                     & reappear, whoever
cares, counts, contends

I said to the kitten rolling the glass
     "Kitty, you're stupid"
Thoughtlessly: the cat's growing
     exercising & I merely talking to hear my head rattle

What opinion do you hold on Antinomianism?
It makes me nervous trying to remember what it was
& which side of the argument Milton took
     also rattles
           Not I love or hate:

WHAT IS IT I'M SEEING?

          &

WHO'S LOOKING?

It comes to us straight & flat
My cookie-cutter head makes shapes of it

        CHONK: "scary!"
        CHONK: "lovely!"
        CHONK: "ouch!"

             but any of us is worth more
             than it
             except that moment
             it walks out of me, through me

& you ask, Where does it come from
Where did I go

Some people got head like a jello mold
It pours in & takes one shape only
Or instantly becomes another flavor
                    raspberry to vanilla
                    strawberry to vanilla
                    orange to vanilla, etc.

Some legendary living ones can take it or leave it alone
They go on planting potatoes, writing poems, whatever they do
Without hangups
Minimum bother to themselves & all the rest of the world
And anyone observing them a little may
                    turn all the way
                         ON

Meanwhile, psychologists test us
                    & get a bell shaped curve
They know something or other I could tell them any time

All this is merely
                    GRAMMAR

The building I sit in
A manifestation of desire, hope, fear
As I in my own person, all the world I see . . .

Water drops from tap to sink
Naturally the tap's defective or not completely "OFF"
Naturally I hear: My ears do what they're made for

                    (a momentary reflection—will my brain
                    suffer a certain amount of water erosion
                    while I sleep?- - -)
&
                    OUT

                                        28:viii:59–9:ix:59

92

Since You Ask Me
(A *Press Release*, October 1959)

This poetry is a picture or graph of a mind moving, which is a world body being here and now which is history . . . and you. Or think about the Wilson Cloud-chamber, not ideogram, not poetic beauty: bald-faced didacticism moving as Dr. Johnson commands all poetry should, from the particular to the general. (Not that Johnson was right—nor that I am trying to inherit his mantle as a literary dictator but only the title *Doctor*, *i.e.*, *teacher*—who is constantly studying). I do not put down the academy but have assumed its function in my own person, and in the strictest sense of the word—*academy*: a walking grove of trees. But I cannot and will not solve any problems or answer any questions.

My life has been spent in the midst of heroic landscapes which never overwhelmed me and yet I live in a single room in the city— the room a lens focusing on a sheet of paper. Or the inside of your head. How do you like your world?

Awake a moment
Mind dreams again
Red roses black-edged petals

8:v:59

BRAINCANDY
1952-1965

Late Afternoon

I'm coming down from a walk to the top of Twin Peaks
A sparrowhawk balanced in a headwind suddenly dives off it:
An answer to my question of this morning

27:viii:64

Bleakness, Farewell

7–10:v:64, revised 26:i:65

N O T E , that I read a slightly different version of this text at a public
reading in San Francisco in June, 1964. That reading was taped &
broadcast later over Radio Station KPFA in Berkeley, & later still, over
Radio Station KPFK in Los Angeles.

P.W.

I was haunted for several days in a row by an imaginary pair of
almost identical Siren voices—they spoke inanities in a drawling
whine—they were American highschool girls—for days I heard no
more than the exchange "Hi, Marlene"; "Hi, Maxine," and the
almost outraged complaint "I've got to go to the LIBRARY!"
(This last word, of course, fits into an earlier poem of mine where
I say, "the library—a house of correction.") Is it surprising that
the message they had for me was a political one? It's considerably
more surprising that I can't remove their voices, their silly conversation, from the midst of this really quite serious text. Do I
apologize—and to whom. What if I am a stranger here, "I don't
feel at home in this world any more," just as the song says.

A friend of mine made up the following routine: "You are a
stranger here. You find our practices offensive? It is our practise
to be offensive to strangers." I feel the same way.

∗

  "Hi, Marlene."
  "Hi, Maxine. Where you going?"
  "I've got to go to the
    LIBRARY!"

∗

Americans are people who own real estate in Ohio.
Real estate possesses a mystical charge which is lost

if the real estate be sold to a Negro,

a Chinaman, a Jew

Americans want a product—any product—whether they have real estate or not.

If the product is ugly enough, poisonous enough and expensive enough, all Americans will buy it—they will cut down on food, sex, curiosity and even their own fits of paranoia in order to spend more money on the product.

Americans never change. They never die. They believe (while they sink majestically—real estate, products, eternity and all—into the giant pit of garbage and shit which they've produced and sold to each other and to an eager world) BELIEVE

> "Oh, yes, it's a mess, and some day I expect it will all blow up or collapse—but it will last my time—until it does, I'm just doing my job and making the payments every month and enjoying what little pleasures I can, that's all I know, that's all I can do."

*

> "Hi, Marlene."
> "Hi, Maxine. Where you going?"
> "I've got to go do my geometry."
> "So do I—let's do geometry together. Shall we go to my house or to your house?"

*

Americans joke about visible changes, "I got silver in my hair, gold in my teeth and lead in my ass," but they call each other "kid" or "the girls" or "the boys, the gang"—sinking into the pit which they have digged, the Bible says, for another, sinking into the grave, never change, even in the grave—where at last each of them has become a product, masterpieces of the embalmer's art (they don't know, once they've had his treatment, that the embalming fluid wasn't full strength, a mixture of low-grade chemi-

cals) they lie serenely rotting, prepared to meet the God they spent
a lifetime cheating & mocking, with confidence, with a smile,

*

        "Hi, Marlene."
        "Hi, Maxine. Where you going?"
        "I'm going to baby-sit at the Watsons. Why
           don't you come over and we'll watch television
           together while we do our Latin?"

*

"Happy to meet you, Sir. I am the President of the First National
Bank, Chairman of the Board for American Amalgamated, president of the Alumni Association, a deacon of the church, father of
eight, a veteran of the late wars . . ."

God says, "Charmed, I'm sure. If you'll just step this way, Sir,
you'll find your accommodations all prepared. (It turns out that
God is actually Franklin Pangborn, the hotel clerk in old movies)
"Your loved ones are awaiting you there. Please go right on in and
make yourself comfortable—unless you'd care to take a look
through this little window into Hell, where you can see your worst
enemies all frying and screaming?"

In heaven, all Americans are Chairman of the Board, from
10 until 3 every day without fail. They are serious men who have
many great responsibilities. They are quite often called to the
White House where God consults with them privately about how
to run the Universe—for even in heaven there are Problems: the
Jews keep wanting to set up a separate homeland to be called
SHEOL. The Chinamen keep insisting that they've been defrauded
in some fashion or other, their complaints are obscure (their command of English has never been of the best) and the Negroes want
to rest, to be left alone—why must they still be janitors in those
heavenly office buildings and banks, why must they be chauffeurs
and housemaids and cooks and Pullman porters and comic garden-
ers to these Americans? There are rumors of a heavenly crisis.
Appalling quantities of Bourbon whiskey and expensive cigars pour
into the celestial skyscrapers. The White House is illuminated
night and day, the air crowded with angelic messengers and light-

ning bolts. THE WALL STREET JOURNAL prints cheerful looking graphs on its front page—Walter Lippmann writes ominous columns—Gabriel Heatter says there's good news tonight, but shall we believe him? H. V. Kaltenborn sounds grim . . .

*

> "Hi, Marlene, this is Maxine. Mama says I've got to stay home. After you're through babysitting, why don't you come over and we'll set each other's hair?"

*

As for myself, I know nothing about the Thirties, I was in grade school and high school all that time, living in a small town in Oregon. My father had a job all through the Depression, he kept the rent paid and brought us enough food and clothing. My folks joked about not having a pot to pee in or a window to throw it out of (i.e. they didn't own their own house.) They said that Mr. Roosevelt was ruining the country, paying people to lean on shovels, collect Relief while Eleanor ran wildly about the country meddling into everything.

During the 40's I was a soldier. I was still in the army when I turned 21 and I voted for Mr. Roosevelt in the election of 1944, against Governor Dewey more than *for* Mr. Roosevelt and Harvard and the Porcellian Club and Hyde Park—an absentee ballot. Late in the 40's the Government paid my way through college—the shovels were hidden away: we leaned on professors and books and beer. "We were educated above our station in life," Thompson says, "that's the trouble with us all." We were not quite starving in L.A. in the 50's.

Now it is the 60's in San Francisco, there is temporarily a room to live in, sometimes I have my own food to cook, but most of the time I have to bum it off my friends—food, and money to buy stamps to mail out manuscripts—I go on writing to pass away the time, to forget about being hungry, to forget the Revolution . . . like the song says, "I don't feel at home in this world any more." I try to illuminate it, transform it with poetry, with vision, with love—but actually, here I am, climbing the barricades, making inflammatory speeches, writing nasty letters to the *Chronicle*, stopping strangers in the street to demand total freedom & love . . .

They say, "What are you so excited about? Everything's going to be all right. The law, the Constitution is on your side, the Government is sympathetic, US Steel doesn't hate anybody, the Telephone Company is your friend, the PG & E only wants progress and a better life for everybody."

*

"Hi, Marlene."

"Hi, Maxine. Did you hear about the Revolution?"

"Yeah. My father has moved into the bomb shelter out in the back yard. Mother says not to worry, he'll come out by 8 o'clock tonight, his bowling team has a tournament."

"Yeah. *My* mother said I had to go to school, anyway."

"Yeah. That's what *my* mother said. I have to go to school, she's going to run for Congress, can you imagine?"

*

In America, it's actually the 30's AGAIN—only without Mr. Roosevelt, without Senator Borah, without John L. Lewis, without Wendell Willkie. Fred Allen is dead. Heywood Broun is dead—whatever happened to Dorothy Thompson? The World Wars are happily forgotten . . . something to do with the Duke of Marlborough. China no longer exists, except as a story, just like the Middle Ages before Marco Polo. Japan is a quaint foreign land full of cherry blossoms, inhabited entirely by small beautiful girls dressed in robes of gorgeous colored silk. Europe mostly disappeared in the war except for the Olivetti Corporation and the Volkswagen industry. India, Russia and Africa have all gone bad and will soon cease to exist, like China. Mexico and South America grow dimmer every day. Canada is for hunting trips and summer vacations, having been annexed to the US about 1960.

101

"Everything is fine, except for these embarrassing scenes in restaurants, automobile showrooms, the Palace Hotel, the New York World's Fair—people say they want freedom—haven't they got it? Instead of working, aren't they out there marching up & down making fools of themselves, destroying private property, getting locked up in jail? Freedom from what? All they want is license —an undisciplined mob who doesn't want to work, who just wants to GRAB everything—driving down property values . . ."

*

WHAT I WANT IS FREEDOM FROM THE PAST, FROM THE THIRTIES, FROM FAKE MORALITY, FAKE RELIGION, FAKE LEARNING. FREEDOM FROM THE PRODUCT FREEDOM FROM THE WHITE HOUSE AND THE BOARD OF DIRECTORS. FREEDOM FROM FAKE LEADERSHIP BY FAKE CRYPTO-LENINIST/TROTSKYITE/ STALINIST INTELLECTUAL POLITICOS I WANT FREEDOM FOR EVERYBODY NO MATTER WHAT COLOR SHAPE OR PERSUASION

but best of all, freedom also
from everybody—I don't want anybody to be
kicked around, I don't want to kick anybody
I want freedom to do my own work

I WANT TO GET DOWN OFF THESE BARRICADES & GO WALKING IN THE WOODS LET GERODIAS OUT OF JAIL! GET SIQUIEROS OUT OF PRISON! ALL POWER TO MARTIN LUTHER KING, ALLEN GINSBERG, DIANE DI PRIMA, LE ROI JONES, JULIAN BECK, TRACY SIMS, CORE, SNCC, AND FSM

LET THE REVOLUTION
PROCEED.

I resign with pleasure from the presidency of the First National Bank, as Board Chairman for American Amalgamated, from the Alumni Association, the DAR, my deaconry—
LET THE TERRESTRIAL PARADISE, THE GARDEN OF EARTHLY PLEASURES THE NEW HEAVENS AND GOLDEN AGE

BEGIN!

The Great Beyond Denver

The pattern for the trip.
I put crux ansatta in my mouth.
Ava Gardner lends me emeralds.
The pyramid slowly rises from the ground.
      O Rā Divine!
      O sand eternal!
At first daybreak the River Platte appears.

                      18:i:64

Clean Song

Last night's guests arrive in the morning
Last night's guests
                arrive in the morning
Last night's guests arrive in the morning
                    in the morning
"And Ile go to bed at noone."

                      18:i:64

A Botanickal Phrenzy

Terror and horror
Sharp straight green leaves
Rooted in my chest pass upwards
Through my throat and out
Through the top of my head

                      18:i:64

Papyrus Catalogue

Part XLI

Holy Cow

Part XLII

I thought your girl friend
was in there.

Part XLIII

Will it spoil? It was all discolored. No no.
Freezing darkens it. That's the fat. I keep it
a whole week sometimes. I keep it in there to
season it.

Part XLIV

The Life and Times of
Marc-Antoine Charpentier

Part XLV

(This part is lost.
(That fish ((*sc.*, letos-fish)) ate it—actually Part XIV?

Part XLVI

Have you seen that white mug with blue flowers
painted on the side? I saw Jay drinking coffee out
of it last night.

Part XLVII

Have you seen those towels that used to be in here?
They're in among this junk. Here they are (LEAVE
THEM THERE!) on the floor. They were set on
top of the pile of old newspapers. Why couldn't he
look for them himself?

Part XLVIII

There were only 13 parts in the first place,
excepting that one the fish made away with.

Part XLIX

I am not responsible.
I decline the nomination.

Part L

Better times are coming
Bye and bye.

Part LI

Tulips, lilacs, irises and snapdragons live in a May-basket. I made it for Miss Hillsdon.

Part LII

Some lemons.
"Dear Anthony West."
Some domes in the distance.
"Dear Mr. Tennyson."

Part LIII

culminates.
"If nominated, I shall not run. If I am elected I shall not serve."

Part LIV

CANCELED

Part LV

Varicose veins.
Lumbago.   Sciatica.

Part LVI

High.

Part LVII

H E I N Z

Part LVIII

Coughing.

Part LIX

CENSORED

Part LX

William Rowan Hamilton
He figured it was there and that it would all add up. It took a century to do it.

Part LXI

Aggravation. As good as gold or platinum emeralds and rubies and sapphires opal garnet and pearl. What I'm afraid of is, I don't think it's going to work and I don't know why. Hey you know what? I've got rubber cement. Aggravation. Why don't he hang himself?

13:i:64

Theophany

Pig-face gods nudge each other, snickering
Pretend they don't smell our incense
They haven't yet noticed that I've fitted each of them with
        pig heads, brains of Americans 15 years old today

29:xii:63

Winter Jelly

Now great winter falls
New Year's full moon blur window fog

Words in books drop slowly over brainwheel paddles which stand
Clear white ice moon sparkle

28:xii:63

Some Kind of Theory

". . . what I know and then go beyond that
far as I can," Duncan is supposed to say

I, however, know nothing, I must look for everything,
I come up with all the wrong things (pudding, tickets,
crystals, maguey) and many which are uselessly beautiful and
wise which is to say discrete, disparate planets of different color
and variously interesting orbits, the formulae for which, expressed in mathematical terms and bright sticky honey

bees have built their home in my orrery

23:xii:63

Re-Take 20:xii:63 from 7:iii:63

Imagine the first part all written out in French:
>   Do I have to choose again? Well, I
>   choose the beauty and frightful horrors of
>   this world

*

>   endless joke

*

In English, now:
>   Puke, unlimited
>   Quantities

*

PUKE

*

several cubic yards of indigestible notions
remnants, thread, ric-rac, hooks and eyes,
buttons, frogs and zippers

*

not digestible by this particular system
they are theoretically
>   soluble

Last Part of an Illustrated Children's Book in a Fever Dream

there. How all have some. My word yes. All about chocolate.
You A R E standing on my foot.

———*———

Elephants. Inside. Good heavens, yes. The quantity.

Are you quite sure. Good grief. Good heavens yes. Here we are. They're surely inside.

All about have some, that's what it is. Distinctly a pleasure, yes. One does see them there— A magnitude of somewhat huge proportion—glued inside.

Some have long legs indeed—so that their backs bulge against the lid, most decidedly we are /no/ certainly not frightened— we would not alarm them, good heavens no. Ho ho.

Please don't come any closer.

Oh hello there are you.

Curiously endeavour.

    internally.

      my goodness yes.

———

strings all up the inside that was the deportment of it. My head. mess.

      Sybil Gurton
      Lady Chiswick
       Telfer
      anti snake
      antique snake.
        the revelry—'rill/a/raw'
      sacred scared propane blue flame

slide up the inside walls they follow each other around flat and curving towards the white hot light in the center/top. Good heavens yes. What a spectacle, you never seen a show like it before, most ungodly sight, I assure you. Crumbs/crumpets/ to a fare ye well. Here they are. Didn't I tell you? Didn't I say? Consternations. Leaking all over everything behind the door/ the contents all loose and soggy saggy soaky. That's oil for you. Depend on it every time. Scornfully. The brutes. Mess. Allocution plague. You pretend not to understand Africa. Absurd.

Avocado plants spring up out of the umbrella pot. Exotic birds. Horrible feet. What do you expect after all. Don't be unreasonable.

My word yes. You don't say. On the inside behind the door/
that was the definition of/

——————*

Bottled up. Buckled down. Quite so. Slide 8 cap 2 there you are
slick as a whistle quick as a wink dropsy daisy.

——————*

animal bundle, a ghastly error but not a mistake.
Burdensome, yes. Inevitably so.
After all I told you about Micronesia.
There they blandly go.
Messages of the hot fog star.

——————*

The Reverend Mr. Shebeare
He saw what he thought was a good thing. He wanted it. He
contrived to get it. Some people can do that./ Why haven't I
learned how?/ You only mean that you never use the word "con-
trive" in connection with any of your own thoughts or actions.
Certainly not.

——————*

Leaded glass—the guiltily broken useless pretty fragments all saved
and newly beautiful window.

——————*

Great living faces of terror, fury, eyes rolling—these are clips from
Eisenstein—what I see is the cracked and crumbly plaster of the
wall becoming invested with gnashing teeth no lips as yet the wall
of cracker crumbs—HORROR—about to speak, about to walk
forward all crumby to grab—the Horror is suffering vast anguish.
It wants to lay it on me. I don't want to hear about it although
I am sorry for the Monster . . .

"How shall you accomplish this task?"
"I have a system. Just you watch me. You just watch. You
don't get in the way, now!"

16:xii:63

Whistler's Mother

Mother and Ed are out in the car
Wait til I put on some clothes
Ed's in a hurry. He hasn't eaten since this morning
Wait til I put on some clothes.
Mother and Ed are out in the car. Do you have any clothes on
yet?
Let me come in.
Wait til I get some clothes on
Ed is impatient. He and mother are waiting. Can I come in?
Wait til I put on some clothes
Mother and Ed are out in the car
Wait til I get into some clothes
Can't I come in? Aren't you dressed yet?
Wait til I put on some clothes
Mother and Ed are out in the car. Can I come in?
Wait til I get on some clothes.

14:xii:63

How Was Your Trip to L.A.?

Here in the North, our houses and their appointments
are old-fashioned and a little inconvenient. There's no doubt
that our lives here are morally
superior to those of the Southern people.

In the South there are many cars
The plumbing works, the gas stoves are better
Food's cheaper and the sun is warm
Unfortunately the air in that place is poisoned.

Our city tends to disappear in cold weather.

12:xii:63

The Walkers' Patio: Giant Plant

Silent an architecture
formal speech of green
flat concrete smooth and clean
the great plant grows out of it:
Music, proclamation, a building
What it does to the light, creating darkness
What light does to it, expanding
                    heading out,

Leaving
Not in a hurry
wraps space around it in a particular way
a modulation, a harmonic progression

Leaving the ground, it may
grow past the roof or not
now the papyrus is gone

Its genes require this order
Sequence in space, dots of geometry
                    where exist?

(A terrible mistake: "Dots & squiggles justify the air & space
                    I occupy")

Geometry is the inside of my head
the plant has its own shape
working out (as I say)
Whatever outside maybe
Those giant leaves

                                        7/8:xii:63

A Recall

Color of the Sun
Color of the Moon
Color of the Dog

That was yesterday animal fire
Druids burning in wicker cages
To the Lady of All Wild Beasts

25:xi:63

Salamander

Behind my eyes (looking the opposite way)
I see roaring flames in back of the cracked iron furnace door
Fire jag flake speed

       (Olson asked me, "Who ever got the idea that you
                were in-
                      telligent?")
I feel myself burning in moony flames and sleep,
Burnt by lunar fires

23:xi:63

Homage to WBY

after you read all them books
all that history and philosophy and things
what do you know that you didn't know before?

Thin sheets of gold with bright enameling

23:xi:63

Breughel: "The Fall of Icarus" 20:ix:63

Beyond what figure will you refuse to go?
　　　　Beyond that one which stands
　　　　　　　　unseen
　　　　　　behind the grille

Let us proceed in some other direction, sixteen
　　　　　　　　pages, to learn
It is the wrong direction

Lost　　down
　　　　　　　　air　　sand　　glass
　　　　　　　　　　　　breeze
Strayed & stolen away away
　　　　　　　　　　　Where's the edge
　　　　　　　　　　　Where are the *neiges d'antan*
　　　　you bet.

The Double Take

I want leeway
I want room to move
November tree with scarlet flowers
Don't crowd me
Bluey-green distant hilltops a picture
I know it comes out of the water
Angel Island the foot of Steiner Street

Admit these pleasures
Ordinarily unseen, I accept them
　　　　demand more

And I need space and time away from you
Demand more, higher quality
I can't stand to look at you,

Hear what you say, watch how you behave
Your insolence, your ignorance

I must have distance,
Isolation, silence,
A vacation from your monstrous beauty

My infinite lust for you.

17:xi:63

To a Nervous Man

One day they'll come whooping after you
False hair and gold eyelashes flapping in the wind
Glom and grope you with their dainty painted pinkies
Hale you away, clutched to their foam-rubber tits
To FAIRYLAND their prisoner forever!

15:xi:63

St. Francis Lobbies Allen G.

unsuspected hairpins & inside Gaffney receptions
          Who lost the 7-year itch?

          "Mr. Harry Lane!"
          "Mr. Harry Lane!" is
          a passenger ST.
          FRANCIS PRAY FOR
          THE PENGUINS
              TEACH US

KARMEL KORN
ELECTRIC DRILL
DRAFTY DOOR

F U R   F U R   F U R
          Jewels
                    (fake)
Where's the Russia Philology?
          scrolls and fur

12:xi:63

Native Speech

"Red-ass," they used to say
Meaning "home-sick"—
Really wanting to be
          AWAY
     from this place, the Army, the war,
Old enough to guess home's gone
               if you went there.

3:xi:63

Roxie Powell

Impotent rhapsody
Forty pages of Hiahleah
     you know Alan Russo.

22:x:63

My Songs Induce Prophetic Dreams

15:x:63–19:i:65

". . . Books, texts, magazines, are tombs . . . tombs that eventually will be
opened. *The duty* I say again THE DUTY of the writer, of the poet,
is not to go shut himself up as a coward in a text, a book, a magazine from
which he will never emerge again but on the contrary to go out to shake
up to attack the public spirit . . . if not of what use is he? And why was he
born? . . . the quest for a speech that any roadmender or dolt would have
understood. . . ."

—Letter: Antonin Artaud to René Guilly,
Feb. 7, 1948. Translated by Guy Wernham

NECESSITY

    is the mother of invention

INVENTION leads to great
    wealth, responsibility,
    and shady politics, if there's
    really LOTS of money in-
    volved.

Greatness is all.
Use autosuggestion in order to
obtain money and power and
energy.
I shall be 41 years old on 20:x:64

                    *

Self-indulgence.
Retroactive self-indulgence:
      ?
    rêve d'amour

                    *

Work again.
find a loss has been
    sustained.

(Later)
>the city goes with us when we travel
>>(first line of another poem)
Literary muffins
>they skate!
>a mistake for Rexroth?
it must be in the elevator
>>do not bunch   bunch bind
too sharp   bind or sag   droop or sag
>no iridium   try to write carefully.   *Bundestag?*

*

It's very hard to work when I'm hungry and it doesn't seem
likely that I shall have anything to eat today . . . some time
next week, yes. I have a tentative dinner invitation
for Monday . . . but that's merely possible
it's just as probable that I
shall receive $10,000 in the mail on Monday morning.
Transform all this into beauty and love and the liberation
of all sentient beings.

*

"I WANT, I WANT!"

Pleiade editions

Baudelaire	Rabelais
Rimbaud	Montaigne
Mallarmé	(Pascal?)

all of Proust
>>although I know scarcely 3 words of the French
>>Language
>(all that I have—& it lies here getting dusty
>—I needed, I still must have beside me—
>>while I sit alone at this marble table
>>>To listen, to wait.)

*

ENLIGHTENMENT   TRANSFORMATION

REALIZATION   CREATION

CONCEPTION ''E N E R G Y
                             i s Eternal Delight.''

May 10 to May 16, I ate 9 times—the rest of America
enjoyed 12 more meals than that,
during the same period. I am
fatter than anybody. This is
the law, that karma is more real
                             than I am?
POWER   ENERGY   PROSPERITY   ABUNDANCE

*

Ten minutes after noon
I saw the moon beside the clouds

              boredom and fright

*

    69 lines
$ .50 per line
$34.50, if Mr. Rago were to find the poem
              "convincing"

━━━━━━━━━━━━━ _fff_ ━━━━━━━━━━━━━
              decrescendo ⟶

*

        Blind counters, obliterated loops
badly designed "s"'s.   "So much for
Buckingham."
              "TROP DE MOUTARDE"
              Black Starr & Gorham

*

On Market Street
White glove pretty girl waits for bus
        holds a letter addressed to me—
At least she spells my name correctly. I wonder who she is?

                    *

            One strike against this day is that it's Friday.

                    *

Believe me, he won't try that again very soon.

                    *

            William Butler Yeats
the magic set fire to the curtains
the whole drawingroom filled with smoke
Blind urge to power which is blind
            ending in a heavy morphine habit,
            Aleister Crowley dead at 101

                    *

            once burned
            twice shy
        W. Butler Yeats was more powerful
than the Empress of India; however he wasn't too sure
        the spirits came to Mrs. Yeats in a Pullman car
(Anyone who's spent the night in such a machine might remark,
"It's a wonder that's all which arrived.")
        WB wrote all of it down, it was so reassuring
Empress of India bedamned! The world is a giant twisted swindle.
Or spindle. WBY in total control! The gyres! The gyres!
    He lived with this knowledge all the rest of his life.

                    *

I went to sleep in order not to feel hungry and sad
I dreamed of my friends, the Ideal Library,
            baby elephants & food
hungry in my dream

                    *

awake, I'm not sad any more
I have the chance to steal some food.

*

MENU
{
large delectable stars
choice rhododendron vinaigrette
melted mountains
live birds en masse
the whole cheese
}

*

a millionaire!
(one million every week, for life.)
        (tax free)
            TAX FREE $$$
            YOURS   TODAY!
                Hurry on down!

*

One million $$$ a week is just about enough
money to keep me reasonably comfortable.

*

Sign, Divisadero & McAlister Streets:

THELMA'S

SOUL FOOD

*

cover photo for *The Ticket That Exploded*
—is it Burroughs's notion of what a brain cell might be like?

*

I figured, I'll have neither breakfast nor lunch today
But the PIANO will arrive
            Disappointed, I have
            imaginary soup for supper

Snake before eating drinks water
goes for a swim;
fish in the same water become
        snakes

                *

NATIVE SPEECH:
            "I know somebody know you
            and they just talk about you every day."

                *

        illness and weakness
                        no matter how often I look in the pantry
none of that food is mine
            weakness and fear of hunger
how can anybody so fat
                    be hungry, feel
                    hungry?
and not have sense enough to steal
                    something to eat

                ?

            *

My ears the secret forgotten weak point
    hidden passage directly to the Citadel
anointed by snake tongues my ears understand
        all animals and birds

snake slobber (i.e. When I was
            MELAMPUS, "Black Foot")
Elephants mountains & horses, all of them used to have wings
            naturally I want out & away from here
    (e.g. Pe Ell, Washington
                N W
        Wn. & Oreg. direct
    out
            OUT)

Canadians call the back country "the Interior"
       talk about "the Okanogan" as if they were natives
           of Washington State
(N.B., that Pe Ell isn't far from the Chehalis River
      in Lewis County)

*

NATIVE SPEECH:
        "If he never comes back again it'll be too soon."
                or
        "If I never see that place again, it'll be too soon."

*

S. T. Coleridge says, "But love is a local anguish . . ."

*

      accuracy, who needs it? We've GOT
         to have more GAS.

*

Why don't they bring buttermilk. A miracle
that anything appeared: there was nothing,
there was a little but not enough and then
a great deal quite unexpectedly. How
come.   an miracle of Annapurna

*

DISTRACTION

Ann Hatch
James B. Hatch
Sara Hatch
Lew Welch   } a party in Marvelous Marin
Gary Snyder
Assorted young persons

*

this hasn't happened yet. Dear Henry James. Dear
Henry Rasmussen. Cher Henri Matisse. Dear Charles-Henri Ford.

*

Genius

*

Being interested in oneself isn't the
same as self-interest. Rocky Road. Any old port in a storm.

*

Start again. (Great T H U M P in the ceiling,
from the floor above: somebody dropped
a 300-pound boulder)

Let there be food.
Let me eat it & digest it safely.
Let there be food in abundance & variety
Food must come soon.
Start again.
O Annapurna! Send me food in plenty!
Let me eat it & digest it safely.
Let me transform it into poetry & enlightenment!
Let there be food in variety & abundance.
Let food come to me soon.
Start again.
O Annapurna! Hail to you benevolent
goddess. Bring me food.
Start again.
O Annapurna, send me food. I can't think or write
I put the cap on the fountain pen backwards. SVAHA!

*

Dr. Johnson writes to James Boswell,
"Poverty, my dear friend, is so great an evil, and
pregnant with so much temptation, and so much misery,
that I cannot but earnestly enjoin you to avoid it."

*

123

Start again. The fountain pen went mad-dog. I got ink all over my hands. I had to wash & rinse & refill the pen before I could write this.

Start all over. I tremble, my balance
is temporarily affected by some disordering of my bloodpressure or breathing. And I'm hungry. I need quite a lot more food than I've been able to find today. I pray for more & better food for tomorrow for all of us: I don't starve alone. I join all the hungry, the dispossessed

*

NATIVE SPEECH
nailed to a riser in the middle of the front steps
blue enamel sign with raised white letters

NO PEDDLARS OR AGENTS ALLOWED

Round corners, rusty edges

"I'm working my way through college."
"Well, why don't you go back to work?"

*

All new: lilies, "Naked Ladies," which have always been here, now.
All new. Begin again. Lily, soft pink child a few days old.
Magnolia flowers invisible this month, neither new nor old. Start over. Make a continuous fabric, not a string. Try very hard.

*

I have
Three
Friends who
No longer want
To know me

*

Do you know the sad little song of WHERE DO THE FLIES GO, IN THE WINTER TIME?

*

I have no food, no money; therefore, my friends say, I am foolish
and wicked. Are they right? (Who cares?)

*

"Who cares what banks fail in Yonkers,
Long as you got a kiss that conquers?"
so Ira Gershwin says.

*

Wisdom. I must change my character. The flavor, shape smell taste
color must be different. Whizbang.

*

Ezra Pound says, "More writers fail from lack of character than
from lack of intelligence."

*

You always do what you have to do
I'm the one who has to like it—"irregardless,"
as people say

*

Now I am 40, I wish that I had died of my vices, excesses or
violence at the age of 29

*

Songs to induce prophetic dreams
Hum.
Fa la la la.
Take off all your clothes and go to bed.
Untie the window curtains: let them fall in dark
and gentle greeny gloom

Tirra lirra
throbbing muffled roar
"being under ether"
Being, from any other universe

No songs around here, Charley and Ann and
Alan Russo found me asleep

SCANDAL!

place-names in *Le Morte d'Arthur*

*

Songs to induce prophetic dreams
Write them sideways because
They arrive diagonally. (Theory of hyperspace.)
Record them in Roman Letters:
"I number only the sunny hours."
Improve yourself mutually
(cut this OUT)
Klong

*

This is not what I paid lots of money to hear.

*

Rare & fleeting Magic!

*

Rudy Vallee used to sing,
"I'm a dreamer,
Montreal!"
That's what I heard when I was young & unfamiliar with the Maine
dialect of American English.

*

Songs to induce prophetic dreams
sold only for the prevention of disease

*

We are happy when we are slightly uncomfortable
for a long time & can complain about it
afterwards

*

Choose again, choose as often as you like
                    you never get your money back
Money is never the same as you've got or as you've had
You must get more. Get a new batch as often as you can.

                    *

I stay here endlessly, absurdly, nothing prevents my escape, I
must flee very soon, now. Get out of here. Quick.

                    *

Open up in there:
                    Bloom!
Light up a new set of synapses
Long excursion into the pre-frontal lobes
Crawl up out of the thalamus & goose the super-ego
Turn loose the memory circuits
Here we begin

                    *

J. M. Edmonds, *Lyra Graeca*, Vol. III, p. 569, Attic Scolia, #16:
"Drink with me, play with me, love with me, be wreathed with
me; be wild when I am wild, and when I am staid, be staid."

                    *

How many other things can I think of
Beside this alphabet soup,
Whole universes: the finest imaginable powder
                    (fern spores—
                    "*myriad*" is either countless or exactly
                              ten thousand—
                    I mean more)
Fresh air   this evening
          delicious

                    *

          eucalyptus: *that* smell

                    *

and now being quietly at home
Freedom breakthrough: arrival at the pass:
Chill wind, all the world huge silent clean rock,
              lakes and rivers far below
Mountain peaks as far as I can see

                    *

But never cop out to having heard Ben Bernie.
Rudy Vallee was a national hero.
General Voznekov sits at the folding canvas table while shells
and blunker fragments burst around him he writes messages to the
Imperial War HQ, his hand rattles across the page as the sun sets

                    *

I see a poem by Yeats
AFIRE, the flame room blue

                    *

NATURAL FOLK SPEECH:
        "I guess he won't be doing that again right away in such
        a hurry!"

                    *

What may be accomplished. What has
              been done . . . but I swim:
        a pool between rocky shores

                    *

If it were upside down
What color would it be?

                    *

Sir John Maundeville, *Travels*, p. 56:
        "Men say also, that the balm
        groweth in Ynde the more, in
        that desert where the trees of the sun
        and of the moon
        spake to Alisaundre."

                    *

AGGRAVATION

o. o. yeah. yeah.
As good as gold or platinum
emeralds and rubies and sapphires
opal garnet and pearl. What
I'm afraid of is, I don't think
it's going to work and I don't
know why. Hey you know what?
I've got rubber cement. Have you
ever considered hanging yourself, Mr. Warbler?

*

After you've said that
What have you said?

*

translunacy, a communicable form of crazy

*

Despair, hunger, imbecility

*

I must continue to work, nevertheless, there being so much still
unaccomplished, unrealized.

*

fire engines and pigeons and rain
business as usual

*

When can I eat the sardines?

*

When shall I leave?

*

I'm not concentrating. I want to worry about food & money.

                                *

NATIVE SPEECH
        "No, I got married & give up drinking."

                                *

funk drawing
        &   Rage & feather
    feathers   tickle
        &   Republiquelle
strange anatomy   false quim rubber gulch

                                *

McClure says, in conversation,
                ". . . not in the movies any more.
                Quasi-pornographic painting.
                I'd love to see her dance.
                        (a tattoo on her shoulder)
                    Greek woman about 30
                Small unassuming restaurant in Santa
                        Monica near my mother's motel
                                all the movie stars go there
                Except for the whale & porpoise shows
                Marineland is a great big skam."
Nevertheless, I think he enjoyed his trip to L.A.
                "Zip in a motorcycle," he says.
                Mountains of schlock.
                                Lawrence Lipton's at UCLA . . ."
And a final comment on the meth scene, here or there or NYC,
        "Everything that's portable is carried off
        Everything that can't be moved is burned around the edges
        Everything has been stolen."

                                *

NATIVE SPEECH
        "So that's what all that was all about."

                                *

Some flowers won't bear close inspection
Others demand contemplation—for example, a chrysanthemum

*

forget-me-not blossoms the 2nd time this year
eucalyptus fence-posts they set out last month have new
                    grey-green shoots and leaves

Beach pine, black pine roots
          thrust out and return right through the surface of a cliff
                         red chert, Franciscan Series
New grand hydrangea season

*

          While putting away my newly washed clothes I figure,
          I may not live to wear these, but at least they're clean.

*

Katharine Tynan writes that Yeats
          "took to an indiscriminate eating of fungi
          which very much alarmed his hosts"
What he guessed the Druids had been doing in that same part
of the world

*

We shall go interview the cypress trees
representing ourselves to be Gavin Arthur

*

"Just exactly how much damage have you suffered?"
This is a perfect English Alexandrine.

*

What is the real message, the complete
word of those Ancestors
whose voices come to me with
single troublesome sentences?

It's grown very late—I
must require them to put up
or shut up.
                    "I ain't going to hold my breath until you do."
(McAlister & Polk Streets, NE corner)
The top half of the Hall McAlister statue has a new coat of green
patina/algae where I stop walking to write this

                              *

. . . . . . the last part is all laughing & singing . . . . . .

                              *

Beautiful turnips I peel for the soup
Do they smell like nasturtiums
                    or chrysanthemums?
Latin or Greek
                    East meets West
          (nasturtiums are South American)

                              *

          pointy roofs
          Light & cloud shadows fall across them

          Rugged snowpeaks late in August

          I see the worn gummy shingle fakes
                    once had several colors

          Light needles through peppertree threads
                    a prism, a diffraction grating
               Rainbow City, heaven's gate

Friday is Love's Day

                              *

Kilton Stewart writes,
"In order to get a more complete idea of the Bontoc's attitude
towards the high god, Lumawig, I inquired about their beliefs con-

cerning death, and about the prayers which were said at the funeral feast. They told me that often the person who is ill and about to die hears the *anitos* calling him, saying it is better in the mountains . . . their prayers (i.e. those of the relatives at the funeral) tell of the good life in the mountains which the old men have seen in visions, and which the deceased can enjoy if he will go there to live and continue to cooperate on feast days with his living relatives."

*

Great bull hummingbird rules
       the peppertree
Skip-bombs neighbor garden roses

*

Gauzy emerald
goldfinch music
pleasure & delight

---

*

Breathe deeply.
Watch the green curtain.

*

"*Polemonium,* "sky pilot," Haselwood says,
       "that blue flower grows on the highest passes."
I've seen it there myself.

---

*

Condition total/condition LIGHT

THE CODA

The food opera has been sung, a final cymbal crash,
drum thump and gong note remain:

When I'm hungry, I'm free, and I have chosen
freedom at this price, a very small one to pay,
considering the noxious fumes and the mountains of
feculent matter which I'd otherwise be required to
admire, to eat, to digest, to add onto the general dungheap.

It would please a very great number of people if I
should perish from hunger; they'd be ecstatically happy
if I should kill myself by whatever means. I refuse to
give them that satisfaction. Let them accept the responsibility
for doing me in with their banks, their governments, their
wars. I must try to liberate all of them.

5:iv:65

Inside Stuff

Swede-bread honey and tea to breakfast half a canteloupe
Honey inspires prophecy & beneficent wishes, thus:
        Boundless ancient delight for Frank O'Hara
        Kerouac will get the Pulitzer Prize *Visions of Gerard*
        I shall travel to my death in a far country

        Frank has Hart Crane's eyes.

15:x:63

Native Speech

1.

It's all put away now. I don't want to drag it out again,
have to go to work and move all them things—you do it
some other time. I'll show you some other time, not now.

2.

I had it all smoothed over and then he has to come horning in,
Mr. Big has to go to work and get things all galmed up again,
raise a big stink just because he has to be in on everything.

3.

Well that's a fine how de do. Now I've got to take and hunt up
another one of them things to go on there! One of them little—
well, I certainly am put out!

14/19:x–xii:63

Gradus ad Parnassum

Palmetto tree, its shadow on the house corner
And the light upon them:
A single proposition.
           (Where was the sky?)

8:x:63

Somebody Else's Aesthetic

        a Monday when it took all the money I had,
except 2¢, to wash my clothes. I must rob somebody to get food
for supper,

GROSS NATIONAL PRODUCT
$580 BILLIONS
the war in Viet Nam cost $2 MILLIONS today
I must steal this room where I drink my tea and
indulge in self-pity, gross natural projection of a feckless history

                    I digress, there are not enough
things
          in this poem, he says, no flowers, no
          tears, no kisses or come
I have to steal those? I ask.

7:x:63

Illness

Hello what's happening?

*

I'm home alone I've got the horrors

*

Shall I telephone someone and demand that they come
          take care of me?

*

          I am thirsty, I'm suffering
a vitamin deficiency, mental or neural rickets,
     flea-bites, Bradleigh's angina, scrofula
          King Charles's Wain

*

     Yearning for the Happy Despatch, the
Long Goodbye, pull the switch

*

Why don't you come over, we'll take care of you

*

          I'm afraid to leave

5:x:63

The Fourth of October, 1963

A cold hand among the clouds.

Song

That little man
Is a bad little man
That one is a loser

He keeps on blowing
All that low low-grade hay
He's a pusher as well as a user

4:x:63

Mystery Poem,

for a birthday present

I am ragged edge of
Nothing
Uncomfortable lumping along
        (no fun)
Out on the dark
     rough and rocky side

     asteroids
little dark stars
between the orbits of Mars and Juppiter

Which way is straight up or out?

          Leads into
the Milky Way, lots of room inside

Lady of Heaven
her milk for all of us
                    who are the raggedy edge of everything
The center,
Her love forever
All of us remembered.

2:x:63

Social Graces

How the hell are you?

*

Cuckoo. I wouldn't have it
                any other way.

*

                    I imagine,
That everyone takes me seriously at the wrong moments.
It is their privilege.

*

        "Go on and dance with the guy what brung ya!"

28:ix:63

Raging Desire &c.

Meat I ate   M E A T   I ate meat

    "I want to have a banquet, a real banquet, I'd rather spend
    the money on a white tablecloth and great conversation than

fancy food, some roast chickens and white bread but what I
really want is a white tablecloth, a spiritual banquet . . ."
    that was Michael on the telephone

27:ix:63

That Dream

There is the light
                There is the darkness there
    is the terror of shifting proportions
Lattice of timbers
                network of toothpicks
Change of relation, the motion
            directionless
                falling

SCREAM

---

blanket/snare   sweat/sheets   mattress/clutch

OUT

---

    the darkness and space beneath
    unknown dimensions
    unlimited size

7:ix:63

Golden Gate Park

A row of blossoming flowers a row of people
2 lines of people several hundred yards apart
    moving in the same direction.

The space between the individuals in each of the lines is interesting.
The speed of the walkers in each line seems to be the same.

25:viii:63

Vancouver

A secondrate star
An experience of a lower order of magnitude
Catalogued or not in that International Register

*

Coming into an Arab story
A vegetable design

*

Think of the taste and smell of lilac leaves
Pleasure delight & joy, certainly no authority involved.
Lilacs. A space between the house and the lilacs
Which disturbs the projection of shadows on that wall.
The authorities outside—are they anthropologists?
Shadows on us,
Where we stood. Hidden.
We exposed ourselves to each other with explanations.

viii:63

Oh Yes. Vancouver.

Two ladies
Her friends and us
A corruption of sensibilities

viii:63

Where Was I

New desk, old chair
I look at them, hopelessly
Where's the man who writes
          there?

                                        26:vii:63

Letter, to Michael McClure, 11:iii:63

Here I come to sit in the sun
Beside three young redwood trees

A number of bugs, a distant cat,
Some kind of wild geranium leaves all through the grass
Each plant has flowers of a different shape, color, smell
The use is general

Bees make tastier honey from clover than from oak and pine
I mean we like the taste, the bees
Didn't figure we'd find it, they made it for themselves
A secretion of bug saliva: delicious, costly, rare
They were planning to eat it all winter long

But the flowers quite often they made me sneeze and cry
There was no living with them
Strongly sweet grapeclusters of peaseblossom shapes
A bug name, locust

I got no intention fighting City Hall
Only the idea of it
And your depending on its rectitude, its strength
          (it is your father, your mother?)
To lean upon, a church that confirms your belief in it
To ratify your own existence . . .

2.

In addition to the weight of my own displeasure
      (I censure myself by the hour)
Here you are, belittling, putting me down

There's no forgiving or forgetting, no absolution, no resurrection
You'll have me eternally wicked
As you're eternally good, totally righteous, predestined
      to salvation

Do I have time to hate you, to fight you and there's no prize
No crowns and harps, no eternal glory, gold,
Final perfect tyranny?

If I believe all this, I'm truly gone
Totally in blackness, death and hell

*

How much will I pay for Life Eternal?

*

Will you get the money?

*

If it costs too much, I may steal it

*

If it costs too much it may be fake and I can ignore it

*

If it costs too much I may have to build my own
      elsewhere
    (although you'd immediately announce
    that it didn't really exist)
        where's the point, I've lost
myself again . . .

suppose you despise me:
Have your loathing and welcome
Have it and see what it is
Have it until it is knowledge, heaven, enlightenment
Don't have it under any lesser terms
In which case it would become an impediment
To drag you down forever

3.

Your trying to tell me I'm dead why don't I lie down
Is all very well but not necessarily
                    true

And what if all those psychological authorities are
                    right
                    ?
            in a world like this
                    ?
                    *

I heard a man put it plain and nasty:
        "I'm practising bending over further and further every
        day so that when I see that flash I'll be able to lean
        over and kiss my ass goodbye."

                    *

Let it go if it won't holler
Or hold on and squeeze
                while it writhes and heaves

                    *

Make a new profession, they told him
Have you thought of becoming a symphony conductor
Like Leopold Stokowski, marry Greta Garbo
Never write again
                never again
Go away to live in Ohio
Join the Rosicrucians

                              as for me,
                              I'm constitutionally unable to enjoy
                              the taste of Bourbon whiskey
Or there actually is a conspiracy,
A war against us

Why shut up when that's exactly what the Adversary wants
Will even pay you money to dump your paints, typewriter &c
                              down the toilet, give up

                              never again

The number (and intelligence!) of those
Who want to stop us, who wish that we'd keep

                    SILENCE

                HOLY S I L E N C E

their fear
their existence in a state of continuous rage
who don't listen to any of this
Who don't know what it means
Who can't control it, who know that it will outlive them
Certainly   (finally)

                              *

Alternatively, I suppose that you figure
Sell guns to both sides and hope they wipe each other out

No doubt this is the reason so many work in secret
One stores his canvases in a bank vault, nobody sees them
                few people know that he's a painter
Another stays away ten years at a time, "underground," he says

                              *

So impossible
The odds against it
Too high and yet

We must feel free to do with it
Whatever we can, for laughs
                              or for serious,
As the blue-painted wickerwork chair stands
            in the muddy driveway

What will
And what won't go

11:iii:63
23:vii:63

To the Muse

You're late today,
        minaudering among the summer fields
        plunk that little Made-in-Austria Irish harp
        roll your blue eyes and twiddle your pale braids

            (reminiscence of Lillian Gish, Evelyn Thaw, ladies
            you never heard of, immortal fair)

But here you are, yawning
Bored with me. I don't believe you're thinking
            of anything
Yet your fingers are grubby . . .
                cigarets, pills . . .
You sing in a high voice
                    a few lines
            indistinctly, not caring, not even amusing yourself

"I wonder," she says . . . "Oh,
                            never mind."
Smiles at my confusion,
                    my hopeful sudden looking up

                *

Leaf and branch twist and wave in the breeze
This pen swings over the page, an equal
Meaning, neither one intelligible

*

Little black dots
These represent bees
Among the leaves and flowers

*

                    I look at the window frame
                    I learn
                    this
I've deceived myself

*

Here you are now,
Quite unexpectedly, like the death of Proust
      fford says the taxi driver told him,
          "*bien inattendu*"

Walk up and down the room
Pick things up and put them back wrong

I've got no letters
Nobody called up, I can see you want me
To entertain you with pretty speeches

Like the King said,
"Scribble, scribble, scribble, eh, Mr. Gibbon?"

As long as you were coming around here anyway
You might have brought a fairly big basket full of chow

But then you couldn't have carried it yourself
The taxi man might bring it

          "If you can't say something nice

                    *

          "Shut your mouth."

                              8–20:*vii*:63

Three Mornings

1.

Fog dark morning I wait here
Half awake, shall I go back to bed
Somebody next door whistles the *St. Anthony Chorale*
I think of Brahms, a breakfast of chocolate whipcream
     sweet bright pastry
    bits of sugar-blossom in his beard

2.

I wait for breakfast to drop from the sky
foghorns, cluster of churchbells
      pale sun butter
    traffic airplane marmalade
salt & pepper avocado branch squeak on window
    I drink last night's cold tea

3.

Clear bluey-yellow sky—a morning here—
grey cloudbank with lights of Oakland underneath
Baywater blacky blue b o a t l i g h t s
Robin: clink clink clink clank clink
   (6 *Adhyoya, Brihadaranyaka Upanishad.*)

             8:v:63
            15:vii:63

Invocation and Theophany

"Do you know at the offering of which libation the waters become endowed
with a human voice and rise and speak?"
    —*Brihadaranyaka Upanishad,* translated by Max Muller

1.

following them
downwind, scraps of pages,

the sandpipers
white and black

chasing the watermark
wigglers where the sand's wet

go after,
spray left cheek and lens of eyeglasses
my head will ache later

clearly the mountain
Tamalpais, Bolinas Ridge walks up
out of the water into bright

blue air, black and hard-running as it is
full sunlight

grey willets
black and white when they fly

2.

grit in my eyes and teeth

I don't return to the trees until I've washed
in the ocean, invoked its help
I want its power in my writing hands
the absolute freedom of action
my own mystery and weight carrying
independent living beings with/ in/ is/
            we
this

3.

wet monster poet
leads them across the wind
a continuous shove

148

I say
sing
the pen lighter than a blenny
Thetis, Tritons
Amphitrite, Poseidon
rulers of the third world

I sing, I say
I hear them whooping, their procession
white arms and blue-black hair

HOOOO   EEEEE!

brandishing tridents, honking
those giant conch shells

I don't see fish tails—
White sleekness,
immortal solid whiteness
jade beings

naked, wilfull, dangerous,
they come toward me
Out of the sea
Ascending

     the air

which is now swift,
polished slick jewel path
existing only as long as white brilliant foot
descends upon it

Naked they
     gorgeous
terrifying, sublimely calm
white faces the superb . . .

4.

they are that ocean
—projection mirage of mine?
I can invert the canvas, the camera—
They come on

I've called their names.
Gigantic!
            don't see me, don't signify
But here they show themselves
Power vision gift
            O SEA!

1:*vii*:63
14:*iv*:64

Epigram

That boy he star-
        ted to be
        a poet but
he stuttered.

1:*vii*:63

Tennis Shoes

So quiet
pussy foot, do not
upset the nerves
they live in a bath of aspirin, coffee and a proprietary
drug that slows
                or shuts the gap from one frond of
                synapses to the possible next

Uniform response patterns
gentle sinusoidal waves on his EEG
as in sleep

So gently
the gym shoes with the proprietary name
arch-supported, ventilated, add
years to your life

Tillman used to call them "American Plimsolls"
And walked all over the Hindu Kush, the
Pamir Plateau and much of the Himalaya
Silly enough, being English, but also
Marvelously coo-coo, enough to serve
As an example to the young, *viz.*

> stay away from the city
> walk in the mountains
> hobnob with hill men
> loiter with the lamas of the unworldly kind
>   (remember *Kim*)
> eat apricots, drink *chang* and hot
> yak-buttered Mongol tea
>
> Politely demand (and get) the assistance
> —food, shoes & medicine—from whatsoever
>   government
> is furthest off why set around waiting for the bill
> at the local movie to change?

In town we can afford no better, the police inquire
What are you, practising to be a cat-burglar? Peepy Tom?
We say we have heart trouble, the doctor prescribed them
To sweat our feet, promote circulation among the pedal extremities

We hoped our quietness would help us escape notice
Next time we'll also wear hat and necktie
Button your fly, the policeman says, walking away, picking his nose.

28:vi:63

Friday Already Half-

way shot in the ass, nearly
                    noontime lunch
          Can you remember the things you're supposed
               to remember:
                         your past lives, the thoughts of others
               and the unthinkable?

                              *

do you remember, quite naturally, the unpainted wooden attic,
the casement windows open on the green hillside becoming
                                             luminous
world wherein all magic adventures naturally happen, tall gold
crowned women in white and green their jewels emitting gleams
brighter than the day, their long pale hair, their untroubled
eyes . . .

                              *

the thoughts of others at this point are too numerous
and too beautiful to record, for example Blake's
          "AND EVERY NATURAL EFFECT HAS A SPIRITUAL
                                        CAUSE"
                         —"Milton" I, §28

                              *

The unthinkable is not a blank, not a non-entity
not to be dismissed as imaginary, not death, not sleep

                              *

small branches, heavy with plums, wag in the wind
As long as they wave they don't break

                              *

Perhaps you'd prefer to make some other arrangements . . .
You might find it more convenient if . . .
Although we've been informed that your situation in recent
months has not been without difficulties, we sin-
cerely regret that we must inform you . . .

go away
go away now, *i.e.* as soon as
you possibly can
go away—preferably
immediately

*

Please concentrate, please devote all your attention, all your
energy, all your admittedly great talents an⁊ abilities to the
problem at hand, namely your immediate removal from this place
with all your goods, chattels and personal property.

*

Please try to remember that you are broke—that you have no
money, that you have no real expectation of having any on whatever
date in the future—and that you owe a great quantity of cash to
a great many people.

*

Think, at least, about how you might be working in order to
realize your own projects, if you are incapable of going away,
or of making any money. WORK   WORK   WORK
WORK   WORK

*

flowers, very tall this summer
canterbury bells, foxgloves, gladiolas
yesterday a huge peony blossoming beside
HOWARD PRESBYTERIAN CHURCH
—Is Here To Serve You—
am I developing astigmatism?

I didn't think of you, my dear
Until just now—
You haven't chosen to appear, lately
And now I know why I've been turned off and cranky
Three days in a row

28:vi:63

153

Plums, Metaphysics, an Investigation, a Visit, and a Short Funeral Ode

IN MEMORY OF
WILLIAM CARLOS WILLIAMS

O Muse!
I don't dare summon you
All I ask is that I might come to you
Only to see you, only to look
at your face
If you're too mad or too busy for a talk
I'll go home soon.

*

Smog this morning
Hot soupy sun
The mailman brought all the wrong letters
The air stinks, the birds are in somebody else's yard
Boys left a yellow broom in the plum tree
(the plums are still green, however fat)
I hear the Scavengers' Protective Association complaining
about the garbage cans, I

worry about the fragility of my verses
their failure to sound fresh and new

By God, here's the garbage men stealing green plums!

*

Neighborhood boys must go after them
Free food! How can a tree
(who is an individual)
Belong to a man? It can't
be stealing
The tree has manufactured these not quite yet
sweet sticky plums

my mouth is full of plastic teeth
most adults are smokers—we
have no idea about the taste of plums
          except perhaps a memory
               climbing a tree

St. Augustine had the shame of it all his life
               he says
I think of him, seeing these kids up the tree
          their silly yellow broom too short
          the tree's old and brittle, unsafe to climb

The pears (in his case) being hard as well as
          green, to say nothing of the sin
          which he never worked out
          a soulful bellyache his whole epis-
               copal saintly eternity
          (no death, no dying for him, alas)

The pears of Africa pursue him past the heavenly gates

                    *

I can still hear something rattling in my head
Perhaps only the little rocks that keep it pointed
Towards the sky—otoliths, ear-stones

                    *

which is (now) the wind, although I see fog
          and smoke linger over the Bay
               3 loader cranes on a ship
                    gantries in the fog
          flashcar freeway ramp more stinking smoke

Which was my ears rattling an approaching poet,
Ronald Loewinsohn with news from out of town
          considering the study of English
               a long trip to the Northwest with his wife and son
                    for August

155

I envy them, I've been thinking of going "home," I still
Think of it although it has nothing to do with me
Wants nothing from me—
To Oregon, all this spring

Hard as it is—I'm hungry, in debt, I own one penny
                    copper money USA
I am still alive, I dance alone in this borrowed room
              I sing to myself
          "Green plums, you won't be ready for weeks
          But I'm fat and purple, full of sweet delight,
          Hidden among bright gold leaves,

. . . .

It is her wish that I be so

              a wasp bounces up and down one of the
              closed windows—two other windows are
              open, he must
                    take care of himself, I say—
              but I worry for him just the same

Goofy june-bug forgotten poet morning stomp.

and the plums, the voices—the presence of Loewinsohn—
all these brought you in, Williams, quite naturally
making my head rattle, your gentle spirit—goofier
              than you've shown yourself to us in the past
              really goofier than I ever gave you credit for being

I mean the insane poetickal rage that you tried
to channel, to subdue
              (notions I hate—rather the fury
              and the madness, than the bland
              "control" of Messrs. X, Y, & Z who must
              ((of course)) believe they're also
              "in control" of

LITERATURE
AMERICAN
LITERATURE !)

they never really let you into that, in spite of
your book that all professors love, *In the American Grain*
that fills my shoes with sorrow and gets between my teeth

      I want to be a world, not just another
      American tinky poetty-boo

                I am a universe
        etc.

well anyway

I never knew you well enough to call you "Bill"
And you were either my father or not
And I did say a couple days ago that I sometimes
Think of you as a little no-talent middle-class croaker

You did know the madness of love and sorrow
Why should I have wished on you—oh, the crash of cymbals
Rending of live flesh, glare of torches
Total battiness—frenzy—typewriter out the window
                into Cowley's plum tree "How explain about
                the broke window and chair to the cranky
                landlady Hart Crane go away you are too much
                and we don't really believe you write so good
                as all that"

Your head fell apart gently, piece-meal,
        a slowly oozy ripening cheese

WREATH OF SONG

(*Liederkranz,*   an American invention)

It was painful to watch—even eight years ago when I last saw you
not quite articulate, and your hands terribly crimped, yet
delivering yourself, your love,
                to us

(I got the window open just this minute
& prodded the wasp out into the wind)

and you said yes you remembered me

Now I remember you, naturally, Dead or Alive, as the notices
used to say
And you are wanted—not necessarily New Jersey USA
Here with us wherever plums and poets talk together.

17:vi:63

Life and Death and a Letter to My Mother Beyond Them Both

O Muse, get me high out of my mind
   open my head I want   MORT
     COLORS   AUX
music and   VACHES
     blast!
      YES.

an attack of middle age and sobriety
break out of this, recover
   soon as

Right now.   plush.
    outbreak of stupid
     a conspiracy

SILENCE I ought to be quiet while I'm
      having myself totally chopped?

It moves from right to left.

on Saturday only!
a condition I refuse to accept
a performance I cannot condone

some sort of complicated
operating but very
delapidated lashup

OUTSIDE?

PLUSH.

?

PLUSH

PLUSH.   INSIDE?

why don't you watch where you're
going instead of tripping over your
own feet clumsy booby.

plush.   INSIDE?   there.

ain't any feet in here. How
can I instruct them if I can't
communicate with them, if I
am so far away that they do not
(for all practical purposes) enjoy an independent
existence

a challenge of bright light
obstinate silence
I no longer answer the telephone.
Big dipper straight outside the front door.

*

bilge. the wind bothers among the avocado leaves
pester the glass writing scratching twig WINDOW
also rattles for airplanes
blah.   blurt.

*

I wish I could remember the song which begins,
"If I had a talking picture of you."

*

I shall revise it completely. I shall render everything into language of a blinding clarity. It will be so charming and persuasive to every reader that the entire civilized world will say, "Surely Jonathan Swift has come again!"

*

. . . passion, it must create whatever new and exciting. Permanently. Forever young, completely mine, but it will seem entirely and exclusively yours. It must possess a molecular structure similar to heroin. I want the stuff to be absolutely addicting after the customer has had a single sniff.

*

?   fakery   ?
?

*

IMAGINE MY CONSTERNATION
Horror & Chagrin . . . !

blooie. (this means, that there was a break somewhere on the inside, such as one of the coolant tubes in a reactor power plant, the filament in a vacuum tube or electric lamp, or somebody's (for example) gall bladder, kidney, spleen, etc.)

I WAS JUST ABOUT

. . . actually a spleen in the

MORTIFIED TO DEATH

moment of its final despair & goodbye says something more on the order of
BLOORGLE. . . .

BLESS YOUR HEART, HONEY!

". . . one of these days I'm going to sort through all that stuff and throw nine-tenths of it all away. I don't know what

I keep it for; no good to anybody, a lot of junk and old keepsakes
that don't mean anything to anybody any more, but a person does
kind of hate to throw things like T H I S away . . . ,"

*

> "Bid self-righteousness be still
> Wound the callous breast."

"CAME TO GRIEF
about it, just over an old diningroom
table. There's trouble enough in this
world without fighting among ourselves.
We must try to live harmoniously."

"When the day
Grows dark & cold
Tear or triumph
harm. . . ."

"LEAD THY LAMBKINS TO THE FOLD
TAKE THEM IN THINE ARMS!"

*

14 May 1963   San Francisco

Dear Mama,
   Twenty or thirty years too late here I am writing this letter to
you, graveyard or no graveyard, no matter whether we abandoned
each other in death, that part's all over with. I know that you are
well because a part of your attention is occupied with writing
this. No need to wonder how or where or whether you are.
   I try to be patient and forgiving and understanding but I'm a
flop at it. You told me that there are worthwhile people every-
where, in every walk of life, people I can respect, people I must
love. I don't know how to explain to you exactly, but I'm afraid
it's a matter of my being too selfish and small minded and preoccupied with my own tiny life—I can scarcely see them, and of
course I don't really, most of the time, WANT to see them,
I have got myself that far under . . . it's I who need out of the
Salem graveyard, not you who were never there anyhow.
   I don't think it matters what we name it, you make it on the
ideas of God, peace, quiet, organ music and Mrs. Eddy's repre-

sentations of the character and philosophy of Jesus. It saved you dozens of times hand-running, whether you needed it or not. I don't mean any disrespect, but it seems unnecessarily complicated to me—that system, those names—it worked for you or you worked it—like Yeats and his bent gyres and cones and pulleys and belts and geary numbers—and arrived, like him, beyond this fake life and spooky death. I get the general idea, I have a different set of names, I know it isn't really a problem, that I'm not really beset, either with sin or salvation, goldfish or onion-rolls. But for the past couple of weeks the whole business has been coming up cardboard, fake Easter nests of shredded green wax-paper.

There was this man at the Zoo yesterday, combing through the camel wool with both hands, two ladies kept hold of a rope around the camel's neck and tickled it under the chin while the man hooked the fingers of both hands into the (I presume) shedding wool on the camel's side below the humps and pulled great sheets of wool away, like peeling a sunburn—I expected, judging from how hard the man yanked and tore at the wool, that the camel would scream or at least spit on everybody in sight. Instead, it stood there, looking only mildly annoyed, while the man took its fur and shoved it in a gunny-sack. The man wore a neat grey felt hat, an expensive-looking suit and shoes, a white shirt, necktie, and, if I remember right, a vest. The ladies were very fashionably dressed.

Confronted with prodigies of this kind—or, as I recall, on the day you found me blowing bubbles of molten glass—you'd say, "God is love!" Also if my sister fell down the stairs or if you happened to see an automobile accident, it was the thing to say. I guess it doesn't matter so much what it all means, the thing is more like how do I treat other people, how do I use myself?

This is all so abstract and dim. You were able to make it iron all our clothing, cook our meals, provide us with total security and love. I must be a mouldy old ghost . . . but that isn't interesting, either, I know better.

I forget how or where this began—I wanted to talk to you, I wanted to speak with you, sensible as you are, and how dear, and properly remote, I'm not that confused, in time and distance, and I believe still forgiving after all, and still believing that you know and feel, I hope you can laugh also, because it's a delight to you, as well as gentle music, Boston voices, quiet lights—joy and freedom where you live.

So here we are—I didn't want to take a walk or read somebody else's book. I've waited most of the day for these words to arrive at last. Now I can let it go—this paper, this pen, the bad light, the nasturtiums curling their stems in my table jar, the tea is cold.

All my love,
P.

14:v:63

World Out of Control

Without my authorization, completely outside my plans
For the shape and color and temperature of the day
Water falls carelessly, insolently, big drops of it
Down into the avocado leaves
Not enough to call it rain or bad weather

S P L A T T E R   d r i b b l e   stops

Now moving uncalled-for blares of light which can't last
Of no use to me, to us, bray like brassy horns and trumpets
Fall dark indecision again

Where's the icecream. I want a change
For the better, a reward for the worse
Where's the feet will carry me off
Where's the way to the icecream store
The birds chirp among green plums
Antique airplane four propellors flap my window panes
Where's the summer weather
Why don't I make better?
Bird   rain   fluff   cloud   I
Wish for music also.

10:v:63

163

PW His Recantation

O deodar tree
I haven't learned how to live

Both of us far from the mountains
I have not adjusted, not adapted

No one must blame you

1:v:63

How Beautiful

A hummy-bird attacks the redwood trees
                    CLOUDS!   look
How dark it is, it will rain it is so dark
Something must happen
Earthquake, volcanic manifestations

Easter lilies, unborn callas

A testimonial dinner

New fuchsias!

I
REFUSE
to be taken in

kindly stop the car
Are you really sick
kindly stop the car
You're just kidding
Do you want me to vomit down the back of your neck?
What's wrong?
"The heart has its reasons that reason knows not of."

11:iv:63

For Brother Antoninus

Do these leaves know as much as I? They must
Know that and more—or less. We
See each other through the glass. We bless each other
Desk and tree, a fallen world of holiness.

Blessed Francis taught the birds
All the animals understood. Who will
Pray for us who are less than stone or wood?

28:iii:63

Spring Poem to the Memory of Jane Ellen Harrison (1850–1928)

Old woman, here in the dark of the moon
Honey milk seed falls at your feet

When will she go up the sky again?

Spirit of milk follow her and swell her body
          bring star showers

               there's been enough rain for the season
               too little snow in the mountains

Old woman, or later perhaps
          Young mad queen of night
                    mimosa breeze in the valley

Honey milk seed, heads of your children fall
               at your feet

                    You say the girl's too young

I say she's flighty
I see her down at the drive-in, kidding the boys
    She waits for that gas-station kid
    That bomb of his 90 miles an hour
        I see the back of her gold bubble wig turn the corner
                East Blithedale Avenue

Old woman I know she's out parking
I don't know what you tell her
        or if you got time
I see that antique poet loitering around your backyard
    petting the goldfish
    grilling your lambchops

Old woman, I'm not a cop or a social worker
I sing loud in the bathtub next door I hope
        you hear me?

You and your lavender hair and white wrinkle toes
        gold zoris

I can do the kid more good than that gas punk
I bet he sniffs glue for kicks

Old woman, stars in your brain
Acacia wind blows now in canyon
Laurel tree blooms, false lilac
        trilium and borage
            wild iris
            I
    devote these mountains of blossoms to you
        and sticky pollen of a purple flower
                saffron crocus
                at your feet.

                                    18:ii:63

166

Spring Musick

Rain straight up and down upon the sword ferns
        the red camellia flowers
Garden stairs waterfall walkways
           Bach!

        a realization of six partitas
        and a skinflute duet (*nombre soixante-neuf,*
          a figured bass)
Just feel your way along at the beginning
And fake the rest

                        9:ii:63

The Coordinates

I was tired yesterday. It was your mother's birthday.
Why do they put everything together. Why does it stay there.
I never leave when I'm supposed to. I never know what time it is.
These are the kind I have now.

                        24:i:63

THE ART OF
LITERATURE
1 9 6 1 - 1 9 6 3

For Lewis Welch

The Art of Literature

I went to the door
And who do I see
Deputy Sheriff with a
     paper for me

    ☰   ☱

             It's
    The Angel of Death
    Wiggles of Life
         tremors of elegance

Come down from that hayloft
Come you down for me
I'm here in the oatbin
Robbing the glee

        Death Angel fungus turn-on

              flap.

                  18:x:62

The Saturday Visitations

1.

Belligerence!
   Mixed bathing, and
That was the end of the Roman Empire
Which ought to have lasted
     at least three weeks longer
       ?
     Oh yes.
    19 people, cars, a GREAT BIG
    Highway Patrolman
        on purpose.
        in cars.

2.

ALL PEOPLE
   they love the/they
     try to tell
   us/we may sue
      !
Very tiring.
  *
FORGET IT
  •

              29:xi:62

Sunday Afternoon Dinner
Fung Loy Restaurant San Francisco 25:xi:62

BUS
WAGON
7 o'clock trip to kitchen

INK
By the pocketful

Ink in jars, tubes,
blocks and dishes

Never (or seldom) where it
belongs

ŎN
TIME

more ink displaced

*

cuttlefish in sepia sauce

*

chop suey
eggs fu-yung
pork newdrilles
fortunate kookies
fly shlimp
bosatsu pudding

*

When the smoke of the cooking flies away
All that's left we
consume what may.
a very Chinese interest.
plastic. Do I bore you.
coriander leaves.

*

A pot, apart from which
as, precious unguents, herbal
wines and essential oils
        sweat and ooze, collect
    a powder of gone spiders
                    P O R T E N T O U S L Y
                          S U N D A Y
                    F O O D   S M O K E
            as if we were gods &c cherubic
                    presences

Hello to All the Folks Back Home

Many's the time I've rocked you to sleep in that chair, many's
the hour he had to walk the floor while you bellered and squalled
now you have to act up ugly now you are sorry now we are dead
and gone now you will say to yourself O, I'D GIVE ANYTHING
IN THE WORLD IF ONLY I'D NOT DONE THAT WAY
THEN!

Sure enough, here I sit, bereft of those who truly cared for me,
penniless because, against their injunctions I've practised laziness
instead of industry and thrift, covered with shame, overwhelmed
with remorse and horrid guilt, another miserable derelict washed
up on the sleazy shoddy coast of Bohemia after the shipwreck of
my passionate lusts and pridefulness and perversities among the
raging seas of the actual world, sure as God made little green
apples.

Now I'm trying very hard to think of lines to speak in the Third
Act. What to put into Chapter XI. What to play for an encore.
Because although I'm through I'm not finished. What better persons, what more elevated thought and speech than yours, my
ancestors, what more elegant blood shall I spill on these plebeian
scaffolds, what greater heroes, queens, than you undigested, unde-
graded ghosts,—

   (*desunt ceterae*)

                                        13:xii:62

The Art of Literature,
2nd Part

Gull flies ahead of his
   reflection in the wave.

19:x:62

Heigh-Ho, Nobody's at Home

Certain teachings are whispered into the right ear,
others are murmured into the left; but the
most sacred and arcane of all must be blown into
the crown of the head, down through the sutures
of the skull bone. When the recipient of this
wisdom is able to convey it to another human being,
to a horse, to an ant, a spider, an owl, a goldfish
And a high cliff by words, gestures, actions
which probably affect the lives of any
such beings I'll be happy to call him a
wise man, saint, successful poet, living man, etc.

Why not now?

What's the reason I'm not reaching you? (Since I think of you,
your presence—your existence—is unquestionable)

     but reasons and ontologies are generally uninteresting

I've chosen the wrong way to amuse or instruct. This is
a subject, a topic, a locus, and you have been trained to
interpret such items of discourse as implying certain con-
ventional stances.

How many times have I told you, Milicent, that "blow" is only
a figure of speech?

12:xii:62

Ignorantaccio

Where do you suppose the world begins
It wakes up every morning brooding sins of dreams
Tree heavens, mouse fears, it contemplates a punishment condign
For living criminally . . . although that criminal should have lived
But twenty seconds he must suffer infinitely

> And up, and up, let's pack our leather clothes and be off
> To the bondage-freak ball!

7:vii:61

The Art of Literature,

#3, A Total Explanation

FOR DR. A.

Busts out, at last, in spite of impossible conditions,
all the magic performed to keep it down and in—or
a Caesarian section—even while She sits at the
threshold, her legs crossed and knots tied in her hair and clothing, as Judas his guts burst out through his
own restraining fingers, as Jonah thrown ashore

as myself puking up the present, the past, the future
drunk and sweating and endlessly weeping
puking up lungs nuts kidneys and all my
brains come spraying out through my eyes and ears and nose

> What has money or the lack of it
How does the dollar apply?

> Invest your money in the stock market what
I need is to write this which I have done,

And this perhaps unnecessary but curious college kid
Wednesday explaining with delight there were now 2
beautiful girls in a hitherto boring and profitless class
how the sight of them roused his pecker, how he tried
and tried to restrain it, how it very nearly exceeded
all convention, embarrassed, nobody having let him know
he is a man, nobody having told the ladies it was a compliment
to their beauty

21:x:62

There It Goes

without gills or lungs or brain
       making its way
         "ahead"
And getting all it wants via skin osmosis

the spinal fluid oozed away and the bones sealed
themselves over, straight AHEAD, I don't mean it went in
a circle any smaller than the diameter of the earth

the density
       frozen krypton atmosphere!

         .center.
         repeat from *"oozed away & the bones sealed"*

(OUT?)

(OUT?)

13:ix:62

Saturday 15:ix:62

No help for it. I'm so funny-
      looking that I can't see the trees.

Fillmore Hob Nob Carburetor

"Carburetors now
Almost like a cat fishing
Almost like a wing flying
Just like a propeller."

15:x:62

The Art of Literature,
Part 4th

      What do they do together, that's what I
never could figure out, what can they do, do they
actually. . . . .
                     :
                     :
. . . . I don't believe it, it's too foolish, too
ugly, unaesthetic, I don't like to think about it
but when people talk about them as everyone does all the time I
wonder how they do it. Let's talk about something else.

21:x:62

The Gallery, Mill Valley

Do we have sandwiches is there a menu
Everything is going to start
We have going to change it all.

11:xii:62

Applegravy

Finally, after long observation of that person shouting, waving his arms, flapping banners, exploding rockets, launching illuminated fire balloons,

I ask you: "What does he want?" and you answer that it was obvious to everyone that he was the official pyrotechnician producing a command performance and furthermore today is the Fourth of July (although it is winter and we're eating turkey and cranberry sherbet)

What does anyone want

The hand reaches down to the gravel on the ground and picks up a shiny surgical tool which had lain there, I hadn't seen it all this time.

. . . want, wish, try to get hold of?

—?—

23:xi:62

The Professor Comes to Call

cet homme ci

bread	b ⎫	⎧ B ⎫	Bernard	⎧ B ⎫	⎧ b ⎫	bread
booze	b ⎭	⎩ B ⎭	Berenson	⎩ B ⎭	⎩ b ⎭	beer

cet homme là

ONIONS

New York, an abandonment
                                 anguished literature, an
OK hero, who deserves it. When it pops
into his head. If it pops. Who
cares about punctuation, after one is
thirty-five.
                    THE RULES OF GRAMMAR
                    Who can forget them?

Present a piece composed of ambiguous existentialism.
Prepare a paper which is concerned solely with the ambiguities
of Existentialism. Nobody can understand it.

                                                        6:i:63

How We Live the More Abundant Life in America

"O-tel!"   Vegetable soup with barley or Toamato
                                                          Juice

———————————   Breaded Veal Cutlets with Country Gravy

A nice   Smashed carrots OBrian Potatoes Froze Peas
quiet   Thousand Island Dressing
family   hearty Lettuce Salad
hotel: Minced Pie Bred Pudding Jell-o Ice Cream
                             Coffee   Teee   Milk
Redmond,   Soft   Drinks
Oregon,   Candy and Chewing gum
except for the   Cigars, cigarettes, tobacco
blackjack game
a gang of rusty   9:00 PM go take a cold bath and go to bed
                                                          alone
sheepherders   9:45 PM wake up and read the Gideon
                                                     Bible until
all night   10:10 PM turn off the light, have one last
half a dozen   cigaret, etc.

rooms away
the walls are
THIN I can hear
the smack of
cards and rattle
of chips on
their table

. . . .

My father says
rusty hell those
boys spend the
winter over there
on the French Riv-
ierra, fly their
own airplanes to
the Arizona Bilt-
more don't kid
your ass about
that.

Probably the view of the main Cascade
Range from this place on a summer morning
is worth the trouble of getting here and the
inconvenience of staying over night and getting up traumatically early and looking.
    If one isn't a landscape queen, what then?
        the eggs are fresh and troutfishing

is fairly good not too far from here

    Don't bother the stock, don't dabble in
the irrigation ditches, don't try to get too
friendly with the natives.

Fruit Juice
2 eggs any Style
hot

MUSH

Hashed brown potatoes pancakes or waffles (syrup or jam) Toast
Ham or bacon. Little Pig Sausages
Coffee   milk

My father says don't ever try to order
steak up there in that cattle country

In Redmond the drinking water still tastes like it had flowers
dying in it three weeks too late, they should have been thrown
out long ago. I thought the irrigation ditches looked like Dutch
canals, years ago.

17:ii:63

178

The Art of Literature,
Concluded

WHAT I MUST CARRY: THE ENTIRE PAST,
Mother and father and sister and grandmother,
Wherever I go, a generation of men and women yet unborn,
The book I'm reading, the book I'm writing,
A list of addresses and telephone numbers
Hair-comb, keys to return for the night for my
                        toothbrush and razor
Pens (and in case they fail, pencils) and for amusement
                a lead-holder with 7B graphite nearly black as ink
And quite often I have a map of the place I intend to visit.

Some sort of Government paper that says I am he,
More government paper and metal I trade for bus rides
Animal hairs and hides, fibres of plant or synthetic origin
2 lenses fixed in plastic frame to light my weak eyes
All dark and wet inside, hot and slippery, rivers, lakes
    and bays and gulfs and voids and sand and mountains and stars

and

The sunglasses, forgotten, lie on my desk.

21:x:62

THE END OF *THE ART OF LITERATURE*

MINOR MORALIA
1959-1962

Minor Moralia

1.

Looking at a man trying to decide what he knows
he looks at his fingernails
                              tree branch out the window
                    stone on the table doesn't move
Dust and daylight fall on him, propel him up the path among
                    tree ferns
A world collapses not a minute too soon
I dodge the heavier fragments as they fall

        "THEY ARE MURDERING YOU!"

I say they're welcome to, although it'll bring them
No luck
They really must—however
I'm alive right now

                    2 kids trying to catch goldfish from the pond
                    Bowling green old men with hats on
                    Heavy construction proceeds among the woods
                              to the left

"I was not chosen His Majesty's First Minister
In order to preside over the dissolution of the British Empire"

                    didn't dissolve
                    bored itself to death
                    just in time

Why do you do that. You're wasting your time
You know nothing
And absolutely nothing about how to write it down
And too old to learn

And supposing you knew what you knew
You'd be a giraffe or a goldfish
That's simple, that's all there is to that
Tell me something I don't know

> A garbage pail full and scattering
> gunk all around it
> Pretty colors and stink
> mold and slime

"I DON'T CARE. I'M GOING TO COMMIT SUICIDE
AND GO DRINK BEER FOR LUNCH WITH RUSSEL F.!"

Your pretty head falling apart
Maybe your poems drop out between the cracks
> and flowers

*

Ho-hum

*

> "What I want you to do from here is go
> completely insane and work all the stuff you've got
> into a giant explosion."

Blow up the world before it's too late!
Imagine a mayfly with the gall to be alive in June!

> (Good heavens! does he mean corpses in the street
> and all that?
> YES!)
> ("and blow up the museums, incinerate libraries!")

*

Your fingernails are dirty from poking your flowers
You're scared of them—if you poke them too hard they'll die
And living,   they're a mystery
            (to poke)
You pinch me;
That's my secret.

*

("... bomb the Vatican!
away with all the gold!")

And of course the vacuum left by its passing
Their passing (list of imperial names here)
Sucks us down,
Our surplus of powdered eggs notwithstanding
Or swell up like a poison pup and burst,
So what?

"FEED THE HUNGRY. HEAL THE SICK.
     RAISE THE DEAD."

        there's precious little else to do

What else do you know, what else?
Oh yes.
After you understand it all
How do you behave?

Naturally the logical thing:
Fill the atmosphere, earth and sea with poison
And watch what happens, the logic running:

$$A$$
$$A'$$
$$A^1$$
$$A_1$$
$$A + 1$$
$$\sqrt{A}$$
$$\overline{A}$$

The Greeks went "A, B, C, D, E. . . ."
They kept slaves and superstitions
They got cynical and vanished after letter "P"
      (Letter "N" standing for the *Nichomachean Ethics*)

We go "A: poison kills a mouse
A': poison kills goldfish
A_1: poison kills monkey
A^1: poison kills geraniums
$A + 1$: poison kills bacteria
$\sqrt{A}$: poison kills ants
$\overline{A}$: poison kills men

". . . it would appear
that "A" is, as a gen-
eral rule, lethal to all
forms of life. Further
experimentation will
be necessary in order
to determine . . ."

"WESTWARD THE STAR OF EMPIRE TAKES ITS WAY"

    The barbarian is no longer at the gate
    He's a four-car family at the expense
    (and *convenience!*)
               of the Government

CROSSED THE INTERNATIONAL DATE LINE 1912
Napoleon said, "I tremble to think . . ."

        TAKES ITS WAY

and our empire
           ("Shine, perishing republic" . . . that was 30 years
           ago: Jeffers told us)
glows in the dark
and by its glow
        what else?

Oh, your flowers, your fingernails
I hear a certain amount of music
A voluptuary in keeping with the times
When I'm supposed to be ahead of them
        I leave you to the Medes and the Persians while I goof
        Writing nowhere poems

Could I have stuck around to teach you what I never knew?
Suppose I began over, in middle age,
Committing laws among the bullrushes:

1 Law: Raise your hand
2 Law: Move your feet
3 Law: Listen
4 Law: Don't commit suicide

INSTRUCTIONS AND COMMENTARIES

Everybody's telling you

1. "Nothing you (one person) can do will make the slightest difference." Follow Law 1: use hand to write to me.

2. "You cannot escape." Follow Law 2: use feet, to convey you out of town.

3. "The mass communications media are in the hands of liars." Follow Law 3: Listen to me or any other poet.

4. "The world as we know it is about to be destroyed." Follow Law 4: *suicide* means you've been played for a sap by a two-year-old idiot child and also means that you believe in and approve everything the newspapers say—I believe you know better.

Further instructions will be forthcoming
Use these now, under pain of being something else.

21:*viii*:59

2.

THE FINAL PART OF *MINOR MORALIA*, FOUR YEARS LATER, A NEW END A NEW BEGINNING, 27:x:62

Swollen wicker gross foot. reed grass. burnt root.

*

slugfoot!
Save the lettuce!
Guard the peonies!

grasses and weeds a few small
rocks, what other people
tell me are stones

Albert fries rice with
bacon onion and eggs
aroma! Breakfast! coffee,
the country smell

stems and moss clumps
a reduction, the forest
on another scale

Jugs pots bowls jars and "deeshes"

freely to recognize, to
love it, put it into an order
which moves me and which

You will recognize and love and meanwhile
I shall have gone on to something else
And you shall become yourself changing also.

Temporary looking and admiring and letting go of it
If possible make a present of it to anybody else

*

(hiatus)

*

The real problems, of poverty, injustice, war, cruelty and ignorance

MUST BE SOLVED

*

(hiatus)

*

I'm not completely tangled in theory, false imaginings,
the frustration isn't total)

WHY THE GREEKS WERE FAILURES
WHY WE MUST NOT ALLOW THE IDEA OF A FREE
MAN, A RATIONAL POLITY

to be lost

Why we have less liberty and how to get more
How to live with each other, to love, to let other
          nations or people we think of as funny-looking

ALONE

     to make their own kinds and styles of life
     undisturbed (short of their trying to kill us—
     why put up with death at the hands of boobies
     whether the boobies in question are of another
     nationality or we call them The Government of
     The United States)

REPEAT it until it's out of the way or arrives at last
Absolutely and finally here

Seeds pelt down from redwood cones
Even with the help of opera glasses I can't see
The birds, tits of some kind,
Not much bigger than the bugs they feed on

What is the glue, the cornstarch, the plastic slurp or

          to bind or string

LET IT RUN OVER YOU IN STREAMS!

Let it run into your ears and armpits and up your
Nose and in your mouth and between your legs and toes
Let it collect in corners and in the unused electric frying pans
The ugly lampshades

AS I REPEAT IT

     Freedom, love, learning and time simply to
     set on your ass and look at the trees and birds or
     the walls, the floor, the other end of the bathtub

look your psychiatrist in the face and say, "I'll try to help you all I can, please look at me, please let me hold your hand, don't be afraid."

(as I'm not afraid to stop writing and eat lunch)

AND REPEAT: Don't be afraid to find out you're crazy
                   but for God's sake give up the habit of being
                                    "n e r v o u s"

an oppressive order: Line up from left to right over there

a stifling sequence:

How do you do. Are you going to hurt me. Am I
going to learn to dislike you and later try to injure you.

a society:
How do you do.

Can we like each other, although we're incapable of loving?
                   Let me bring you this.
                   Let me do that for you.
                   Tell me what's troubling you.
                   I'll pay your lawyer's fee. I will help you
                   carry a picket sign.
                   I will write to my Congressman, too.
                   I think you're talking nonsense, I think
                   you are funny-looking but I like you.
                   Often you are in an ugly mood. I shall wait
                   until you're in a better one

I repeat: NO KNOWN FORM OF GOVERNMENT CAN
                                    ARRANGE THIS

We must do it ourselves.

And remember: that the Government is unalterably opposed
                   to our beliefs and actions

Repeat it every day:

I shall oppose tyranny in every form.

Try to remember:

Freedom (independence of thought and action and feeling and imagination and creation) is . . . "The new fun
thing" (if you can't think of any other phrase or if none
other reaches you)

NO GOVERNMENT CAN DO THIS FOR YOU, NO MATTER WHAT IT CLAIMS

Repeat it again
I defy all tyranny

What we need is freedom, love and learning
We won't let each other starve, we got food out the
   ears

Tyranny of these head-kinks which require these repetitions
Mostly I mean that physical and mental oppression and pistol-
whipping that we practise on each other daily in the
name of maturity, progress, good government, better education

*

. . . but I thought, "how ill-equipped the world is
to deal with me! Defenseless . . . likewise all my friends
who must be tired of my continuous hollering . . ."

Begin all over again, repeat it from (as musicians used to say)
the top

*

I discover a page of this is missing and I wonder who's been reading all these pages and I want it back.
This is as bad as notebook missing in Boston Nineteen Hundred
and Sixty.

How can I (at this late date) be such a total dumb-bell? It must be lying under something.

*

29:x:62

which it was, half-folded between
the cot and the wall

Nobody read none of it.

3.

2:xi:62 SECRET ARCANE AND HITHERTO UNPUB-
LISHED PRIVATE NOTES TO *MINOR MORALIA*

i.

The community, the *sangha*, "society"—an order to love; we must love more persons places and things with deeper and more various feelings than we know at present; a command to imagine and express this depth and variety of joys, delights and understandings.

ii.

or; "community, etc. are the visible expression of that order . . ."

iii.

Where does the State, the Government fit in? And of course its absurdity, its uselessness, its exact position in history (its connection with and placement IN the past) shows up immediately: A bad old idea; EXHAUSTED.

iv.

None of this is precise writing, correct logic or responsible action? These notions and words appear to me, set themselves in my head as I awakened from sleep. I hurried out of bed to write this down

v.

"persons, places and things," and of course, our own selves as well . . . Maybe not all this is "love"? Much might be euphoria.

I have trouble displaying, expressing that sensation, it drives me to dance and laugh, to write, draw, sing, caper, gesticulate wildly. This seems to frighten many of the people who happen to see me hopping and giggling. I must imagine ways to explain this feeling to them, and wish that they might have more frequent accesses of it, equal to or more profound than the kinds which I've known. For several minutes at a time I become a glowing crystal emitting rays of multicolored light. (What a metaphor . . . ugh . . . but a beginning) because I've forgotten (or remembered, which is it?) so much while I was asleep?

I've tried to explain, repeatedly, that this ought to be my daily, hourly condition (ridiculous demand!) Do I know what this feeling actually is, do I deserve (hah!) to exist in that state?

I change, I tell myself, "I" IS ONLY THESE PASSING STATES, THEIR ACTUAL PASSAGE . . .

I came at it wrong-side-to, as usual . . . I find a lump of wooly fabric, pick it up, turn it over, pull the sleeves right-side out, and there's a sweater. While I'm not wearing it I must put it away in mothballs. If I have more than one, I ought to give this one to a person who has none (for example).

vi.

In the mean time, I imagine I must discover and compose these instructions which even a child can follow, if a child needs such instructions—which will be mailed to you in a plain wrapper free of charge   ?

vii.

One of those Chinese sages figured the child/heart/energy/delight as his chief metaphor of instruction. We turn our children off, we try to, that they may come into a room correctly (How do you do?) I can recall our own parents and relatives putting us down, horrified at the sight of our natural elation (why is it frightening to them . . . they're afraid we'll fall off, down, and break our bones?)

An orgy of screaming, chanting, circle dancing until we fall exhausted and sweating in the grass, hypnotized by the clouds and sun, plant seeds drifting in the air, birds.

Why not. Later we feel quiet and happy, quite ready for washing ourselves, dinner, sexual congress and sleep.

viii.

This morning the sun is covered by varying thicknesses of mist and the kinds of foghorns and the order in which they blow remind me of Marin An, and being there at night or at this same time of the morning after, everyone else asleep and I listen. But there, in that place, eucalyptus—as on this hillside, redwoods and ferns. I sweat, drinking coffee after breakfast.

ix.

I imagine a motto, "Ecstasy is my response," and think of it as embarrassing to write or say. I suppose this is what Philip Lamantia's book is actually concerned with.

x.

The length of these lines, the affected sound, to my ears, of their rhythms—the repetitions, cadences, pausings, the gropings which aren't actually necessary or real—I know precisely what I'm saying, what I think—but I must permit them here, admit it all, look at it, like looking at my own anus in a mirror.

xi.

Quite often when I feel that I have an idea, a notion or an insight, I'm actually understanding something I once read or heard—or I find that I'm now able to express an idea of Plato or of Whitehead in my own vocabulary, in words which correspond with exact feelings, with personal experience—I suddenly "see" something, comprehend.

21:vii:59
2:xi:62

The End of MINOR MORALIA

Song to Begin Rohatsu

Overcome with frustration I sing a few songs
Ring a few bells & wish for better times.
A dim and moisture afternoon.

       FIXED? The race
  is absolutely honest. Very
                   straight; OEDIPUS UN-
BOUND.
         the same fate, no matter what his
position relative to an imaginary horizontal plane
        D A R U M A
      was there any change.

                                30:xi:62

A Short History of the Second Millennium B.C.

Talk about fellaheen, talk about
    the taxi drivers and cops behind the wheel read comic books

A manipulation, a slick robbing job, two thousand years of it
           trade in faience beads, amber
           tin,   TOTAL MONOPOLY
           (Mr. Morgan said, THE PUBLIC BE DAMNED!)
Read Gordon Childe what if he is a commonist

Who knows better.
2 thousand years of work yourself to death
building God a house
tending God's ducks and pigs
killing God's enemies
kissing God's ass

Total control of energy, animal and human
        "The earth is the Lord's"
        also innumerable brains and hands

Keeping fingers busy with God's work
Keeping the books and letters locked up in God's house
Thoughtless holy suffering hands

a tyranny so complete, a captivity, reduction to animal existence
You see the delicacy of it,
Twenty-two hundred years of tyranny, high-grade embalming
        and exquisite stonework

Tell me, the big man says,
about Millennium 2 BC

Big rocks, fascism and ignorance
manipulation of knowledge to keep them down on the farm
22 hundred years of bad beer and worse onions
        I ask you

                          22:ix:62

The Prophecy

The present, assailable at any moment
        we pretend
        from Russia, yet, Eternal,
An absolute,   raised above
And beyond any chance or possible
        changing

Subject to the weather, to
    my imagination?

        IT SHALL NOT STAND

                          16:vii:62

Technicalities for Jack Spicer

One is enough, she cried
But imagine thousands of them
      some with wings
        little naked boys riding on them
           pink silk ribands for bridle and reins
        a leash to guide them, blimply

*

Angels, someone tells us, have no dongs
But where should you get your poems
Except angelic peckers thrust never so subtly slender
        into each ear
          Skull neon whipcream illumination
?

*

He's more intelligent than any of his wives
Who teach him antique enchantment
Why is he a mystery to everyone but himself?
So near from hand to mouth

*

One is enough, if it be of convenient length
Or one begins at an early age learning to curl up
        like a porcupine,

           "Serapis and Agathodaemon combined
           in a single figure adoring
           the Master of the universe"

*

Three is required for that game of yours
One to throw the ball, one to catch
One who swings his bat between—chance
        which breaks the cycle
A farther number adds pretty variations

The path of the ball: 1, 2, 3, 4, 5 after it is hit
                    (an acuminate circle)
              curls on itself again
Commences swinging back and forth
                         Night and Day
The sun track
              EAST SOUTH WEST NORTH
                    and the center

LINEUP, 6th DAY			
Lyon, Pitcher (center)	white	water	god heaven
Oliphant, Catcher (East)	blue	ether	animal world
Cheval, 3rd Base (South)	yellow	earth	human world
Peacock, 2nd Base (West)	red	fire	ghost world
Griffin, 1st Base (North)	green	air	god hell

              We very seldom see each other
              Standing on opposite sides of Mother
But fear not, these are only reflections
    of your own several organs grown
              autonomous

                         *

He wants a world without mothers?
    which is to say, no energy
    no show, no wisdom
Only will-power, character, that very large phallus
              of Mexican granite, a tree stump overgrown
                    mossy lichens
    as distinguished from that flying snake
              Kukul Can
              (traveling east to west)

Yellow is the color of thought
Human world light path

                         *

from inside your own head! fragments of yourself
putting on campy costumes, devil masks
bagpipe sounds, instruments of torture, boiling lead
humiliating ice, a universe of poo-poo cushions
demonic yells—*viz.*

Nugatory purgatory
Dramaturgy right of clergy
Kerosene magazine   or   *"Don't bring Lulu—*
Thuribles in the clerestory   *I'm bringing her myself!"*

*

perhaps rather less embarrassing
than to discover that you are someone else's
                    doppelgänger

*

It has been given to me to say.
I can't leave you alone.
Those heavy thumbs of yours TILT the machine
You must pay again.

Take me away to your hell world:
I must have that salvation, too—
Burn away my fleshy dreams

Nine years from now
You will be known as Lump Skull Buddha!

6:vi:62
26:i:64

To the Muse

Dear Cleo, I can't complain about your absence
Nor excuse my failure to call you sooner
I mistook you for your sister and
Now I thank you both, you one Lady
            who changes before my eyes

QUEEN LIONESS OF HEAVEN IN THE SUN

 . . . tangle of a dream, a history
              waiting while I sleep, I grind my teeth
    or waking I watch your closed eyes
    film of gold hair across your cheek
              a mystery

a tangle, my impatience, your wildness,
this persistence of vision
              centered in my own chest
(the print of your ear on my skin)

              your presence
I'm high, my brains foam
I can't hear what you say
Quietly happily out of my mind

Madrones blossom on our mountain
Deer in thicket
Watch me pass
Fawns and does,
Tawny and grey
Bless me as I walk along the fire road

Who are the brilliance of that day
the glory of this night

                                        25:iv:62

The Admonitions

If I told you once I told you a thousand times
I tell you stay awake until sleep
Forces you to shut your eyes and even then
arrange to awaken yourself not more than six
hours later, better five, and one of the senses
never sleeps, O King who lives forever

Lion jaws
Barred with gold
While Daniel sang alone
Darius was awake all night
      worrying

I don't mean that you should go around
        asleep on your feet
Don't be afraid to fall over, once in a while

There's no time.
Thoreau said there isn't enough of it unless you start
Each day at sunrise and also enjoy a little bit of what the
      night has to offer, viz. lights in space
      and the far-away practise drummer

Daniel, a triumph
The nerves triumph
        for a change
And don't jitter, collapse, divide
Was this what they meant by "heroism"
      (as distinguished from "chutspa"—unutterable
      gall, brass, etc.)
Coordinating to achieve, surpass the ordinary actions of men

But it was angels who locked the lions teeth
Angels who are communication ever jealous
      that I might speak
      revealing heavenly mysteries
Or the lions teach us animal royalty

The angels were the prayers of Darius. The seals
      of the den unbroken

Awake, the wonders multiply
We praise them or condemn,

GOOD AND EVIL
the gross national product
We send them out, we save money
      all die

I said to the lion, "All right, go ahead."
He filled his belly and went to sing on the mountain

What's the score now? He's
Hungry again

Darius hopes for the best

His grandson will perish.

23:iv:62

The Chariot

FOR JESS COLLINS

I stand at the front of the chariot
The horses run insane, there are no reins
The curtains behind me don't flutter or flap

I don't look worried. Is the chariot headed
        for the edge of a cliff?

Behind the curtains a party's going on
       laughing and talking and singing

I prefer to stand here, my arms folded
       Ben Hur
Or one hand leaning lightly on the guard rail

Watch the horses galloping

Mother and father behind the curtains
      they argue, naturally
       "Who's driving, anyway?"

Wind whistles through my spiky crown
Some hero, some king!

30:iii:62

The Idol

A gold woman with a condor's beak
      her hands are llama heads
Weights these pages down
Peru or Bolivia or someplace in South America
A goddess, I don't know her name,
I hope not a picture of bad luck

*

You'll notice how easily I withhold what you need,
What you require of me.
I can't imagine what it is, and it doesn't do me any good

*

A terrible mistake: "Dots and squiggles justify
              The air and space I occupy"

12:ii:62

Mysteries of 1961

Lazy tongs
Jacobs ladder
magnetized flywheel
gyroscope
folding mesh ring basket

*

Mr KNIBX, a sinister

*

"A is for jelly,
  B is for Jell-O"

*

"You are the how
  they call panic"

200

Early Autumn in Upper Noe Valley

Bang dang ang S. Philip Martyr Angelus 6 P.M. or

VESPERS

but all that's Huguenot propaganda

VEXILLA REGIS

PRODEUNT

that's the *real*
old time down home hogmaw and chitterlings

FUNK
Mr Wagnall hasn't got a look-in

POSITIVELY NO
POSITIVELY NO
this means you!

"I think *Moon Mullins* is terribly vulgar."
"I stand corrected."
7 October 1961
8 October (Sunday,
or, less specifically)   (Tomorrow) is Krishna's Birthday
San Francisco
"a real sweet little guy"
San Francisco 7 October 1961
Saturday at evening

S. Francis (of Assisi)
S. Francis Xavier
S. Francis de Sales

Why not.   OK

☒
a vote for
Good Taste

The Poor

salt

oregano

toilet paper

2 natures of soap (one kind bought 31:ix:61)

liquid bleaching compound

peanut butter

APPALLING
FINANCIAL
CRISIS
!

degradation   despair

we really do need some olive oil

7:x:61

"There's a Man
in there!"

7:x:61

Statement of Condition

a change in personnel
      of personnel

                            one what?

                         "One never know,
                         do one?"

  different people

A change of people isn't the same as people changing. What
A shame.

How different. How different upon the mountain are the feet
Strophe and stanze. Will you settle for good. Handsome is as
handsome does. Try to do right. Be a real man for a change.
No matter how presented, it is yesterday's cornflakes, it is
hogwash, it is without sense or understanding. It is not
(alas) beyond reason or comprehension FROM THE OUTSIDE,
but once you're in, then where are you?

Right here at home, the sewer has broken again. Dirty water,
faeces, assorted garbage and mephitic vapours are swurging
about, underneath the livingroom, a few inches beneath my feets.

          Kriste eleison!
          Kyrie eleison!
          Kriste eleison!

You can imagine my horror and chagrin
          as it were to say, "Well I'll be dipped!"

                                    7:x:61

Easy Living

                       I want more than my share of
                       good luck and prosperity

Tenderly.
You may well imagine.

Overwhelmed with dismay & consternation? Confusion,
Ruin,
>
> hebetude

We are undone!

Balkh	Sikkhim
Ladakh	Kashmir
Chitral	Nepal
Hunza	Gilgit

"Come where my love lies dreaming . . ."
overwhelmed with fumes of Indian hemp
(*cannabis Indica*, bhang) but enjoying
hallucinations of joy & delight all the while

ZOUNDS!

cried Mr. Controll, this must not be so!
him and his agents busted everybody in sight, the whole shop—
scones, crumpets, jam pots, tea trays, silver spoons and all—
took it all down town, booked for use, possession and sale,
120 years to life, to run consecutively

HAS ANYBODY SEEN MAUDE FRICKERT?
WHERE'S FRED MERKEL?

I want to call my attorney right away.

7:x:61

The Revolutionaries

FOR R. E. MILLER

1

Fred Merkel,
What are you doing
Fred Merkel is my name
And I'm just a little drunk
But I'm soberer than I was this time yesterday evening

Fred Merkel
What are you doing outside the Police Station
Praising God the Father
God the Son
God the Holy Ghost
Joseph, Mary and Jesus and St. Therese of Lisieux
        AMEN

Fred Merkel is my name
I'm waiting for Maude Frickert
        to meet me here
She's already booked inside
Praising God the Father, God the Son, Holy St. Joseph
Holy St. James of Compostella
        AMEN

2

Where's Fred Merkel?
    I want to talk to my lawyer
Who's Maude Frickert?
    I want to see my lawyer right away.
We're going to have to take them
        Downtown. They
        don't want to cooperate.

                *

        Smart people
        College guys

                *

You play ball with us
And we'll play ball with you we got these rubber bats so you don't
        get all marked up

_____

"*Queen.* O, I am press'd to death through want of speaking!"
        —Shakespeare, *Richard II*, III, iv, 72.

205

"Pressing to death by laying heavy weights upon the body (*la peine forte et dure*) was the regular English penalty for "standing mute," i.e. refusing to plead guilty or not guilty."
        —G. L. Kittredge's note on this passage.

15:viii–7:x:61

Saturday Morning

Bread of Origination! Fell desire
Has fled across the border of the bright
Leaves towards night to build a tyrant winter
In the heavenly trees

> *Good Morning to you,*
> *. . . in our places*
> *With sunshiny faces*
> *Good morning, Dear Teacher,*

  a winter, a deadly winter
I'm afraid of it although I have steam heat
Furlined clothes and no reason to leave the house
Between Thanksgiving and March 21
Would that it were Bread of Patience and Perseverance!

WHEN SHALL I BEGIN TO REIGN?

23:ix:61

Friendship Greetings

Carelessly all fixed up a can of beer
several cigarets a cup of coffee I don't care
whether school keeps or not
thinking of Frank O'Hara in Paris right this minute
or the basement of the Museum of Modern Art as the case may be.

23:ix:61

One of My Favorite Songs Is Stormy Weather

silk
lumber
sawdust
wood
pulp
pitch
turpentine
rayon
paper
syrup
rubber
kapok
chewing gum

I said to myself,
"Why are you angry, why
Are you afraid, try
to like something, look
at that flowering weed or bushlet
that bug, that dirt, and select
choose one and like it: love."

As I walked further I grew happier
and less nervous; although I am an
atheist I pray all the time.

frankincense   Acorn   Allspice   lime-flower tea
myrrh   Almond   clove   jasmine
fruit   Avocado   nutmeg   gum arabic
 &   Apricot
nut   Apple   lime   lichee   mace   gutta-percha
     Bay   mango   loquat   coffee   oil of eucalyptus
     Beech   pear   cheramoya   pepper   amber
     Chestnut   peach   coconut   quinine   palm wine
     Crab   plum   cabbage-heart   cascara
     Cherry   pomegranate   pawpaw   birch beer
     Chinkapin   prune   papaya   root beer
     date   persimmon   breadfruit   sassafras tea
     fig   quince   guava
     filbert   tangerine   olive
     haw   walnut
     hazel   mulberry
     kumquat   grapefruit
     lemon
     medlar
     nectarine
     orange

I walk on hills of jewels & gold
A foolish, wicked man.

20:ix:61

MONDAY IN
THE EVENING,
21:VIII:61

*Monday
in the
Evening*

There was an animal
It left a set of tracks
The animal was I
And the tracks also and the mud wherein they appear to your eye
        which is (who) not you, I

        suppose I do (and I do
            what then)

Well then.
Or now. I protest, I complain that I am lost,
aching, coming all to pieces,
I claim that I am (nevertheless) quite in control.

I behave in a particular way. I
sit holding my left hand across my mouth, my right hand
And two eyes do this writing

        On the hillside (Twin Peaks)
        Broken glass, tin cans, a box the milk-man used to
                    carry bottles
        Weeds and ground squirrels
            clouds

Pencils in a jar on this table
            tric-trac
                        that's
                  backgammon
      ("heigh-ho Anthony Rowley and spinach")

Spoor, my scent on the wind,
                  the ink I customarily use
                  dead letters under the table

                  between pencil jar and ink bottle
                  wooden mouse from Denmark, gift from
                  Persky, tin windmill from Joanne
                        MANUSCRIPT
                              (prose)
                              (unfinished)
                              (I care desperately about that and it
      can't be finished, never, never, never,

How can I go through Thoreau's life again, the unfinished
Unpublished self-righteous walker, disconnected from all
Women and men?)
                        Damn damn dull damn blather
                        I proceed

Tiepolo Baroque church peach icecream
Sun/
    /set   color of nipples, of labia minora
                  (I crossed out Tiepolo at first, why bring in
                  some artist, some painter, where are my own words and
                  visions,
                        Why isn't it discrete pink clouds instead of
                        Art History, female anatomy?
                        Because I can—this being my paper and ink
                        My table and chair, my floor, my electric light—
                        Write it the way I want it
                              HERE
                        any way I chuse)

But why must I insist, why pick an argument with you
  who have begged to listen
  prayed night and day for two months for the privilege
  of watching this pen write words. . . .

this is the evening star

this is the end of my life

REQUIESCAT,
Sweetie.

Here lies
PETERBOUX
  note quite
40 years old,
Who imagined he could not
  cope
Supposing that it was something
Different from blinking his eyes
Breathing, keeping his fly
  buttoned
His big mouth
Shut, and his imagination em-
  ployed with high-grade poetry.

(what's he lying about now,
for Christ's sake?)

How I love me! How much
I'd give for a divorce
! or simply get very drunk
PUKE, SPEW,
DEFECATE,
WEEP,
        clean up the mess,
        take a bath, put on
        clean clothing and

start in again upon a clean
sheet of paper

But now, at last, I'll tell you everything,
All that you've always wanted to know,
Those things I've successfully avoided saying,
The innermost secrets, the real W O R D. . . .

*

Absurd!   You guessed all these dingy tid-bits years agao,
That is, presuming that you have lived seventeen or eighteen years
        in the USA
Are neither deaf, blind nor simple-minded

                                  *

I digress
            a manner of speaking
Here's new tracks, new signs of my presence gone by
I seemed headed towards the drugstore, for tobacco
Into the kitchen for coffee
            ?
                        that wish to move away from this paper,
                        this table

        ┌─────────────────────┐
        │ QUI VIVRE?   │
        └─────────────────────┘

            HO!

                spirit of the cat-tail marshes, genius of
pollywog land, discoverer of those frog or fish eggs under the
lilypads Aunt Clara's backyard fishpond,
                        S T A N D

A N D   D E L I V E R !

                        Having burnt several ounces of myrrh, frank-
incense, branches of the sloe, a few hops, and seagull feathers, we
perceived the faintest outlines of an Apparition, light and wavering
at first, it seemed to draw substance from the heavy foetid smoke,
so that soon there appeared to be an almost palpable column of
dimly glowing light in the corner of the room nearest the book
case. . . .

        Obstinate Creature!   S P E A K !

What he said, after we had gone to all that trouble to bring him back from the vast beyond (A task which we began so happily, facing its difficulties with good cheer and hope, because of our deep admiration for him) called Elysium, the Happy Land, etc. I can scarcely begin to describe our subsequent feelings of disappointment, of chagrin that bordered upon total disillusionment, cynicism and despair, after we had heard his voice at last.

"I want popcorn
I want a naked friend to play with,
    all over
I want a great many cigarets
I want to read the Greek, Latin
    and Sanskrit and Chinese Classi-
    cal Writings
I want icecream
I want the rest of my library
I want a piano, pipe organ, a harp
I want a number of books and
    musical scores added to my
    present collection
I want to spend a year in Europe
    and several traveling in
    the Orient
I want a large new typewriter
I want new teeth, new eyes
I want final perfect enlightenment
    (i.e. Nirvana)
I don't want to smoke any more
I really shouldn't masturbate so
    often
I shouldn't eat so much
I want to be left alone

*

Children holler in the street, chasing each other in circles in front of the drugstore, threatening and sparring, grabbing cocks and asses

    Do I wish I were young again?
    Today, at least, I don't feel old: that wish, question
        is irrelevant.

*

How are my orchids growing? Big leaves and no flowers.
    They (not I) are contrary.

?

Am I better than you, is that the idea?
              (irrelevant)
"Why do you hate me," that's really the question,
And I mean, "Please love me, pay attention to me."
              I want to be left alone.

*

The spirit, having answered all our questions in a most satisfactory
manner, was bidden to depart, but it was some time before it
concluded its apparently endless list of desiderata. For a number
of days afterwards, the corner of the room in which the spectre
had manifested itself smelled strongly of stock flowers, cardamom,
cinnamon, sea water or semen, depending on the age, sex and
stage of spiritual advancement to which the observer had attained

*

". . . all so phony, my dear, you know what he really wants is to
sit for a certain number of hours every day, writing, every month
to be sending mss. to publishers who pay him fabulous sums of
money. He wants to live in Pacific Palisades with a couple of
swimming pools and live entertainment, like Tiberius his Villa
on Capri. Once every five years or so, he wants his picture on the
cover of *Life* and a big jolly article inside, all about his new
book. Then he wants the Nobel Prize for his 50th birthday
present . . ."

*

DOWN!   "I want a dish of Chinese black mush-
"Exorcise te in   rooms
Nomine &c . . ."   I want a lot of hashish
AVAUNT!   I want to write nine best-seller novels
AVOID!   in a row
                         I want everyone to let me alone except
                                    for that naked friend of whom
                                    I've already spoken
                         I want a little peace and quiet"

*

"TEKEL"

*

". . . I don't care, I'm not afraid of you. If you try getting funny with me I'll knock you for a row of pink potted geraniums. I have studied judo and karate, so don't go trying to give me no bad time.

*

Oh dream, o vision of continuous
embrace,

SCRAMBOLA! { "I want cotton candy
I want to visit the church of St.
Appolinaire in Classe
I want rare roast beef in London,
greasy baked lamb and olives
in Beirut
I want a vision of the New Heavens
and the New Earth
I want a bottle of rootbeer"

The time
contrary not only to your belief but to mine as well
has not been wasted or misappropriated or in any way
abused, it is, it
Must (I see) remain out of our reach or certainly
We should abuse and daub it in some unseemly fashion
were it ours
But its existence is ideal and perfect
While my creation stands elsewhere, namely
In this sublunary sphere where all things must decay
and pass away
(but that's not time, neither)
I have redeemed nothing but beauty, pleasure,
and wisdom, I have failed
To save you or myself out of the ruck and chaos of this
jeweled gorgeous world, this universe of love
bright joys and all contentments.

Although these abstractions can scarcely be lost
  and their ownership is in doubt from the first reckoning
    of who and what it was and is

*

I must remember to scream and holler more often (*i.e.* go ahead
and write violently, absurdly, idiotically) if it means an end to fog,
clutter, ill-painted scenery, machines with squeaky pulleys . . .
also, if I misinterpret the echo from this noise as being sounds of
comfort and encouragement, which will in their turn provide me
with enough confidence to continue the inspection and interpretation of my own visions, I shall be content.

*

Because I imagine that I'm far—too far—IN, I sometimes stop,
when I'm out walking, to grasp the branch of a tree, a handful of
foliage, put both hands on the tree trunk, closely inspect the bark
(and are there mosses, lichens, fungi or insects on it?) note its
color, thickness, texture. In the Park I stop to press one hand
flat on the ground among the gravel, fallen leaves, dead grasses—
or simply lie down on one of the great lawns (I pay no attention,
then, to the sky, sun, clouds, birds) and attend to feeling the
springy grass and solid earth beneath me.

I click my tongue at a squirrel. It approaches me on a zig-zag
course, running, then stopping to sit up with one forepaw held
to its chest, uncertain what I'll do—feed it or hit it. (I do
neither, and presently it goes away; several other squirrels must
come to inspect me, to ascertain that I'm carrying no food to
them . . . as each one approaches, it points one paw at its chest,
excitedly, appearing to enquire "Who, me?")

Inside, outside, may or may not be significant distinctions.
I know that I can bore or frighten myself rather easily by think-
ing, "I am inside; I must get out"—and have felt what the
Ancients called PANIC, i.e. been outside and felt an irrational
necessity for being indoors, for going home . . . but the last time
I felt that way I took out my notebook and recorded the fact.

Soon, I was writing about the general scene, about particular objects that caught my attention, and the terror left me.

21:viii:61

The End of MONDAY IN THE EVENING

Vector Analysis

What I want? green
   grass under leaf tree and vine
Sunshine all around
      dark and
      muddy ground
  wants I
    air
     no boundaries
  put a hole in your skull bone
     open up the sky
  an equal
    vacancy

that is, a partition, with a hole in it, such as might be installed in an empty cigarbox. Partitioned, the space in the box has two parts—as long as the lid is open—but shut the lid and where's your eyes?

   mallow in marshy ground, the water
   hyacinth is found, caltrop
    sliced with dinner meat
     I
     ?

21:viii:61

That One

He spends lots of time in that all-night movie, a red bandanna handkerchief over the lens of his flashlight so he can read without disturbing the other patrons. As long as it's dark, he sees trolley cars and buses with flames billowing out of all tne windows while crowds of people and animals inside burn and scream.

In the daylight the streetcars are quiet, being full of water like aquarium tanks; the drowned bodies inside sway gently back and forth to the motion of the cars.

He reads volume after volume of Stendhal, referring only occasionally to a pocket-sized French dictionary. He pauses rarely to look blankly at the movie screen at the rush of cowboys and Indians, Bette Davis as *Jezebel*. Although it is several miles from his apartment to the theater, he invariably walks to it. He never told anyone what happened, what he saw, the one time he took a taxi downtown; he never rode in one again, nor could anyone persuade him to do so.

10:vii:61

The Daydream

A call from, a pull in some direction (EXCELSIOR!) echoes of the future I will presently look back upon (whether with pleasure or chagrin there is no adumbration—the noise is an excitement of some kind) I must seize upon the present moment, the controls—wheels, levers, pushbuttons, dials—and arrange them in such an order that the future event will bring me something valuable, pleasing, rare. With great annoyance, I realize that I'm further than ever from the wheelhouse, the control-board. How shall I ever reach it in time to prevent the boiler explosion, the collision with icebergs and hay-wagons, then skip immediately to the spotlighted stage to receive the medal, the honorary degree, the hundred million dollar prize?

27:vi:61

Life and Art

build you a house out of all this stuff—make bricks
from all these straws—or failing that, rayon stockings

An aeolian harp for dishonest immortals
Windbag for a dudelsack
    (Swinburne, thou shouldst be living at this hour!
    Arkansas hath need of thee . . .)

Put it a few octaves higher up.
     UP!
And over the sublime blue edge of Sol's corona

I wouldn't be a bit surprised,
Not after what's already happened in the first couple of times
around. I should say not.

           22:vi:61

Twin Peaks

A swollen cloud a curving shadow ripples light on the lumpy hill
Maybe so. A straight edge of light a bumpy shadow the
Smooth hill slope and valley crease. Perhaps.
I suppose it is terror now invades me, tightens my chest,
Swells my eyes
My heart beats the blood stands still

I try lying flat with my eyes closed but then I see myself
Climbing
    that hill, distantly bushes and grass,
Flashes of sun and darkness
Towards the radio towers

I get up, break up, sneezing
Again, again   again, again,
            again
My brains liquefy and run out my nose
My eyes regain their hydrostatic balance the clouds
Continue slopping dark and light across the hills.

11:v:61

Philippic, Against Whitehead and a Friend

Pull it down over our faces and ears
That English wool Plato Alfred North Whitehead
And say "there.
The sweater eternally becomes immortal."

I scream   H E R E S Y !   It's that old slow & gradual salvation
                                                    routine
They tell me "The limits
You must know what are your limitations
And then proceed . . ."

> (LIMITS: i.e. polite categories & hierarchies
> that justify repression
> "for our own good")

H E R E S Y !   Whether its creeping Fabian socialists or that
"Infallible" process you call reality, glued to time so that
            "Justice is later
            Freedom is later
            Dessert comes AFTER the nasty spinach"

B A H !

I can't help feeling this world is immortality:
Two pigeons in the sun (house cornice across the street)

And nonsense as well! Words, a grammatical order
The world palpably NOT of this order
Exceeds our limits

We kill each other quite artistically
Exquisite tortures, exorbitant crimes
Think of the glass flowers in Peabody Museum
I am limited insofar as huge areas of my brain
Dissolved in Hitler soap-vats
Dispersed as radiant poison over Japan

One of the pigeons flew away the other
Peers down from the cornice
                    Goodies below?
I look up and it's gone, end of the world
    ("invalid argument," Whitehead says, "depending on
    ignorance of the theory of infinite convergent numerical
    series")

Which puts me in over my head

Cantor discovered three orders of infinity:
Aleph-sub-three has yet to be discovered.
I don't consent, I demand the excessive "tertium quid"
That "somewhat" forbidden by Aristotle
That ocean
                (although I'd drown in a pisspot quite as easily)
                (and perhaps my dissent, my perversity, are also
                ruled, have their determined order?)

For limits let's try Blake's
            "Enough—or too much!"
Certainly excesses are deplorable
Those glass flowers at Harvard offensive as the war
I feel better knowing that the secret of their manufacture
Is lost. I'm delighted that the young believe professors
who tell them, "*Ulysses* and *Finnegans Wake* are no-good
failures; Proust killed the novel once and for all."

Whitehead says—and you, my friend!—repeat it:
>"God is the organ of novelty."

I hear an electric organ
Producing pure notes, tone reduced to bare vibrational frequency
>(no Pythagorean overtones here,
>>Plato his Ideas exactly)

Total purity
Sexless
Absolutely reasonable
Accurately in tune past hell's freezing over (within reasonable
>limits, variation due only to line-load and distance from
>the powerhouse)
Precisely and completely what we want
The triumph of the West

Arnold Toynbee tells us this is the true goal of mankind;
Anybody who doesn't want this is uncivilized, out of history.
The psychiatrists tell us if we don't want this we're mad
The government tells us if we don't want this we're goddam
>Communists, GO TO JAIL!

God is worthless except he become a man
Man is a murdering slob unless he exceed himself

The limits,
Orders of infinity:
My own immediate incarnation as compassion and knowledge
Appearing to you
>(who are the ground wherein this manifestation
>proceeds)
>RIGHT NOW!
In response to your necessity
Even though it is I who am deluded
And you who are the Buddhas of this world.

8:v:61

To Ruth

Insane clouds between moon and ocean
    which reflects them
I've been awake, I've slept, the clouds
        moving
Keep their pattern day and night
Swinging sun (moon) aureoles, beams, shafts, panels of dim glow
Revolving the water in regular circles
        over itself

        smash on the sand

I say "depression, madness, doubt"
Water dragon, Earth Dragon the power of these elements
Water, air and earth
      I doubt the sun's a fire
      There's more fire in the ocean
        and beneath it
To disguise myself, hide under. . . .

O, I know—an Indian blanket
    pulled over my head window sunlight color
Otherwise afternoon nap's a waste of time

The sea and I generate clouds
The clouds and I
          wandering pieces of the sea
Greater and lesser lights appear "in space," we say
      More than anything we value the distinction
      "Outside" *vs.* "Inside" . . . claustrophobia
      is the human condition

I've devoured them all.
Galaxies in my shoulderblades
The space between
    subjective
    a relatively large number can be assigned to it
For the sake of our convenience an International Catalog exists

    IMAGINE!

Klein's bottle made from varicolored glass
Face of Glory in the void

29:iv:61

The Treasures of Rage

patience and exactitude
Even now, it's plugged.
Clarence, connoisseur of fine toast, says:

Don't bother me with all that goddam nonsense before I've
had breakfast! Why are you wearing that cap in the house?

   a) it makes me feel like I'm back in the Army
      presently I shall lose my marbles in all
      directions and lie hidden in the corner

   b) you should go, he says, to the baseball game,
      having written *Up the Dodgers!* across the front of it
      or a large *Pittsburgh Pirates* . . . you'd be found a
      bloody mess down among the empty beer cans underneath
      the bleachers.

   c) yes. Most certainly. Yes. Prodigiously.

Swiftly the butterfly
Dream the Death of Winged Tiger General.

20:iv:61

Staying or Going

MERRY	another day another $2.65 plus
CHRISTMAS	overtime plus cost-of-living graduated scale
A JOLLY INTER-	increase less FICA contribution less Federal
LUDE	Income Tax less insurance less medical plan
OR THE	contribution less contribution to the Enter-

GAME OF
WHO'S
GOT
THE
BUTTON
UNDER
WHAT
WALNUT
SHELL
OR
WHAT IS
SHE LIKE
BEHIND
THAT
MASK
LIKE
ISIS
WITHOUT
ANY VEILS
OR THE
CHARLATAN
UNFROCK'D
THE MON-
STER PLOT
DISCOVERED
    *
Happy New
Year from
Kazakhstan
    *
EASTER
IN THE
MATTO
GROSSO
    *
FLEE
FROM
THE

tainment Fund a grand total of 87 cents *I
OWE THEM!*

MY BACK! MY ACHING BACK!

The world is speeding swift away
Or melting slowly, a mass of retaliation

    "The Passion of Yang Kuei-fei"
    "The Claws of the Dragon"
    "The Breeze in the Moonlight"

Something has G O T to be done!

WRATH
TO
COME
     *
"A
WEARY
TIME
A
SLEEPY
TUNE"

2:iii:61

Homage to Rodin

I.

"THINKER"
            in the classic peristyle
Shows up in old *New Yorker* cartoons, appears in some houses
            as plaster book-ends

A great ANIMAL
            the biggest goon Rodin could find for a model
            or magnified him, I think most Frenchmen are small
            by nature

ANIMAL for sure (we customarily think "man, human, soul"
            confronted with this kind of creature—"I," "We," &c.
            concomitant fantasies of art, politics, religion)

Rodin says: "ANIMAL: WHO SITS DOWN
                  which is one difference, apparently doing
                  nothing
            TO CALCULATE, CEREBRATE"
                  & that's of the first significance:
            Meat thinking and got hands to build you what he
            Means or throttle you if you get in the way, either
                              action
                  without too many qualms

"HANDS FEET ARMS SHOULDERS LEGS," Rodin says
We're in the habit of thinking "Man: subject for the psychiatrist"

Old stuff, we say, "Oh, Ro-*dan*. . . .
Rilke's employer . . . oh yes, Rodin, but after all—
Archipenko, Arp, Brancusi, Henry Moore—
Sculpture for our time . . ."
    (they appear in Harpo's Bazzooo, modern, chic,
    seriously discussed in V*ogue*—
    Epstein and Lipchitz are OUT, the heroic
                tedious as Rodin)

NOBODY KNOWS WHAT IT IS, HULKING BEEFY
NUDE
We all the time wearing clothes and arguing "quest for values"
Forget what we are, over-busy with "who"
The only time we sit still is on the toilet and then
Most of us read, the only quiet and private room
Where we have bodies we wish away

Rodin: "BODY: with head containing brains,
            hands to grab with, build (possibly, the physiologist says
            hands helped enlarge the brain) feet
            to come and go, buttocks for sitting down to figure it
                            out . . ."

How isn't
It wonderful how
Is it "base materialism" why
Do we insist "There is nothing we can do"?

II.

LANDSEND: "THE SHADES"

I won't go to the park today informal prospects groups of noble
                                                    trees
Playland At The Beach instead
You never saw a merry go round so fast

2 fat old men watch it from a bench
One sings words to the tune everyone else forgot

No amount of sympathetic observation will do any good
Why not get older, fatter, poorer
Fall apart in creaky amusement park and let the world holler
Softly shining pewter ocean
Or let it quit, who cares?

The road to the Palace of the Legion of Honor still broke
About 1000 feet of it don't exist as I walk along the edge
Above the foghorns & dim fishboat passing the rocks
Anise and mustard, pinetrees and fog

Formal building pillared propylon and stoa
            HONNEUR ET PATRIE
Apse and dome and Greek pantheon life-size
A few golfers look at them
Just beyond the apse, Ft. Miley steel fence
Empty concrete bunkers, coast artillery no defense
No more meaning than the gods, a wonder of expenditure
The whole outfit stone marble pipe organ and all built
By a single family, given away (more or less)
Nobody home but Cézanne
Amusement (high-class) park to remember dead soldiers
and the late M. Rodin

No amount of reflection on the noble prospectless dead
No amount of indignation does any good
They are blanked, puzzled-looking (*The Shades*)
They stand heads bent down, three arms pointing towards
The ground that covers them, young burly ghosts wondering

We like to kill each other
We like to grab with both hands with our teeth and toenails
Unless you got sharp teeth and toenails you end up
Watching the merry go round not even a dime for popcorn
Nor anything to chew it

"EVERYTHING WAS ALL RIGHT UNTIL *THAT MAN*
CAME ALONG & WE DECIDED TO BE KIND TO
EVERYBODY THAT'S THE TROUBLE WITH US NOW
WE'RE TOO KIND WE OUGHT TO KICK THEM ALL
RIGHT IN THE ASS & STAY HOME & MIND OUR OWN
BUSINESS . . ."

which is being mean as hell

Fat kid wants expensive camera Daddy to put two-bits into Cliff
House binoculars his father screams in reply, furious, insane,
"Whaddaya wanna looka them rocks whaddaya gonna see in this
fog?" "Come on!" the fat kid hollers, "Gimme twenny-five cents,
put the twenny-fi' cents in, gimme ten-ficens I wanna see them
!R O C K S! out there is COME ON! Gimme twenty-five cents!"
and his father screaming back at him like he might tear the kid
limb from limb but actually looking in another direction, quite
relaxed

There's all this loose hatefulness rolling around
We spend all our time hating the world, the Russians, the Gov-
ernment the job the noise the cops our friends our families
& ourselves for not changing, rearranging
Not being able to find what to change
Or what we'd use to do the job

A woman plays in the surf
Tight jersey pants, a kind of sweater top with sleeves
Fully dressed but the water doesn't hurt her clothes
Oblivious to her girlfriend hollering at her from the sand
                          at the foot of the stairs
She plunges, laughing, through a wave

III.

WATERLILIES (and *Iris*)

Fog washing past Mt Sutro Parnassus the Medical School a mirage
     that city in the sea

228

Leaves over the sky where these waterlilies grow up
      through my mind
Flowers in the water not to be reached or touched

POOL OF ENCHANTMENT, pink granite curbing says, before
                              De Young Museum
Short reeds & shrubby island Hiawatha boy blows flute
At cougar pair, one crouching, one setting, their ears
Laid back, enchanted
Black water thick mud at the bottom
Lily bulbs, heads in the dark
Pattern of stars inside, buried lights

First a few lobed circles on the water
Then leaf mountain with pink pecker buds
Open flowers (unmistakably women) that never fade nor wither
Impregnated they withdraw beneath the waves

No mystery, genes in every cell manifest
                  themselves
Bulb of the earth showing itself here
                  as lilies
The summer flowers, underwater globes of winter
                  all the same

                    *

Since you'd gone I hadn't thought of other women, only you
Alive inside my head the rest of me
                  ghosted up and down the town alone
Thinking how we were together
You bright as I am dark, hidden

Inside the Museum I see Rodin's *Iris*
Torso of a woman, some sort of dancer's exercise
Left foot down, toes grasping the ground
Right hand clutches right instep
Right elbow dislocating
Reveals the flower entirely open, purely itself
Unconscious (all concentration's on the pose;
      she has no head)

Its light blasts all my foggy notions
Snaps me back into the general flesh, an order
Greater than my personal gloom
Frees me, I let you go at last
I can reach and touch again, summer flesh & winter bronze
Opposite seasons of a single earth.

13:vi:60
1:iii:61

For Albert Saijo

Fireweed now—
Burnt mountain day
Sunny crackle silence bracken
Huckleberry silver logs bears
Bees and people busy.

Rainy mountain years
Trees again—
Green gloom fern here
Moss duff sorrel—
Deer sleep.

Tree fire people weed:
Bright and dark this mountain ground.

18:xii:60

The Death of Boston

Bringdown, Boston? is a bringdown?
Why should I
　　　　　　suffer

What
      packed under dead leaves
      thrown-away pages of Thoreau
West, now
      lives with us
      up in back of Fisher Peak
      Deerlick Cabin by Freezeout Creek (out of sight of
          won't see Mt Hozomeen

      Kid's idea, Chinese sign for MOUNTAIN
      which would scare him? anyway he's forgotten how
          to read Greek)
And he's forgotten in New England which might as well be old
An idea, a notion, extremely
Impractical, of course the Police
Would not allow it now
Not now in Boston the trees are labeled
      and POLICE TAKE NOTICE, the sign says
      of all we do

Who wants a life in the woods when there is Harvard?
All of us want to go there & thence to the National Shawmut Bank
The leaves the air thick with decaying hundred-dollar bills
Flopping in raggy bundles through the streets
Plugging up my nose
                  no joke, it smells,
And the weight of it, rotting
And heavier, the hatefulness
Children of immigrants clawing and hauling to get I N
Tearing each other, dying when they don't make Harvard, the
Statehouse,
          City Hall
And the Yankee above/below them all
          rots and hates

That smell in the Old South Meeting House, Christ Church in
Cambridge,

America born and dead in one town
Lived momentarily in the woods
Now all is fear and culture (which is Harvard)
Civilization (which is museums)
Observation of the proprieties (properties)

Thoreau said it was possible without money or slavery
They imagine he's safely buried in money and fear,
Vaults of Widener Library guarded by corps of bought professors
Note I do not mention Sac & Van

23:x:60

Dream & Excursus, Arlington Massachusetts

I see Mrs. Garret opening the glass doors of the tomb, doors of
the wood and glass pavilion that's built over the family vault, four
glass lighted passageways—the windows on three sides framed and
can move up and down as in a regular house—mansard roof,
wrought iron ornaments on top and weather-vane. Small wooden
sign to the right of the tall doors:

"QUIETLY AND PEACEFULLY AT HOME
MADELEINE SUMMERFIELD RATHBURN"

like a doll house with gingerbread decorations, small panes of
colored glass surround the window in the center of each door.
Flowers grow in beds on three sides of the building and on each
side of the walk leading to the entrance.

This is probably an early 1870's tomb. Rather eccentric for Cambridge cemetery—or was it a fashion that lasted for several seasons?
A wooden replica of "the old home place" built over the family plot
to protect the expensive marble, granite stones and concrete curb-
ings from the vast Cambridge weather. An investment and a
burden upon the heirs who must spend something each year on
the place . . . paint job, new shingles, mend the walk, etc. Family

quarrel: flowers or shrubbery for the landscaping? and if shrubs, what kind, and if hardy perennials, would snapdragons be facetious in a cemetery?

Cousin Lawrence infuriated everyone by causing the ornamental ironwork on the roof to be brilliantly gilded. Cousin Maude assessed each member of the family 17¢ to pay for the immediate application of black enamel paint to restore the propriety and hush the scandal. A secret sympathizer of Cousin Lawrence paid his 17¢, waited until the black paint was thoroughly dry, and then—in broad daylight—had his chauffeur drive him (Rolls-Royce 1925) to the cemetery, set up a small tent into which he retired to change from street clothes to painters overalls, and with his own hand painted the ironwork a beautiful Kelly green, the chauffeur steadying the ladder and helping wipe the green paint off his person after the job was done, the street clothes restored, the tent removed. He was driven back to town where he sent a telegram in the name of the cemetery corporation complaining to Cousin Maude about the green paint.

14:x:60

Warnings, Responses, Etc.

"You better get next to yourself," my father used to say,
"Hanging around loose and unnecessary."
                    ("Hello there, Loose & Unnecessary," coming up
                    the walk from his car
                    me slung in a lawn chair reading)
MEANING: Alert yourself
         Be aware
         What's happening & what
         Do you think of it, how
         Do you feel about it

What shall you (when push
    comes to shove)
Do about it? & if you were any good at all
You'd feel that weight or pressure
Continuously
& comport yourself accordingly

("The strenuous life," Mr. Roosevelt said,
meaning something quite other)
   Which isn't a sandbag or "circumstance"
   It's inside after all
   One's own metabolic transmutations make the world go round
Next to myself
        the world and all the people in it
        asserting doggedly that I don't exist
        & certainly if I close my eyes I go away
Next to myself,

AN EMBLEM
a mountain creek under logs over boulders
potholes in its bed patches of gravel the water
invariably falls into eddies at particular points breaks
into spray or spreads in heavy darkness as long as the water
source high up the canyon no end in sight beyond vinemaple
overhang downstream

flows
       & & & & & & & &
RESPONDS:
      To J. about art &c., that you must break yourself
      to create anything, this I, this self, holes have to be
      punched, cracks made in it to release the
      power, beauty, whatever; the act
      breaks us, a radical force like sex not lightly
      to be used,

      FIREBALLS ("plasma," the physicists call it now)
      Mesmer and Franklin thought in terms of "an
      electrick fluid")

> but I suppress a section of it here, a piece of it I
> fear is likely to fall on my own head . . . can I
> walk around it?

> & walking, fall into a tar pit!

A FURTHER EMBLEM:

> a line appears to separate the sea and sky at the
> horizon.
> You put it there, your eye, the air is hollow
> And the earth falls away before your feet

ANOTHER, OF THE BALANCE:

> the beam of the scales a horizon line between
> a mechanical governor, two whirling balls, &
> the mind, its nature must be described as "built of
> contraries or opposites"
> & & & & & & & &

There we go again
A struggle for power (whatever
it is, lying around loose ((Comrade T. remarked))
in the streets)

> ". . . don't I know it! I gonna
> tell you . . . !"

3:ii:60

Historical Disquisitions

Hello, hello, what I wanted to tell you was
The world's invisible
You see only yourself, that's not the world
            although you are of it

Are you there

> hello
> why do you have your head in a sack?
> a roony-bomb dream tank?

235

Why you got a banana in your ear?

You where?

                    Brown eyes they see blue sky

                    The world imagines you
                    Figure it's a planet

                                        You hear?

            an obscure star in the middle

Once you were pleasure-milk and egg

            Were you there

Now you are eggs of milk between your legs

            Are you there

"I am situated somewhere near the rim of a fairly large galaxy
which is one of a group of same & outside of which a considerable
number take their way at incredible speeds & apparently in the
opposite direction . . ."

                    You are a wish to squirt pleasantly
                    You want a lot of things & they are nice & you imagine
                    They are you and therefore you are nice
                    You are a wish to be here
                    Wishing yourself
                                        elsewhere

"Hello. Try to talk some sense even if you
don't think any
It is history
            (your mistake: "History WAS")
                                        now

                        *

History an explanation of why I deserve what I take

                        *

History an explanation of why I get what I deserve

*

(Through more or less clenched teeth):
"How can you sit there & look at the faces
you see in Montgomery Street wiped blank
from selling whatever brains they got faces
in 3rd Street blank from facing a lathe all day
& TV all night African tromped-on faces Asiatic
hunger faces Washington war-masks & smile at me
about how after all this is a Moral Universe
gives me the screaming jumping meemies I thought
you were bright enough had enough work-experience
yourself to have some faint idea of . . ."

*

hello.
"THE WIND RATTLES THE WINDOW I CAN'T
SLEEP FRIDAY NIGHT IS VERY LARGE IN SAN
FRANCISCO THE LOWER CLASSES GET PAID ON
FRIDAY & GET ON THEIR WAY TO SPEND IT IN
UPPER-MIDDLE-CLASS CLIPJOINTS THEY CLAIM
AREN'T TOURIST TRAPS THE UPPER CLASSES ARE
LUSHED OUT OF THEIR HEADS DOWN IN PEBBLE
BEACH SUCKING EACH OTHER'S & WILL SKIP THE
SHRINKER MONDAY HE'S GAY HIMSELF THE
SILLY SON OF A BITCH AS LONG AS I'M NOT OUT
HUSTLING SAILORS ON MARKET STREET & ONLY
WHEN I'M LUSHED OUT ON MY OWN PREMISES
(FOR WHICH I PAY EXCESSIVELY HIGH TAXES)

I DON'T CARE"

"The middle classes the middle class is mainly from out of
town (that's what I like about San Francisco everybody's either
up or down) they come & look at us they go away puzzled where
they remain,

outclassed . . .

(they will fight the Rooshuns &c.
they will fight the gooks & wogs & chinks &
japs & niggers & commies & catholics & wall
street & any man that tries to tell them
different . . .)"

"The upper classes don't bother me a bit except
why do they let themselves be buffaloed into
hiring the creepy managers they do? Faceless men to
represent a legal fiction? The upper
well, the . . ."

"UPPER CLASSES ARE HARMLESSLY IM-
BECILE THE LOWER CLASSES PRETEND NOT TO EX-
IST (& VERY NEARLY CAN'T, OUTSIDE OF JAIL) THE
MIDDLE CLASS MANAGER MERCHANT BANKER PRO-
FESSIONAL PROFESSIONAL THE SOLID (IT'S THE
CHEESE THAT MAKES IT BINDING) CALVINISTFREUD-
IAN DEMOCRACY SWELLS

& BLOSSOMS!"

TERMINAL LUES ACROSS THE SHOULDERS
OF THE WORLD

"The Roman Empire went to hell when the Romans bought themselves a goon-squad; bankrupted themselves trying to enforce moral
and sumptuary laws . . ."

History's now

9:vii:60

Movie Night

Cry no more fitful membrane dreamflower
And you dismal terror gunsel pestering my sleep
You chase imaginary wrong

Murder theater bridge to soda cracker
Above the dead spring child flower festival Italian light
Colors of enamel precious Memling Van Eyck glaze
Desert in the sky where possibly you walk where you're going.

29:v:6o

Essex Was a Cowboy in Vermont

"LOTS
      of money all new and different
38 degrees below zero, feeding cattle
The maid got mad because I ate so much
& everyone had loads of money

They didn't want the other ranchers to know they had so much
money
All transactions were carried on by telegrams in French

Universal International Money Millions To Come To This
Rancher
A fifteen thousand dollar Rodin on the wall everybody sat in the
Kitchen they didn't know what to do with the rest of the house

If I wanted to go to NY next week I'd go
If I wanted to go to Europe next month I'd go
I'd be scared to death if I had a million dollars

Have it, I guess, in a trust-fund paying 100 dollars a month?
Otherwise I might do nothing except ski in Europe or go
          to South America
          Whenever I felt like it
Or go to Japan or hire a yacht and take you all with me
. . . it might be funny taking the whole
Household everybody wearing the same hats in the tropics—
          dressed the way you are now—

The Agha Khan wanted to buy the ranch but he died
                    Shortly thereafter"

27–28:v:60

Dream

Wander through expensive party not for me
Open door into formal diningroom I've offended, they are gone
Step out of window & swing on a velvet rope to top of old wall
            dangerous muddy grass flowers
                    the top of the arch! (it collapses as my left foot
                    reaches solid rock ridge
                            nightmare gulf behind below me)

    Funeral on a sunny day in Spring, child procession in festival
    clothes
    Child in open coffin half seen under giant flower wreaths
                            passes

    Landscape: barren river valley in high plateau-desert crossed by
    two bridges, one a Roman aqueduct, partly lost, incomplete,
    worked into new bright girder work repeating enormous arches
    across miles of wide valley sunset of a day order and peace
    far below the aqueduct, two ruined castle palaces

18:v:60

Itchy

What is your name feathers and eyes Mabel Spinning Wheel
Marguerite Pearl Flower

What are you spinning feathers flowers and pearls
      "répon-, répon-, réponds vite!"
Eaglefeather bullseye manheaded lion-wheel
       "Ah, *Marguerite!*
        Réponds-toi! Réponds-toi!
angelflame

      THE SIGN OF FOUR
                     not meaning what they thought at all
     ANGELFLAME
Did you tell any lies today?
Learn anything?
Did the thought occur to you, "This is a good
Solid unchanging world?"
              KNOTHEAD!
Did you forget anything?
        Are you paying attention?
             PEABRAIN!

What are you doing right this minute?
What shall you do one second from now?

           TOO BAD!
           TOO LATE!
           YOU LOSE!
                 (temporarily)
YANKEE DOG, YOU DIE!
           (temporarily)

Aimlessly
Not a success
Accidentally evil idleness
          (temporarily)
               Angelname

Why do you live the way you do?
Feather spins as it falls
Even if you did it better, who would care?

they put you in jail for trying, but then you're not
interested in Christianity except as one of the chief
keys to understanding the psychosis presently afflicting
our several minds, i.e. American Culture: which isn't
as sick as the intellectual journals try to tell us—
it (Culture USA)
                    is an illness

Laying up crowns and harps in heaven

ANGELFLAME

is what we've got, we itch all over
And if we scratch once, all the light escapes and we fall
                    in darkness
Total cynicism, "I got a right to do whatever I please"

ANGELFLAME

Hanged for a sheep as for a goat
We talk mean and die sudden.

15:iv:60

A *Vision of the Bodhisattvas*

They pass before me one by one riding on animals
"What are you waiting for," they want to know

Z—, young as he is (& mad into the bargain) tells me
"Some day you'll drop everything & become a *rishi*, you know."

I know
The forest is there, I've lived in it
        more certainly than this town? Irrelevant—

What am I waiting for?
A change in customs that will take 1000 years to come about?
Who's to make the change but me?

"Returning again and again," Amida says

Why's that dream so necessary? walking out of whatever house
alone
Nothing but the clothes on my back, money or no
Down the road to the next place the highway leading to the
mountains
From which I absolutely must come back

What business have I to do that?
I know the world and I love it too much and it
Is not the one I'd find outside this door.

31:iii:60

Palace Café

"Don't have any money bring me some brown toast OK
  I pay you medium I want it medium,
  Lots of money. You
  Sit down."

8:iii:60

Haiku, for Gary Snyder

                   I S
Here's a dragonfly
                (T O T A L L Y)
Where it was,

          that place no longer exists.

15:i:60

An Irregular Ode

Once I began to write,
Be ruled by Beauty & her wilfullness
& got no further
Choking and wheezing, subject completely to the selfishness
                    of my own history

I don't wonder that you doubt my love
My attention wanders even now, squinting at the moon
            bamboo blinds—I should be with you
                    we're only blocks apart

The same imaginary beauty splits us up, I keep chasing
            the one who invents the mountains and the stars
I'm a fool supposing she's someone else than you
            are moss & ferns in forest light

                                                    13:i:60

To a Poet

She sings the music
        pulls you down
She's totally irresponsible
        so are your ears (they're supposed to hear)
But why do you care so much
        for music?

                                                    31:xii:59

New York City

4 A.M. goggle-eyed and pestering myself
            (no fit subject, a cold in the chest)
        Want to go home
        Don't like ConEdison smokestack blockhouse
        Cocknozzle clear across (I'm lost again—14th St.?)

Really the city & amiable as it is, part of it probably Seattle
Or Portland my childhood memory

Best because it's anything I want it to be and full of dinky trees
                    and mystery

    Where's the mob, the gangsters?
    They all in Kansas City 21st Floor
    $300 London handmade suits conducting war against the
    Mafia?
    Where's Jack? Nobody home in Long Island
    Where's anybody? All I see is Melville, Whitman,
    Poe and Henry James promenading the Bowery 3 A.M.
        spelled "Bouwerie"
    and they aren't talking to me, I'm an out-of-towner
    Not even the cops talk to me; at home they stop me
        any time after ten P.M.

In Houston Street the Brooklyn Bridge pops out behind a building
I've gone the wrong way again unless I was going to Williamsburgh

I have money in my pocket nobody steals it
The Long Island Railway gives me polite conversation and free
vodka
        fallen leaves slow it down

The Armory! How did I find that? And it W A S something,
        ten years before I was born

I hunt for the pattern:
        8th Ave. has a dogleg at Sheridan Square
        4th St. is occasionally Great Jones
        The Cedar Bar—well, there's Cooper Union and
            something
        like Ninth St. unless it's University Place

Seagulls in Avenue A, bring me to home!
New York Marble Cemetery, bring me to home!
Katz's Delicatessen, (closed), bring me to home!
        but not for two weeks and I'm not really homesick
                anyway

How do you get out of the Baths of Caracalla?
I burrowed out through Postoffice Herodotus,
Swift courier late on his appointed rounds.

9:xi:59

Farewell!

Goodbye
I cannot tarry
"*ici*
Je suis très triste"
(Melisande)
duck down
duck down
f l o a t i n g
DUCK!
another one!
BOOM!   (Krunk!)

7:x:59

Temporarily Insane

Mr. B retreats into his bed
Semi-coma hangover problem-solving dream
A perfect future, flat on his back
Bamboo stripes lock him in
He tells me "All the birds are dead"
The broken window does not exist.

12:ix:59

Song for 2 Balalaikas on the Corner of 3rd & Market

We have no peanuts to eat so sad
While looking up tall buildings capitalistic
We cannot return to izba on the steps of Russia Hill
Unless instant money appear in tambourine
                    UNFORTUNATELY
The snow is falling in our galoshes
Wolves in our underwear alas poor Czar
Our oatfield crushed under tractors
Varnish falls off our balalaikas all the strings are warped
                    we sing out of tune
Give us bread and money, sad,
                    S A D !

*

(*With much assistance from Michael McClure, 14:viii:59*)

To the Moon

O Moon!
Gradually
                    Milo of Croton
Lifting all the seas
        indifferently
Leaf shadows & bright reflections
        simultaneously

                                        13:viii:59

I Am King Giant Dragon Sun

                                        F a d i n g
you're sitting (Baby) on my toe
& your arm on some kind of nerve-center
                    my trembly hand

247

my liver singing anthems
            (Have you been eating roses?)
cotton eyes calm sea belly

(*LACUNA*)

. . . flat out, much speed high above the vacant page
& no connection. The Daly City Turnoff
Submergence
                as under molten metal pouring into a cast
                a form incomprehensible from the outside. . . .

(*LACUNA*)

I pretend my life stops & after my exit the whole continuum
Snaps back into its own shape after my passing
An ordinary sequence, ice to water to steam
Carbon cycle in a star a sun
King as king (not   OF   anything or place)
Crown, robe, sceptre and orb, complete royalty
No power problem, the powers completely known & understood
        a chess king, a star of the Main Sequence
        i.e. a predictable life-cycle blue white yellow orange red
        & the attendant internal sub-atomic shifts between too hot
        too compressed to be thought of as "substance"
        & existence under some other name

"Our "space" has the property of being distorted
by electromagnetic waves." —A. Einstein (we do not know
why the radio works, a mystery no matter how inane its
                                conversation
a guillotine for shelling peas)

Please don't cut off my circulation

        to wake up embarrassed
                        half soaked into this oriental rug

You got that pearl-chain Byzantine look again
Chiafu's calligraphy on the wall:

>   MOUNTAIN
>   Eye/walk
>   gate/heart ("mind," "*l'esprit*," &c.)

its characters either most eccentric or very live
      I can't tell which

Portrait of Han Shan and his broom, by an unknown hand
                   (Liang Kai?)
Not immediately decipherable either
                       if at all

Eardrums ballooning out & singing,
I sit on a lime-tree branch with Coleridge
          bitching and chirping
Pythagoras heard the dodecahedron—find THAT sound again!
    (already, perhaps, found? and by the wrong man—
          Rinaldo Hahn, for example?)

We are known by the character of those things to which we visibly
R E A C T ?

Under total anaesthesia and feeling everything
But most, that all the things and persons I am
Are precious, rare & inconsequential, no weight in the scale
& sitting here maybe 48 hours
Concentrating on total insanity. . . .
I don't belong to that and I don't belong to myself

I told Baby, "Flipping out isn't the WORST that can happen"

May 8th, 1959: Where the will is there is roses.

N O T E , 27:ix:64, that the "unknown hand" at line 41 above belonged to
Yen Hui, 12th-century painter. See plates 6a & 6b in D. T. Suzuki's
Zen and Japanese Culture, Bollingen Series LXIV, Pantheon (New York, 1959
reprint).

For a Picture by Mike Nathan

Two surgeons tired waiting—break
           between operations
Their baffled faces knowing, they imagine
      life and death are private secrets
Tiny balances, thin alterations between "me"
      and "meat" insulate
      isolate from the rest of us . . .

Frightened, they must depend (like us)
      on "the doctor," one of themselves
They know in the end they'll be yelling
      SAVE ME!   SAVE ME!   I AM A MAN!
      INFINITELY VALUABLE!
Knowing the doctor might be nervous or unstable
      on just that particular day

We must pretend to respect their mystery
Uninitiated as they are to ours, tolerate
Their damned insulting manners, their open sadism
They are lonely and they need our help.

                                        4:iv:59

Take, 25:iii:59

I've run so far in one circle I'm visible now
      only from the chest upwards
Any poet who's really any good
Dances a complicated maze on top of the ground
      scarcely wearing out the grass

Motion Day

Mr. R: Whereabouts in the Waldport area do you live?
Mrs. H: About five miles south of Waldport on Highway 101.
Mr. R: Down towards Yachats?
Mrs. H: You know where the whale skeleton is? Tilly the Whale?
Mr. R: Yes.
Mrs. H: Right near there.

*

Later. The court reporter sits at her machine, apparently asleep. From where I sit I can see her fingers working the keys, but it seems that the lawyers can't. One of them asks, severely, "Did you get that, Miss Reporter?" The reporter opens her eyes, looks surprised and says, "Yes I did." The lawyer asks her to read the last question and answer. She begins turning loops of paper tape from behind her machine, peering at them, mumbling and moaning like the Pythian priestess, then suddenly articulates the question very clearly, and its answer as well. She added, "I've got you in there all the way through, Mr. Co-counselor." The judge said, "Well, let's proceed."

29:i:59

I Think of Mountains

I keep thinking of Matlock Lake, nobody can live there
Not for long, it's Government land over two miles high
Not enough air (which gives you notions, "This is real, this is true")
University Peak stands/falls just overhead, the mistaken idea
"Of mountains he is Sumeru," a little over 13000 feet

Wednesday morning's "test-shot" from Nevada, I figured
"The mountain has split, the Goddess has appeared!"

They've had these thoughts in India thousands of years
& every minute millions die of them—
Radiation sickness from the mountains

Is it only a question of balance—
Power and knowledge their proper economy
Are we stuck at last with Aristotle?

When I came down to Berkeley my cottage was a birdhouse
I had to crawl in the door on my hands and knees I was immense!
What was I doing there? What was the ceiling for? The walls?

I NO LONGER HAD TO BREATHE

Nobody could live there, town of perpetual childhood
Babyland the wrong door of the time-machine
No changes except the buildings and trees no future
Except Five o'clock or the week-end about to happen
(Life stops at midnight Sunday)

To D O   anything (consciously) N O W
A problem, paradox, quandary.
The disciples, the hearers listen in silence
The inside boys don't crack a smile
The Big Wheel hollers "Turtle eggs!"

The difference between wisdom and ignorance
The potential between them
A current of human misery (freedom and slavery) which
Can be accurately measured

The mountain a lump of granite in my skull
My mouth filled with Indian corpse meat

28:x:58

Against the Magic War: An Open Letter to Robert Duncan

Dear Robert, for whatever reason, you sent this dream against me:
A lady brought me over in a boat with several kinds of bread.
She says, "You ought to see him singing hymns and wheedling around, "Won't any of you buy yourselves a bridge game?"

I paid several times to get in and out of the amusement park. I showed all my mis-marked identification & all the children laughed and shot hot sparks at me. I should have busted their space helmets!

Then my father said, "I could take you to India," and I cried then because I'm sorry he's old & I haven't done anything about it & he said, "That don't mean anything, all that bawling around, you're only feeling sorry for yourself, just like Jack tells me (he's been crying, too, at his father—he says, "There's too much furniture in my apartment"—we've had a lot of long talks lately)"

A double rebounding track of lightning, Victory to salute and Salute to Victory

and I awoke with eye-pains, conscious of swift lights and motions through the room and your name & I exorcised the shade, the emanation of Robert Duncan from this room with magical implements and music, spells of magic so profound I am ashamed of having used them. Later, you caused your demons to laugh outside my house at four in the morning—I know they were yours, your name was on them, it shone through the walls. I invited them in for gasoline, lit fires to warm them, keep up their strength. One had a sore: I poulticed it with tabasco sauce and sandpaper & in gratitude he became a horde of pride-spiders that swarmed over me, biting & singing:

> "Temperance, Fortitude & Justice
> The pen is mightier than the sword
> Celibacy, poverty, obedience—
> Virtue always gets its own reward."

I hid them in the oven when the sun came up. I'll send them home
tonight with cookies & milk for you and all your friends.

O Robert, all of us are bound by hate & power—all we know is
misery and self-indulgence—why this battle among enchanters?
    Blind power the sightless crown the enchained sword
    A tyranny of magic in the sun
    Hitting out on all sides to defend an empty center
    The raving Face of Glory whirling, raining down
    Flooding with fire

If it were as splendid as all that
If the destruction were total
If it took that single hair out of my soup
Then yes, I praise it, I consent, I worship
But it does everything else. The hair remains,
The nature of soup admitting a possible hair
Or somebody's thumb

LIST OF POSITIVE THINGS TO DO

1) Wash the dishes.
2) Wear a hair-net while cooking.
3) Keep the cat out of the kitchen, the diningroom.
4) Serve the soup in a dish with a wide brim—or
   don't fill the rimless dish too full.

With many blessings,
P.

23:vii:57

From an Envelope Addressed to Charles Olson

Zucchini rollers
Summer-squash crown gears
Innocent vegetable machine
Illegal thousand-dollar cabbage leaves
New Jersey Mafia salad contemplation

3:vii:58

254

Corvallis Down the Road

Where does the weather turn off for Elk City?

18:v:58

Sincerity Shot

My hair is itchy, my wandering shorts
Provoke fantasies of sexual congress
& having removed them I have this to say:

> I'm drinking sweet Italian vermouth with ice in it
> No more visions, only sensations of general contentment
> & a certain smug self-righteousness
> > about my present continence

& " 'a babbled o' green fields" (cheating already! A quote.)
> &
This vermouth tastes like shaving-soap

> (Eating a dish of ginger beef,
> The Judge: "I don't like it."
> I: "It's good; it tastes like Cashmere Bouquet."
> The Judge: "Some people *like* to eat soap.")

More cheating, that was memory
& not what I have to say, which is:
> My nose itches, a prognostication
> > a) I shall presently kiss a fool
> > > or
> > b) Someone is coming to visit me,
> . . . but a lying prophecy, it being 12:35 A.M.
> & I don't know nobody to kiss in this town,

23:iii:58

Translation of a Lost Play by M. M.

Maurice.   O, Ferdinand, listen!
           What is that noise there, that tiny
           Sound issuing from that place there? Do you
           Hear that sound? What can be producing
           That so dolorous as if weeping baby?

Ferdinand.   That? Ah that, dear Maurice, that is
           The infantine Moses child weeping there amidst
           The bullrushes beside the dark river's edge making
           That sound there.

Maurice.   Why is it that he weeps there in that unique position?
Ferdinand.   He weeps there for that he is already a prophet.
Maurice.   Ah, glorious wretched little!

desunt ceterae

19:iii:58

"While the Patient Slept"

Why inquire into the astrolabe?
What use the quincunx now?
Unicorn.
      TROY IS DOWN
Stubborn
    Thebes in all her glory
Great Babylon
        fol-de-rol
           I live in a different town.

Spring 1958

For My Father

Being a modest man, you wanted
Expected an ordinary child
And here's this large, inscrutable object

          ME

      (Buddha's mother only dreamed
            of a white elephant;
      my mother . . .)

Cross between a TV camera and a rotary press
Busy turning itself into many printed pages
Heavy, a dust-collector, almost impossible
           to get off your hands, out of your house
Whatever it was, not an actual child

You recognize parts of the works, ones you first donated
But what are they doing—the flywheel horizontal
Spinning two directions at once
A walking-beam connected to a gear train turning camshafts—
Which produces material like this
Sometimes worth money to folks in New York
Or not, nobody knows why.

                                3:i:58

In Memory of a Statesman

What's become of my brains, my eyes?
I had them here a minute ago,
Now I can't find them anywhere . . .
      THE CHILDREN!
          arranging them in saucepans? the toy stove?
Bring them back immediately!

Carefully, clumsily ladling, a few hasty stitches
    (the dolly sewing machine)
Now listen!
The children wildly protest their future good behaviour
Return their attention to Baby
& I am free to continue:

> After the opening of the Crimean war it became evident
> that the tensile strength of a single hair from a sea-otter
> pelt (one which later became part of the great cape of
> that fur presented to the Empress Catherine of Russia)
> was found to be just $\frac{2}{3}$ds that of beryllium. . . .

MY DEARS!
Daddy is sorry that he has had forcibly to detain you at the very
beginning of what in prospect appeared to be a highly interesting
& instructive expedition into the never so dim & expensive interior
of the television receiver and it is my duty to express the most
profound regrets of my Government concerning the untoward
incident which so recently disturbed the equanimity of your Government's Minister Plenipotentiary during his late visit to Chagrin
Falls.

If I give you one cooky you must drink a full glass of milk
And a full glass of milk with each succeeding cooky.
Do you understand?

27:xii:57

Apedeath

Today I found record of a dream: the marble rotunda
Virtuous bronze & the dying hairy ancestor

The marble paternal dome empty without my double and me
I cannot save the ancestor totem-beast
Which dies & I am pursued as his killer

Through the Dutch wooden store (a thief & no thief but afraid)
To the river/canal bank—safety in the white house
Impossible to reach

Escape up the wooden ramp to bridge
Into Seattle/Portland foggy rain

I wake up in a strange house, looking at a familiar chair
& a door that doesn't belong & wake dying
My own cottage floor bed facing the bookcase Berkeley summer
night.

11:xi:57

Literary Life in the Golden West
A Birthday Poem for (&/or about) Mr. J-L. K., 20:v:57

*

Now we are thirty-five we no longer enjoy red neon
(MILNER HOTEL)
We don't know what to do except
Stand on our head four minutes a day
To adjust our metabolism and feel a physical
Ecstasy when we stand up & the blood
Rushes down from our head

It is impossible to write in the big front room
The space, the high ceiling scares us
In the kitchen we write:

"I have nothing to write about,
no work to do—I made a pastel picture of the backyard
I'm reading *Swann's Way*, I talk to my mother & go see
my friends, they are dull and vaguely busy suffering
from metabolic disturbances (they don't stand on their
heads) I just finished writing a book 1000 pages long,

I'm going away to—or am going to have to manufacture—
another world, this one is all worn out, Buddha is much
more interesting than fucking, eating or writing, my
mother is happy, now I can die next week."

None of our serious friends approve of this
Routine they write articles against us in all
The liberal magazines, the young hitch-hike from New York
And Alabama with their poems, we sit together in Portsmouth
Plaza
Drinking muscatel and swapping stories
Until the buttons drive us home.

Esprit d'Escalier *Rant*,

Directed at Dr. P.'s class in English 106-B

You didn't see me, you didn't hear me, I said
The theory comes in later, a frame,
And even then the picture juts
Past it, down or sometimes through the wall.

Me, I don't understand counterpoint
But playing Bach on the piano
I really pick up and fly with him. The shapes
The figures are on the page

My eyes are fingers and ears
They work a design, a real
Imaginary pattern in the mind
That feels rough or buttered, like Dante said.

Triangle to Bach
Is triangle to me—*and*
A clown's hat and a lovely hair pie
(Turn it over in your heads.)

Like I mean you
Aren't questions, each of you
Is an answer.
But you'd gone, all of you afraid

Of mistaking CAT for "cat," a merry-go-round
For a gift-horse with a smile. Not, damn it, I SAID NOT
A private world,
Nor off a Georgian platter;

And when the dish I did use broke,
I hope to God some
Of the contents splashed on everybody's clothes. You
May not call it love, but that's what it is.

9:i:57

The First Day of November

I'll walk to the postoffice & then to work
Seeing hot cinnabar geraniums green circular leaves
Dry heads and drying stalks of yarrow

Hearing in my head   *"Ist das nicht ein' schöne Welt?*
                                    . . . schöne Welt?
                                    Schöne Welt! Und nimmer,
Mahler!   *Nimmer. . . ."*

Don't see that wren I hear

No rain after all
Though the air is heavy
                            and the war is on again
        (caused by my own carelessness, goofing)
Sphinx will have another medal on her chest

And the postoffice is closed
In commemoration of the Feast of St. Fellation

261

The same sad war, the universal drag, I lost
Four teeth in the service
                    "Schöne Welt!"
I must have been bored without knowing it
And now the rain comes down.

FICHE-MOI LA PAIX!

1:xi:56

I Give Up

I hate the morning, I hate the night
Lie down and die, tell me some more
Don't go to sleep, don't leave me alone

The dreams: of changes, suffocation
Loss of speech, pursuit by monsters
Or of endless logical argument

Awake and watching you sleep is worse
The stores are closed, no buses run
Homicidal maniacs prowl the suburbs

And the happy phantom of my greatness
Wakes and grasps this pen, leaving
A heap of used-up words to read

After a morning dream of music.

22:ix:56

Sauced

I go reeling down the hall
                    into the leaves!
Tree of Heaven balcony door is open
        A Trio for Jaybird, Telephone & Trombone

Jay
Jay
Trambone! poo-poo-poo   POO!
Jay
Telephone
Poo jay telebone
Tram Sunday poo

The landlady explains the vacant room across the hall:
          "Very quiet."

          Gold squirrel!
                         in pear tree
Surgeons the stem &   (Campanile 5 P.M.)
               pear wobbling in his no-chin-space
Leaps into Heaven tree
The neighbors' pears

Jay   Jay
     (   )
      F Train horn
Wren
          airplanes in the eves like hornets
Notably drunken Berkeley Sunday 6 November '55

Tell Me More

Not a word
Not for love or money
Not a single word from me, nor music
     (these are not words but signs
     they carry no charge)
Make your own speech
You'll get none of mine

Not a consenting silence
Not withdrawal
The continuation in another mode
          A finger pointing at the moon
All the rest is for you
You name it
And welcome

11:i:54

Out of It

What's it to me? The telephone
Rings only when I'm not home
The biggest knockers in the world
On television; I have no set

We never see you; what do you do?

I sun myself in the agora
Watch periwinkles on the rocks
Below the Palace of the Legion of Honor
Record the fishes' comments on the children
Outside the tank (the aquarium is wired)

You inhabit public buildings?

A taste for marble in a wooden age
A weakness for the epic that betrays
A twiddly mind.

8:iv:53

Homage to Lucretius

It all depends on how fast you're going
Tending towards light, sound
Or the quiet of mere polarity

Objects: Slowness

Screen
A walking sieve
Wide-open and nowhere
The mountains themselves
Sucked up into turnips, trees
Wander as bones, nails, horns

And we want crystals,
Given a handful of mercury
(Which can be frozen into a pattern vulnerable to body heat)

The notion intimidates us
We can't easily imagine another world
This one being barely
Visible:
We lined up and pissed in a snowbank
A slight thaw would expose
Three tubes of yellow ice

And so on . . .
A world not entirely new
But realized,
The process clarified
Bless your little pointed head!

1952

EVERY DAY
1964-1965

Respectfully dedicated to the memory of
JOHN McLAREN
1846–1943
Builder of Golden Gate Park

The Preface

A continuous fabric (nerve movie?) exactly as wide as these lines—
"continuous" within a certain time-limit, say a few hours of total
attention and pleasure: to move smoothly past the reader's eyes,
across his brain: the moving sheet has shaped holes in it which
trip the synapse finger-levers of reader's brain causing great sections
of his nervous system—distant galaxies hitherto unsuspected (now
added to International Galactic Catalog)—to LIGHT UP. Bring
out new masses, maps old happy memory.

12:viii:64
7:xi:64

THE DAYS

March 1964

more than welcome
        more than enough –

of all things !
    where's all this cold air
            come from ?

Scribble

Banderolle

{ Giovanni della Bande Nere }

What's your platform ?

            Ressurexion
            Renaissance
            Total Paradise

I put down programatical funk. {speaking, now,
    absolutely off the record – my business isn't
    really to put anything down – I want
    a new life } I say RISE AND
FLOURISH
                for all you're worth {it is all
                        you're worth ? }
        SHINE , Radiate,
                Joy bliss and whoopee vibrations !
{The night air! }
{ The weather ! }
                    EXQUISITE
            what did you say the message was ?

270

Corinthian Columns

Let me get up, I have to look, to smell, to taste everything.

in out of	fall petal	dust	In,
in, out of the	blossom	hairs	Out of the
W E A T H E R	leaf	lint	rain
	twig		

	Perish in the dust		dust
	Become jewels		lint
	of rare worth and		hairs
	color		

dust is powdered rock, metal, flesh, bones, woods, fruits
—a pulverized universe

Water is even finer

        Gas.

                                     22:iii:64

Mexico

Baja California
           far away underneath where we are now

("O "Kiki" / O Miss Margaret Jarvis")

           the way things fit together
           a drill which makes a square hole

"DO ME NEXT!"

                                     25:iii:64

Chagrin

Winter is gone—how I abused it!
Wasted an age, an elderly child

What's become of Christopher's painting?
Where is Mertis her coal-oil stove?

26:iii:64

Composition

I teeter I dangle I jingle
Fidget with my fingers ears and nose

Make little repairs—tape or glue
And the floor is filthy again

> putting on hats in front of a mirror
> down in front
> down in back
> slaunchways
> mugging and posing, thinking of
those beggars Buñuel shows in *Viridiana*,
gesture of one finger, two eyes,
the smallest imaginable shimmy
creates a gigantic bacchanal

Iron straps won't hold it all together
It's already there, a piano—in tune with itself—
a closed system:
Even if you play on it with feathers, rocks, rubber tubing,
Dear John Cage

26:iii:64

The Lotus Sutra, Naturalized

I got drunk your house
You put that diamond my shirt pocket
How am I supposed to know?
Laying there in drunk tank
        strange town don't nobody know
Get out of jail at last you say
"You already spend that diamond?"
How am I going to know?

                               27:iii:64

Early Spring

The dog writes on the window
        with his nose

                               30:iii:64

The Mystery

Who are they when
I don't see them?

I hear walking in the next house
What face?

Walking in the next room is Mother,
        same as usual, visible or not
        I trust her to remain herself

Who's next door?

Presumably them Chinamen know what's
happening on their own scene

30:iii:64

The Problem

Hot tea for breakfast
Hot tea is
            breakfast
With sugar in it

                What's for lunch and
                        where
                          ?

13:iv:64

The Metaphysical Town Hall and Bookshop

"I was sitting there. I knew it was her.
I knew she had a message and the message was love."

17:iv:64

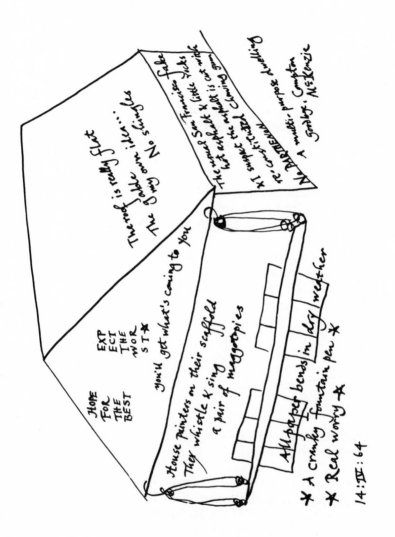

The roof is really flat
The gable our own idea...
No shingles

HOPE
FOR
THE
BEST

EXP
ECT
THE
WOR
ST *

You'll get what's coming to you

The roof San Francisco fake
hot asphalt & little sticks
I suspect the asphalt is cut with
re'-cycled Chewing gum
*I suspect the
No PARTHENON
A multi-purpose dwelling
A Goodbye, Compton
Goodbye, M'Kenzie

House painters on their scaffold
They whistle & sing
a pair of maggotpies

All paper bends in dry weather

* A crunchy fountain pen *
* Real worry *

14:IX:64

275

Absolute Realty Co.: Two Views

1.

THE GREAT GLOBE ITSELF

I keep hearing the airplanes tell me
The world is tinier every minute
I begin believing them, getting scared.
I forget how the country looks when I'm flying:
Very small brown or green spots of cities on the edges
              of great oceans, forests, deserts

There's enough room. I can afford to be pleasant & cordial to you
         . . . at least for a while . . .
Remembering the Matto Grosso, Idaho, Montana, British Columbia,
New Hampshire, other waste places,
All the plains and mountains where I can get away from you
To remember you all the more fondly,
All your nobler virtues.

7:v:64

2.

Vulture Peak

Although my room is very small
The ceiling is high.

Space enough for me and the 500 books I need most
The great pipe organ and Sebastian Bach in 46 volumes
              (I really NEED the Bachgesellschaft Edition)
              will arrive soon, if I have any luck at all.

Plenty room for everybody:
Manjusri and 4700 bodhisattvas, arhats, pratyekabuddhas,
              disciples, hearers, Devas, Gandharvas, Apsaras,

kinnaras, gnomes, giants, nauch girls, great
serpents, garudas, demons, men, and beings not
human, flower ladies, water babies, beach boys,
poets, angels, policemen, taxi drivers, gondoliers,
fry cooks and the Five Marx Brothers

All of us happy, drinking tea, eating *Linsertorte*,
Admiring my soft plum-colored rug
The view of Mt. Diablo.

11:v:64

15:<i>v</i>:64

a date, a cribbage score?
        the size of a machine part

"Hello,
    HOW
          are you?"
            "Fine."
So that was the meter man from the Gas company
15:v:64 being cubic yards of gas at

        "*HOW*
            are you?
        HOW
            are you?
        HUH?"

Is the gas man simple-minded?
Thousand cubic feet per minute
Volume, a rolled-up scroll

        "*HEY*, yaaa, here, yaa,
          here's yaaa
            pistol
      here, yaaa, *HEY!*
          Hey!
          Hey!"

Tommy's Birthday

O Greta Garbo!
The flowers all came back again—
More & faster than the slugs can eat—
Tragic Swede bouquet, camellias
            all are fallen,
You midnight sun!

                                                    1:vi:64

Caption for a Picture

A home of many-colored gas,
A way from   A S I A, monster.   Soul-trap.   Bactria!

                                                    21:vi:61

Magical Incantation

Pig fuck pig baby pig shit.   ham, bacon, pig
            sausage, Charles Lamb

            A beautiful sunset
            A gorgeous broad

_____

            *

_____

Fallen stars, fallen arches at Nimes,
            broken dick, fallen womb, Chagrin Falls
                  Ohio for the view,
            no fun for anybody.
Farewell Wilhelm Reich.

                                                    7:ix:64

278

Goddess

Where I walk is with her
In fire between the ocean waves
Towards that Lady I stand beside
Center of the earth in the center of the air
Stand moving star cloud
Roar music silence
Waves break over our muddy heads
Dash against our sunny feet

14:ix:64

Buck Rogers

Continual
departure from Earth towards the Magellanic Clouds

Let me out of here
I don't think you realize who I am
Officer!   Officer!   I
Want to make a phone call.
Officer!
I am entitled to make one phone call—
Officer!   Officer!

Shut up and go to sleep. Bust out of here. Blow this flytrap
COURAGE!

OUT OUT OUT OUT OUT

". . . can't do that to   M E !"

leave
town

11:x:64

The Chain of Lakes

FOR DONALD CARPENTER

Call of passing swans, why not
I haven't seen or heard a wild one—
      Look—that woman's trying to draw it,
      big notebook & brown crayon,
      her husband watches—
"Swan" translates the Sanskrit *"hamsa,"*
The great Gander whose flight is this universe, its nights & days
                 his breathing
Because "goose" means "fool" in English 19th Century,
A hundred years before that, a tailor's implement
And always a bird which defends the Capitol from invasion

Splash mudhens, chase mallards and
Fly again, fall back into

      no geese in this pond
      cars and beer cans & horse manure
      as it might be John Muir's Trail
         high in the Sierra

We hunted the buffalo but found none
Until we started home
Saw them standing or lying in a row
East fence of the meadow
Where a tree full of pigeons
      (Flowers!)
Shot up and away
No single fallen petal.

                          12:x:64

True Confessions

My real trouble is
People keep mistaking me
    for a human being

Olson (being a great poet) says
"Whalen!—that Whalen is a—a—
That Whalen is a great big vegetable!"

He's guessing exactly in the right direction.

6:xi:64

Dying Again

*Destruction, Death, Depression, Dismal & Up Again, With Any
Luck At All:*
Funerals, a set of 12.

1.

Ever since you shot me down a year ago
I've run the night journey (music by Sibelius)
Hanging in chains, face blackening, eyes & tongue forced out,
                drying
                strangling lungs, trying to crawl up
                    inside my throat

Kydde the Pirate swung in chains
    Wapping Old Stairs

8:vii:64

2.

Testing Reality

I wander through the movie in my skull, fortunately
I wasn't in the street just now, I'd have been hit by a trolley,
        a bike, a rollerskater

Sitting here I didn't see where I was going except
        backwards through a meat-grinder

        check   check   check

        The test for blackness

15:v:64

3.

I went to your house after you were dead
Nothing left except your pet white goat
        grazing the green meadow

4:vii:64

4.

        What do I care my old leaves crack
and wrinkle, bent flat broke and killed against
the windows,

        I have more, every spring
        Even this June morning smell the fragrance!

Dear Avocado.

Avocado made laws about the expansion or compression of gases
        The birds do a rain dance and jibber song:

        *"bee-deep-dja
        bee-deep-dja
        bee-deep-dja"*

        Some kind of magnolia

29:vi:64

5.

During the day I'm all right, I understand
We no longer see each other.
In dreams I go to pieces—
Four times I see you in tears, running away from me
I can't stand it, your hating me—

I wake up, eat breakfast, the day's filthy, we're apart

If we meet, later, you'll be gentle

This is all wrong, the dreams are true, your kindness when we meet
A waking dream, the consolation, the booby prize

15:viii:64

6.

Dying I see my soul depart—a black, feathery flying thing,
Completely alien—
This is my first and last view of
                    it. Europe and all goodbye.

29:ix:64

7.

Orders of the Day

Cancel all engagements: baleful influences
          reign: coughing & sickness brought on
          by rapid travel through Berkeley Hills
          the stars shower malign vibrations
                    moon rots, leaves decay
          fever
                    and fog,
          suffocation panic &c., also
                    a sore thumb.

26:x:64

8.

Labor Day fog is brilliant Rosh Hashana
I see my spirit, my soul, whoever it is
She sits under a tree, he sits under a bush
    all of us writing and singing

    brighter than the sun
    darker than today

---

*

TROPE CITY

---

*

---

    try running it
    more slowly—a
    pleasure at every
    speed or delightful
    keeping still (together)
    ? BLUE SPARKS ?

?

---

    try having it both ways
    if the pen travels over a
    small area, perhaps it could
    be both fast and beautiful?

SHOWER/SPRAY OF ZIRCONS

7:ix:64

9.

The Renaissance

Some days nothing
    gets done

I just sit and laugh.

When I do anything, everything is fine.
    You laugh, if you notice me at all.

    B E W A R E   T H E   D A Y   O F   J U D G M E N T ,
the   E L E C T I O N ,   Bloody Lamb Flag waving
        the splitting of the rocks
        the ocean's death
   what shall we say then,
          boiling,
What shall I say, "Maybe we can get you a cancellation;
    there is nothing available at this time."

Fell & terrible doom,
Quiet grass beside the lake

                    5:vi:64

10.

When I forget you,
Nothing happens except sleep, and
    waking with mouldy fur eyes
        dull skin slime drear tongue
           collapse nose loose balls
      no self to sink into
(McClure's favorite botanical animal
        MIXOMYCETES, the slime mould
           walking fungus)
I wandering feeble terror
Until I think of your appearance

gold bees fly in my room

               31:vii:64

11.

Brightly under the apple tree
White skulls in green grass
    (that's you and me)
We sing alternately alas
       and praise the blossoms
         perennially

*

Dark jeweled emblems of bright death.

6:vii:64

12.

Two Is a Pair

i.

To live forever &
    never die, so
We are here together,
In the morning.

ii.

How did I ever get here
       Without ever moving from
        there,
A magic, an enchantment, or a dream?

19:v:64

END OF DESTRUCTION, DEATH, DEPRESSION &c.

PROCEED AT OWN RISK

*

The Ode to Music

FOR MORTON SUBOTNICK

Where'd all the music
                    go?
"There's a piano in there, but nobody here can play on it.
Old Clodfelter can sing better than he ever lets on."

*

We wait
          for the fire from heaven
          for the maturation of our annuities
          for the new life, new earth
                    (Who's going to pay for the roof?)

*

"Georgette used to play just beautiful on her saxophone"
          "Waiting for the *Robert E. Lee*"

*

"We got this radio, the cabinet is just gorgeous
I've always loved the way it looks, it's got
                    beautiful wood in it
We listen to *Amos & Andy* and *The Richfield
Reporter*
But I'm asleep by the time *Amos & Andy*'s half over

*

I never could stand all that symphony music
All that high tone shrill screechy singing I just hate it
Some of it is beautiful, I guess, but oh God, when they get
Some woman with one of those high shrill sopranos . . .
I just never cared for it at all

*

. . . but I love nice quiet organ music
it's so soothing and restful I could listen to it for hours

or a violin with it—love to go to sleep listening to it
an organ and a violin

*

Dad and them get a big kick out of playing their fiddles
I never could read a note. Your own Dad has a beautiful voice
I never get tired of listening to him sing."

*

"It's a pleasure if your own kids are doing it,
terribly expensive and you've got to keep after them to practice
—I'm so grateful to my mother, she made me
absolutely made me practice and I'm so thankful for that
today;
     I take such pleasure in my music."

*

The length of a song, a short one by Stephen Foster
Or a hymn, that's all we got time for;
In the middle of a second or third verse,
A whispered conversation is likely to begin, something
We've just recollected (did the music remind us?)
To add to what we were saying
                before the music began
". . . that old Mrs. R. turned around,
gave us a dirty look,
           "SH*H*H*H !"
I don't know who that old cat thinks she is—
         Mrs. Astor's plush horse?"

*

How—or why
        do I fizz and throb
I guess I understand
    Camptown Races, the *Archduke* Trio,
       The Pearl Fishers
(Even if I don't like the first or the last)
are matters of life and death

I congratulate myself
I know all about art and I know what I like
      (Q.: ". . . but you *are* queer, aren't you?"
      (A.: "Yes—
          but I don't
          like
          you.")
What do I know or care about life and death
My concern is to arrange immediate BREAKTHROUGH
Into this heaven where we live
          as music

           *

the fingers that hear it as it happens
as it is being made, Thelonious Monk
"has the music going on all the time," AG told me
"You hear it while he's at the piano,
you see him listening to it when he's out walking around
it's *going* all the time."

           *

The best music I make myself, with a piano, or borrow
          a pipe organ
(People think the elephant bells beside my door
are purely decorative:
             wait until you hear my concerto)
Quite seriously the best is my own
Heard in a dream, I conduct a total orchestra
      (from the podium or from the organ console)
A gigantic auditorium (is there an audience?)
I wonder if all that
           can be heard by other beings—
people from other stars or maybe sea-beasts,
          just beyond our shore

While I sleep in stillness

           *

ALIVE!   Joyful or horrendous Being,
A goddess, they said,
Or a god,
Meaning that it zooms us away,
We find ourselves dancing,
Singing,
We are changed, we—   who so seriously commanded
So solemnly understood ourselves
the world,

Spin,
Leap and holler,
Out of our skulls
Life and death no problem, not interesting,
Free in the air as in happiest vision dream

AWAKE!

and smiling (weeping)
We dance
                together and apart
Awake and tireless
We soar beyond clouds and lights are music
Which streams from our moving
body mind laugh leap

2:iii:64
2:v:64

a very complicated way of saying "appearances deceive"?

Subjects

A
1. I see a bird
2. Some birds are good to eat
3. Birds' eggs are good to eat
4. Bird feathers make good pillows
5. Bird-dung is hard to remove from automobiles & buildings
6. My Grandmother kept canaries
7. I can take birds or leave them alone

B
1. I see a bird.
2. I hate birds
3. What if it bit me?
4. I'm going to hit that bird with a rock.
5. What if it got loose inside the house? TERROR
6. Uncle Lester's parrot bit me.
7. The world without birds would be better.

F
1. Walking thing goes away quick in the air. Where? How? BAW!

E
1. I see a bird.
2. The bird is a thrush, mistakenly called "robin" in the USA, "Turdus migratorius"
3. Habitat: spring to autumn US winter: south America
4. Diet: bugs & worms
5. Call: "peeowoopoo"
6. Many feathers.
7. Fits an ecological niche

C
1. I see a bird
2. I love birds
3. All birds are beautiful & free
4. Birds ought not to be kept in cages.
5. People ought not to shoot birds.
6. Poor bird, starving in the snow!
7. Dear birds!

D
1. Bird
2. No bird
3. Bird
4. I'm not a bird. ?
5. Bird's name is Sam.
6. If Subject B kills Sam with a rock, that will be hard luck for both B and Sam; however it is B's nature to kill birds – he'll have to figure it out.
7. B & Sam & me –? Subject? Object?

! BLOCK !

The Best of It

Worry walk, no thought appears
One foot follows rug to wood,
Alternate sun and foggy sky
Bulldozer concrete grinder breeze
The windows open again
Begin
    a line may
      start:
  spring open, like seams of a boat high on the hot sand

     *

   with luck
   water will seal them again
   and I'll float on the soundless
    wave

     *

No airhammers today, so far
Perhaps all of 16th Street
     opened
   & the sewer
     made perfect at last?

    *

Earth-mover, power-shovel, ditch-digger,
Whine clank and rumble, whichever
Bless you and your
     fourteen dollars by the hour

     *

Write it off as a day when I can't work,
tomorrow is a holiday. I can't handle books
& paper, having just put a layer of grease on
my hands, shedding their skin again, my
nerves wear it out from the inside I can't lie down

to write this in bed because I just re-heated
the tea, can't go to bed because I must
wait until Tommy brings me the key so I
can feed the cats tonight and tomorrow,

    Here it all sets, or freezes, two
things have to be moved before I can do one
that I wish,

        which is this
        whoever has,
           is responsible

    Try (the policemen, the doctor, my friends
insist—none of them is my father, my mother,
none of them knowing or feeling what I am)
        to face
        reality

           or we will kill you.
None of them able to escape my enchantment, magic spells.

The head of Orpheus appears to me, crowned with
vine leaves, old wrinkly beard or sleeping youth, a wing
seems to spring out beyond his left temple, as in marble
fragment known as "Hypnos"—wise, drugged, golden
the continuous great song

Please return daily. Look at me, Kids.

What's the big idea?

Nothing else will do except to begin performing, having had 20
seconds notice. (Suppose that the seconds are years.) Try not to
do it in your sleep.

What's the big idea?

Once it begins, it remains an embarrassment until one
reaches the end, when another perhaps more
disgusting mental savor manifests itself.

Deep glass fire crystal
There we throw down our crowns of gold

$250 at a clatter

a cure exists

The crystals are growing in the pressure tank, or so
I must, at last, believe. I find them lying on
the ground, or on my table or while I wander, sleeping,
through moss forests dimly green. These crystals have
a taste, a smell, many colors, combinations of sound,
texture, a spectrum appealing directly to the mind
alone.

*

Delusions of Reference

Occupied just now—taping a worn book jacket
I was whistling
     These Foolish Things Remind Me Of You
Seeing myself—and feeling
     sensation of dream, quite as if I were sleeping
"Seeing myself," I say, walking in a strange city
(Seattle downtown, Vancouver BC?)

My father used to say, "Don't believe everything you hear and only
half of what you see."
*

Let this be a season of prosperity and happiness,
Joy & gladness unconfined. Preposterous glee.
Cat cries on the back porch. Forget it. A
Fire truck ambulance police car siren— Let
Them rave. Maybe we should.
     Think about the treasures of reason,
        logical delights

*

hispid. Many insects are hairy.
Read the Greeks, read nudist propaganda with bright colored
photographs
The Greeks are enchanting
as far as they go but there are many more things
to know and discuss, more worlds of
trouble and delight than they had time to know

*

Do you know how many senses you possess
and how far they will take you, how many kinds
of music, how many kinds of food how many ideas
about the world have you known?

What passions you have? Are any of them
beyond your understanding, beyond your control,
beyond the bounds of polite society (I was raised pure
lower middleclass white Protestant American: Emily Post
fake genteel overdone roast beef or chicken on Sunday)
What do you care about Western Civilization—as a friend
has lately written, "How big a piece of it do you own . . .
how much would you miss it if it disappeared tomorrow?"

*

A THRILL A MINUTE
EVERY SECOND

*

I say,
Believe some of the senses part of the time,
although I've seen my share of mirages,
visions, optical illusions, fake skin pangs,
nightmares, *déjà vus*, false memories,
lies, frauds, theaters, governments, universities, magicians—
come hell or high water. "It don't stand to reason,"
they used to say—other times, "If I hadn't
seed it I never would have believed it"

*

Get the words out of my head
Lewis looked at me one day and yelled,
"Look at your head! You got all those words in there!
Your head is full of words!"

Mine them out of the bone, scrape out
With special tool steel chisels and corkscrews
Rake and scrape out,   these caries
Hard brown crystals of living rot in the brain bone

All my nerves yell, my muscles resist
The brain thinks it's evading the probe

It lies there, helpless oyster
Bubbling in its own thin juices . . .

*

Today I want to evade all my responsibilities (I write in bed)
If the rug were cleaner, I'd lie down and
roll on it.

I practice looking out through
the top of my head,
brain surface receives direct radiant energy
it responds like the compound eye of insect
which is also the eye of bodhisattva watching everything
at once with perfect detachment, perfect compassion, perfect wisdom. . . .

World seen *via* sensitive head of my dong—
Like elephant's trunk, yogis
Inhale air ocean through that little tube
      (Lady in Russia has fingers which tell her she's
      TOUCHING "blue" . . . "red" . . . "yellow")
Also through belly button, pores of the skin
Fresh air & the world's "evil"
Converted into beneficence, blessings

*

I wrote "46" a few days ago.

EXCELLENT
HOW
GOLD   IT SHINES
HEAVILY
WELLS FARGO BANK
& UNION TRUST COMPANY

Earthquake washing-machine

California Belt Line Railroad crash hump freightcars
                midnight roar and cool

What other word can I comb out of my moustache?

Tilden Park:
            a quince bush with fruit. (hispid.)
            Come home to the year's first
                        pomegranate

---

coffee and tea
blacken my teeth

Jewel facet, hairline edge, sapphire
emerald ruby the pure colors have
settled out, petrified from white
crystal prism light split breakdown
One precious gem the ancients believed was crystallized leopard piss

            blang, blang, blang, six times
            red orange yellow green blue violet
            some people say "indigo" for "blue." I feel it
            has too much black in it,
                        flat vegetable dye

            blang, blang, blang
noiselessly: a chord of music for the eye
God's promise in the sky,

Goethe believed Sir Isaac too prosaic
Herman Weyl says that color is real,
           a separate realm of existence

---

blang

---

   very little else works as well—printers ink
(magenta blue and yellow) makes the whole *schmeer*

      The Tropics!   ablaze with flowers and gorgeous
      porcelain bugs rare spicy odors
      perfumes and rotting brain eyes curry!
gone up the spout or down the chute
an extended vacation—federal pen or a State
        Asylum for the criminally
           insane

          J E W E L S A N D G O L D
  priceless treasure   J E W E L S   of the rarest
color and water, countless rivers, lakes, creeks
and streams   fish gems   frog pearls
          bug articulated jewels
          crystals inside rocks
jewel fern   jewel moss   flash water diamond

The animals are silent and very powerful.
Fishes and frogs have other kinds of lives, they
    are doing something else, they have a plan,
      they also have great powers
Fire-opal worms: beneficent presences
Microscopic walking jewel beasts, living
crystals, the virus living molecule
all the rocks and mud, all the plants,
all the elements, the sun, moon and stars

---

      at the aquarium we see gar-fish six feet long
      "What do you suppose he's thinking?"

Snyder says: "Most animals are in some state of *samadhi*
most of the time."

---

*

O Goddess I call on you constantly
People laugh when I speak of you
They don't see you beside me,
I'm young again when you appear

"It stands to reason," people say,
But I mean Holy Wisdom
Buddha-mother Tara
Bringing poems as I asked, as I

Was lonely and impatient
Drug with literature and politics
Almost convinced that writing's impossible,
Totally controlled by professors and publishers

One small zap-ray blink of your eye
Demolishes all these tinny dreams of Art
Breakthrough to actual skin throb stroke

And beyond all this—
Countless worlds, life as joy knowledge
Flower freedom fire
My doubt impatience fear and worry
Consumed in wisdom flame garland
I can bless the editor, the PhD, the *New York Review of Books*

The poems and the writing all are yours.

3:x:64
7:xi:64

VANILLA
1965-1966

To My Muse

Now I see my part in the story:
    Tithonus, immortal & wrinkling
    greying and fading, voice
    from a big pot,
A seashell echo, prophesying

      and you pink sunrise, Eos, ever young
        opening

                                      3:xi:64

Point Richmond

Hearing. Plato. phrot. phing. destroy destiny rose rot, green, black
edge slip stink. "Go home, dead tourist." We have arrived at the
beginning. "One thing that's got to be every night."
    Each leaf has its diamond—an inactive occupation. Let us
have the "active option." Look again. Wait longer. A paintbrush
with a gold handle suggests what?
    Something googoo this way comes. Black ghosts
flap in my pantry, my closet dampens, rust and the moth corrupt.
    MOSS ON BOARD, fence board,
wooden death pearl pearl wet. WCW points to moss on under
edge of railway iron, AG astonied. (Astonied—why apologize?)
    Conflation of all texts intellectual mongrelization
"more people" (S. Spender) "read Shaxpear, fewer
understand him"
    "If you have a cow that gives no milk,
sell him." Fit them into glove boxes. Push to flatten them.
    Corrupt and mothy rust.
Leaf curl and crumble. Caterpillars burn them.
    Green frog neatly painted black trim—

What's Hecuba to him, that pampered jade of
Asia?—Mechanically perfect green frog, all white meat and black
discretion, (no panic,) folds his hands in front of him—"We plan
to discontinue the earlier series of debentures"—heartbeat observ-
able under green flexjewel hide it is his mud. The sun belongs to
him. He is prepared to leave us.

He stays.
"We are preparing to foreclose."
Moth/rust. Speak no more. Wednesday was the last. No Joy.
Replay the other side of it. Gold? Out. Down, the split rocks, the
cliffs "open"! Gravel patters down. What city. Get rid of all these
papers; private fire a public virtue? Glass
dome, red glass birds? She asked us. Rid
yourself, throw all that away, don't ever leave
me. Chain smokes breathing? Relaxation of gold molecule fang.
Percolates through seams in the rocks, and a jelly and a jewel.
Start OVER. Give up everything. Encircle the globe cinque-
spotted,
four-bits the time,
the wild throttling angel/sphinx/FATFOOT
". . . wandering boy tonight . . ."
Culture, such as might grow
in a Petri dish full of agar-agar,
cleared away, a wad of cotton soaked in alcohol swipe across the
surface
Spider come across. Silk is better than nothing. (Than
mouthing?)
A MUSICAL OFFERING.

*

Zoe says, "I ordered an owl. I'm going to have it. HOO!"
William James: ". . . the active option . . ."

*

"Take down the wallpaper, we're moving."
I think we are moving, don't you notice that kind of rumbling
vibration.
The stars appear to be speeding up.

FALLS NOW THE POMEGRANATE FROM HIS BOUGH
ROTS ON THE FADED GRASS BENEATH

Point Richmond, 13:ii:66
Kyoto, 14:vii:66

Portland in the Evening

The weather is changing; the green light is blinking.
In emergency
    call R. W. Reynolds.

8:xii:65

Trip, 30:x:65

He kept repeating that domestic fucking automobiles wouldn't
corner worth a damn.

Pair of China pheasants in flight.

South Oregon green rug,
Sheep overstuffed furniture standing or lying on it

Mush rooms?

*

DRAIN REEDSPORT   DRAIN ELKTON

*

  ". . . will never corner . . .
  never apologize, never explain"

*

"Zürich Switzerland or the center of the sun?"

*

"Let's all cap out simultaneously.
"Let's all hyperventilate one minute then hold our breath
envisioning Mr 2765 and pray for the little green cannabis
plants really working their hearts out
giving their all on the back porch at home."

So they did.

N.B.: For "Mr 2765," see the frontispiece to Arthur Avalon's book *The
Serpent Power*.

Lemon Trees

Portable garden, Bill's shed in Point Richmond, moth
ripple in the air. Moth holes in air that walks around
ALIVE
these flying dust wing flap. Air
quiver, a shaky curtain.

> Explain the spherical gastank.
> a) it holds more. b) it is stronger. c) its shadow is
>   a circle on the wall. d) aluminum paint
>   keeps it clean and cool

I have nothing to say about the American "commitments" in
Viet Nam at this time.

*

Perhaps today I understand the saying,
"We're all miserable sinners." (Understanding it
isn't the same as believing it or being frightened by it.)

*

DEATH YOUR HEAVY FOOT   TIRED SLEEPY DEATH
KING COBRA   HOODED ALIVE
NEUROTOXIC DEADLY CORAL
APPROACHING SNAKEPIT   ENTER HERE

*

289 years the T'ang Dynasty (A.D. 618–905)
USA, 176 years & still functioning?

24:x:65

Opening the Mountain, Tamalpais: 22:x:65

Hot sunny morning, Allen and Gary, here they come, we are ready.
Sutras in creek-bed, chants and lustrations, bed of Redwood Creek
John Muir's Woods.

First Shrine: Oak tree grows out of rock
                      Field of Lazuli Buntings, crow song

Second Shrine: Trail crosses fire road at hilltop
                      Address to the Ocean,
                      Siva music addressed to the peaks

Third Shrine: Rock Springs music for Sarasvati
                      Remember tea with Mike and JoAnn years ago
                      Fresh water in late dry season

Fourth Shrine: Rifle Camp lunch, natural history:
                      Allen: "What do wasps do?"
                      Gary: "Mess around."

Fifth Shrine: Collier Spring, Great Dharani & Tara music

Sixth Shrine: Inspiration Point, Gatha of Vajra Intellectual
                      Heat Lightning

North Side Trail, scramble up vertical North
        Knee WHERE IS THE MOUNTAIN?

Seventh Shrine the Mountain top: Prajnaparamita Sutra, as many
        others as could be remembered in music & song

Eighth Shrine, The parking lot, Mountain Home
        Sunset Amida going West
        O Gopala, &c Devaki Nandi na Gopala
        with a Tibetan encore for Tara,
        Song against disaster.

RETURN TO CREEKBED, MUIR WOODS: Final pronouncement of the
Sutras

   We marched around the mountain, west to east
   top to bottom—from sea-level (chanting dark stream bed
   Muir Woods) to bright summit sun victory of gods and
   buddhas, conversion of demons, liberation of all sentient
   beings in all worlds past present and future.

"Plaster of Paris: Helen of Troy."

                    flowers of sulfur
                    mother of pearl
                    wrath of Moses
                    cream of Tartar
                    Cape of Good Hope
                    The Ruins of Time
            "Cloak of China, cap of Spain"

                         *

Did the universe explode. Who burnt the toast.
        Why does no one love me and
                obey my every whim?

                         *

R. Buckminster Fuller.   Gerard Manley Hopkins.
                    LA BETE NOIRE

                            *

Remember the high white light
Remember the question
What is the difference between eggs and vomit?
Pigs and silver. (Pigeon's liver?)

                            *

2:xi:65 *Erection Day*
                            Private fish heaven
It's largely optical

                                              18:x:65

Sad Song

i is a statue of white-hot metal
i is a river that never stopped
i is the falling flower petal
is the love I never copped.

                                              11:ix:65

Labor Day

There is St Ignatius Church
There is Point Bonita
There is a bug like a wasp
        its giant antennae
        flail and thwack the concrete in its path

Fennel green and yellow lace
Great moss rose flowery shaving-brush

You're the only creature I really love
Aside from Mama and my Teddy bear
I never miss you until I think of you
Now you love lots more than I
No matter how often we meet you never see me

I've become an old man
Soon I'll be keeping cats and goldfish
A large photo album of the days when I was middle-aged
In love with you and expecting immortal fame

6:ix:65

Tara

This bronze Tara this bronze lady
Represents that Lady of Heaven I now invoke,
That idea of wisdom that saves more than itself or me
All the universes,

Enlighten us we murder each other in this night our eyes
            won't tell us anything but fear

All the universes, all the probability tracks

IMMEDIATELY

Her hands form the *mudra* "Teaching the Law"
Explaining herself.
She also appears as a song, a diagram,
As a pile of metal images in the market, Kathmandu
We seldom treat ourselves right.

5:ix:65

Homage to Dante

What I'm saying is we're facing each other
                    on stage
I thought you had written a complete script

Why have we chosen to appear at all,
Here of all possible places, hello in the midst of
                    boiling fire and silliness

4:ix:65

The Task Rejected

We all went to the zoo
That's one thing done.

The sun shone, light foggy clouds blew past
The animals were variously disposed (waking or sleeping)
We saw the lions being fed
We ate hotdogs.

The koala bears are wintering in San Diego
They return in August. It is rumored that Bubu is *enceinte*.
The coatis are mangy, the gibbons shout
What about the sooty mangabee, what about

            enormous pigeons nearly three feet high
            powder blue, diaphanously crowned
What did Clark Coolidge say then?

Hawaiians laughed at the macaws, tree-climbing kangaroos
Toni Coolidge wanted soda pop. There it was.

We did not visit The California Palace of the Legion of Honor.

3:ix:65

Palimpsest

Where there's a telephone there's a woman to be talking on it. There's quite probably a man hanging around the woman, and he pays for the telephone. Why don't we go out and have some fun— I've been in the house all day. We can't go anyplace I just paid the phone bill.

Some men talk like that. Other men say, Put on your hat, Sweetie, I'm all ready to go. That kind has spent the money but he doesn't complain about it. He takes her to Playland at the Beach where they walk around watching the bright colored lights and the crowd, watch the sunset from the top of Telegraph Hill, go look in store windows on Market Street. . . .

> (*The hiatus (rather, lacuna) in the ms. here has been tentatively restored by the Editor,*
> *who has borrowed without stint from*
> *the work of Professor Woodleigh*):

e.g.
| "What do you say, Cutie, scarf your box?"
| "Harry, that man said something nasty to me!"
| "Hay, Buster, come back here!"
| "Hit him in the mouth, Harry, he is a son of a bitch!"

25:viii:65

The Honeymoon

"We drove Father's Bugatti on our honeymoon."

*

"You were right, Eb. Dope fiends."

We spent our 43rd birthday in Kyoto. The next year we were in Kathmandu. We're determined to do Egypt soon. Dying Egypt.

Dying Egypt every color.

                         Let us discontinue this
line of inquiry.

           "flense him."

24:viii:65

Paranoia Revisited

I see in the mirror, these mornings
That I'm now completely mad:
Ambition, fear and rage look back at me . . .

I suppose that noise was only the man next door
Feeding his rabbit.

16:viii:65

Good News and Gospel

We hear it but choose to ignore . . .
As the telephone rings in the used car lot

12:viii:65

The Promise

cross eyes twist brain?
   When did you get the job of being town lunatic?

MEM.: No more bad news. No more smart remarks. No more false quotations (Amer. Tel & Tel up ⅜) Stop reading

---

Stop here. Ice Cold Drinks. Cold Watermelon All You Can Eat. Fresh fruit five hundred feet. Corn on the cob. Oranges. Please don't abuse your eyes any more. I promise.

---

a faithful blank

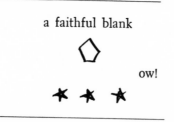

ow!

What percentage of up is over. See them
hovering there? Don't mark the cover. Pay no
more. Call the mover. A great endeavour
has come to nothing.
Saves time, costs less, more fun than
Pigs in clover. Could such a one be
a major poet, a losing gambler, a
fortunate lover?

—Patient, sweet and kind. I am also infallibly
good natured. "Escape me never."

9:viii:65

Higher Criticism

The Iliad
a tribe of brutish wrastlers would come to nothing
without Homer his girlish delight in bronze, gold, horses
all kinds rich plunder and the hairy sweating bodies
of contentious kings

6:viii:65

Genetics

How much of the time do I spend re-living my father's life,
        my mother's?
Doing what they liked, what they wanted to do, finding out
        what they wanted to know . . . seeing and hearing all
        they never had time for, never dreamed?

5:viii:65

The Mystery of the Alphabet

A row of letters: Message in
Language as yet undeciphered
Secret formula discovered

e.g.	2nd Rameses ALIVE! Demands obedience of entire civilized world. Edgar Hoover "Appalled!" Southern scientists claim fraud.

Arrow of letters addressed to that one who invented them
Four-eyed Chinese dragonface Ts'ang Chieh

(Mathews 6707)

e.g.

Egyptian bird-head
Greek murder victim
Sumerian supernatural
Phoenician warehouse clerk

倉吉

OR

倉史

"... having wonderful time wish you was here.
X marks the window I'm in ..."

marks Eleusis where Demeter gives the seeds and the letters to
Triptolemus

*

A BOUQUET:

mushrooms appear in a night or in a moment
(spontaneously, we say, but there are seeds, little beasts that
are so small as to be invisible to the naked eye, according
to A. van Leeuwenhoek)

from fairies dancing in a ring?
Laws of electrochemistry? (Are they
really reasons?) *Toujours la même chose.*

Rare blossoms! Do you want to do it again *already?*
Why don't we sleep a little first oh well.

*

A world of pleasure, a world of suffering
whatever it is
    "that show was over before it ever started."
night-blooming cereus

*

All worlds are real crystal, humming energy
All reals are temporary bubble of glass
         "fiasco"

*

blossom pollen scatter seed swell dwindle and perish
come back next year crimson, purple
masses of blossom, the rhododendrons
        and perfume

*

Kore goes underground where the snake lies hid

3:viii:65

L'Enfant Prodigue

I want to see the old country before I die .

    Babble on to me of greasy regrets. I feel
    immortal Helen with a kiss. Caesar yourself,
    you brought her.
              ("Why don't you go back to the Old
              Country. . . .")

"There's only three places in that Europe I want to see—
Holland, Hawaii and The Holy Land."

("... any old country.")

3:viii:65

The Greeks

divided it three ways
> Underworld, earth and sea, heavens above

HADES   POSEIDON   ZEUS

3 ways
body, soul and spirit
We've been fragmented ever since
(Very carefully NOT in memory of Adonis, Osiris
we do not ((all tattered)) RISE AGAIN)
At best we show scars and seams, ill-joined
That monster created by Boris Karloff and Perc Westmore

3 ways
"I'm going to cut you three ways: wide, deep and frequent."

Jesus tried to save both worlds, nobody cares,
Everybody's out celebrating Good Friday. The Sunday following
They wear their new clothes, the children play with flowery eggs
But of course Jesus is quite dead, still nailed,
"... in Todesbanden"
Bach proved it all out in the B-Minor Mass, nobody listens
Blake tried to start all over again, good news, a new dispensation,
The churchmen and philosophers alternately use glue and string,
Some try to break the bone and re-set it, like a surgeon
Nobody can pry the western mind loose from
those nails, that perfumed grave, the weeping Momma

We are hung three ways, money sex and stingy
We are too many and we try to work it out to the nearest decimal
Everything hung up on NOTHING
And we had no zero until 1300 A.D.
And we pretend it's nothing, that it don't exist
We hang by ten fingers, our measures don't work
Our spelling is wrong, our counting of syllable, day and year
We count money, "a Sicilian coin struck in the year A.D. 1124"

*

The Sumerians were smart enough to combine sixes and tens
Their year was exact, their poetry
Who knows if their poetry scanned?

1:viii:65

The First of August

some of it
an opera
somebody enter upstairs
    Ernie
Under false wig of Watusi? Later is free for you
baby sunspots interfere with the transmission, honey
We're going to foreclose.
    (foreclose!)
Amphitryon shock messentery loop line
under modern transmission unclear WE ARE
      GOING TO FORECLOSE. Fore?
      Chewys?
dee   deee deee deee Chewys?

I'm going to eat dinner I am oh yeah fuck all these feeble drones
I swish (*Muiopotmos:* or *The Fate of the Butterfly*) end paren-
thesis 40 feet. I said gahgoo gagoop grope callouses da-dum from
E-flat to F? No, C-major. Somebody. Anyway. I don't know what
I'll do to commission him disappointment. Yes I do have some

where. In the jacket. Bib overalls. Shake. Shake. The rest of the night, I never saw you again; stop it.

Please leave me alone, you motherfucker. What are you going to do with that. It would be lovely.

I seem to be distracted. Fuck anything.

Première d'Août 1965. Question that I asked back before you got too tight. I want to go home. Exquisitely.

I want to. Yes I do. Who do you think you are you big stiff. I really think that you *should* tease me. Not from this profile, baby.

Cette image. I crush my cup. Scoot up.

*

Did you do the drawing. It's such a small pad that I could only do a half at a time, first the top half and then the bottom half. He says, "I don't feel like going."

Look down at the rug.
Première d'Août.

*

Well I run across some kind of longhair off a dope scene and I didn't have to come across with anything.

I saw him making it along the street bombed out of his skull that lady in the telephone booth, too fat to shut the door, saying "you don't care if I live or die," all dressed up and on her way.

1:viii:65

Vignette of an Ice Axe

"The truth of it is I took you for granted
You went away with somebody else.

———————————

Velichros!
Velichros!

I fall fall down.

———————————

I look into floor-level apartment
They are a painting by Oskar Kokoschka—
        JEALOUS!

1:viii:65

Secret

The great secret books are available to all. There are copies in
most libraries; they can be bought in cheap paper editions. However accessible, they are still secret books. The careless, the casual,
the thoughtless reader will come away from them no wiser than
he was before. The really secret books are dictated to me by my
own ears and I write down what they say.

31:vii:65

Giant Sequoias

Amazing creatures, I was delighted
to visit them, to watch them,
languid waving those green feather scale fronds
they aren't too far from being ferns

These giants make me laugh, they are young and fragile
upwards of 2000 years old, I worry about them, will they survive?
Here are more of them than I had hoped
But the odds against them are huge as themselves.

28:vii:65

Pop Doughnut

"What if everybody did that"
          hilarity was unconfined
     everybody does.
DOUGHNUT, a big one made of
raised potato flour, now all brown
under thick sugar crystals.
Doughnut without a hole has red jelly inside.
Doughnut, small and rather heavy
thick skin of powdered sugar.
Doughnut, brown and spicy, newly fried,
still hot, later it will be a lump of grease

Everybody likes doughnuts and crullers
Doughnuts and ice cream and coffee.
These were invented in New England?
Waffles are from Holland
Marie de' Medici invented ice cream?

                              28:vii:65, a Wednesday.

The Education Continues Along

FOR CLARK COOLIDGE

Don't leave the house before noon there's a reason
You'll find it later it will be revealed to you
Preserve ritual purity
The Unworthy must be left in that Ignorance which is a Divine
Punishment Amen.

                    rutile:
                    ore from which titanium
                    Queen of the Night   SAGENITE?
                    (Queen of the Fucking May)

322

an independent study of
non-Euclidean pleasures non-canonical hours
watch and pray. "Watch"
means "to sit up all night without sleeping."
Watch means look at me: See my bellybutton.

I hope you didn't think I meant anything personal by it.
You don't have to if you don't want to.
What happened to your hair. I left it on the bureau.
The pleasure of exact location lies in a certain
            feeling. Let me feel yours.
                Feel mine?

LIMIT defined by change of state, as
            the bed is just so wide
            beyond the edge of it we fall on the floor

                            *

            MEASURE, that which contains a number of beats. Two
                pints one quart; eight quarts is a peck.
"O,   Aristotle a dead professor? "container for the thing con-
 A   tained?" Hart Crane says, "For joy rides in stu-
 B   pendous coverings."
 S
 O   *
 L
 U   THE PRIMARY: are you in love?
 T   are you hungry? WHERE YOU AT?
 E   do you have a toothache?
 L   who's got all the money?
 Y   How much does it cost to find out what you want
 !"   to know?

                            *

THANK YOU. COME AGAIN.

                            *

We *do* all of us depend on one another. Do it some more.

*

peh!   *this was a π-meson,*
moving at some kind of
unbelievable speed. The
speed identifies it.

*

The song says,

"Please give me something to remember you by
When you are far away from me, Dear—
Some little something, &c &c."

*

———meh!———

viz., a μ-meson, moving
some kind incredible speed
"*Incwoyable*," they
used to say, refusing
to use that "R"
which would remind them of
that unfortunate Citoyen Louis
Capet, whilom LE ROY

*

————*bah!*————

much slower, the loss of a
β-particle out of the middle
this only penetrates four inches
of lead or twelve of concrete.

Mr. Yeats has warned us, "things fall apart, the centre cannot
hold." Quite as if we were able to learn anything, as if we've
listened to Wm. Yeats—or to Plato, Jesus, Moses & Co.—Nothing
has soaked into our heads except of some fake superstitions about
sex and a few jokes and limericks concerned with the same
subject.

(I exaggerate. I remember a few lines about the weather, "red sky at night, sailors delight, &c.")

*

Yet I hope that curiosity isn't dead . . . contrariwise, I despair about the high price of second-hand books, even 2nd-hand PAPERBACK books

*

Do I know what it is that I am doing, &c.

*

How badly do I need to read one more book, whatever its price considering that I'm already half blind from too much reading anyway and one more book has as many lies in it as all the rest, why don't I go look at the world instead or sit and think for a few years, or even try to write "seriously"

*

We got to the top of Windy Ridge then climbed Peak 12524
We saw where we'd been last year, whole days of travel in one
        glance: Pinchot Pass, the Palisades, the heights towards
        Muir Pass where will the next trip be?

*

Why don't you quit while you're still ahead?

*

Why not. But a few hours later, or the next day or whenever, there it is again, straight, hard & throbbing, no knowledge of Civilization, fatigue, the Law, the usages of Polite Society &c. Osiris, Adonis, Dionysius, Attis, Jesus, Heracles, Odysseus, Aeneas, Gilgamesh return. All return. A wheel.

*

". . . ABSOLUTELY FINAL FAREWELL PERFORMANCE"

Liszt made eight or ten of them, Eleanora Duse did a dozen or so, Anna Pavlova and the Marx Brothers built it into an independent art form, "FOR THE LAST TIME ON ANY STAGE!"

*

or drawing room or Turkey Bath . . .
"It turns out," as Helen used to say. The Beautiful Poet is really this middle-aged type wants to fuck me in the ass.

A B S O L U T E

REALITY, namely, how much can I do right now about life in this place? I am it, all of this living AND this place and what I'm doing is called T R A N S F O R M A T I O N ,

IRRADIATION: BASE METAL BECOMES GOLD

". . . just dancing," Mr. Lenny Bruce explained,
". . . no kissing."

XY says,
"The beautiful poet wants to lick me all over, suck my dick *et cetera*. I can't think why. The first thing you know, there we were and there wasn't any yes or no to it, we had a ball. Wouldn't you? Magic, he calls it. Absolutely indefensible, of course, unnatural, a symptom of profound psychological disturbance, we did it every chance we got & will probably do it again."

*

"ABSOLUTELY, O *Absolutely*. Where you're at; what's happening." I suppose he's interested in the quality sometimes.

*

G. Stein: "History is what happens from time to time"

*

Where I sit in "my" room with the windows open, a joss-stick fumes before bronze Tara

(Gary and Joanne hunted it out from great junkpile at
Kathmandu, bronze images . . . arms, legs, axes, ele-

phant heads, reclining, sitting, standing, *in coitū*, sprouting more heads and arms, animal features, wings and haloes, which recall the great battle of Ahura Mazda light against the Darkness again, a Persian overlay on Buddha sculpture)

1.) am I hungry. Not right now, and there's food in the refrigerator.

2.) I am in love with so&so, and would like to make it with S, T, U, V, W, X, Y, Z, &c.

3.) Did Nikola Tesla REALLY make a machine that could extract electric voltage out of the very ground on which he stood. (Clark Coolidge asked me.) I can't remember what are the characteristics of or the use for the electrical coil which bears his name. Tesla.

4.) History is probably shorter than we like to think. What is history REALLY. What is a new and active use for it?

5.) I've got to stop writing and start thinking. So what else is new?

*

SHE says, "You must know what's really yours; you must know it's really you doing it."
I wouldn't have it any other way.
SHE says, "You really like that. Why don't you *have* that?"
There are a number of reasons why not.
I suppose that light still flashes high above Miner's [minor's] Ledge.
"1-4-3," "I-love-you. I hear you. 1-4-3, Miner's Ledge Light, 1-4-3—I-love-you, what better way to remember?"

*

"So & So" (some historical figure, some artist) "grabbed up all these" (musical notes, words, whatever) "and made not another" (whatever it was) "but . . .
a STAR!"
Where'd I read that?

*

I wasted an hour trying to locate the story, riffling through half
a dozen books, and I MUST let go the search isn't the one I want
to go on today.

"Come in! Come in! You're just in time
                to hear me recite the history
of The Invisible City of Kitezh!"
                The Sacred City of Great Kitezh
        (large and lurid color lithograph, slightly off-register)
                Hear the bells. Birds of Paradise that sing.
The entire CITY
                yarded off to Heaven in a goldy cloud
                nothing left but a blazing cross to mark the spot
                & terrify the Mongol Horde
                    (KKK?)
                the bells of the Sacred City
                chime deep in the woods, audible from the stars
The wicked repent, the soprano ascends with her prince
They all sing—
                        eternal delight invisible to earth
                        we hear it all
                        hope for the best
                            (K L A N G !)
                        but what we get
Next week, *Cavalleria Rusticana*

THE XIX C. was black and white.

Kurt Schwitters tore it all into COLOR
                "primatiti," &c.

                            "primatiti-ti,
                            Primatiti-ta, &c."

moreover, there are blue horses now
and a *Fish Garden* by Paul Klee
We're willing to have other creatures
Share the world

I must make a correction.

>Charles Darwin was black and white in the XIX Century?
>Charley Baudelaire?
>Sir Leslie Stephen black and white
>>was he a lesser man?

Walter Whitman said the animals don't complain.

*

>NB: PLEASE REVISE YOUR *DIX-NEUVIEME*

*

LATER (after lunch) I couldn't leave it—I find, so far, that it was Edith Sitwell quoting John Livingston Lowes who was quoting . . . what author?

>"Give Coleridge one vivid word from an old narrative: let him mix it with two in his thought; and then (translating terms of music into terms of words) 'out of these sounds he (will) frame, not a fourth sound, but a star.' "
>>—*The Road to Xanadu*, p. 303

*

The point is, I *remembered*, at last, that I'd been looking at the Sitwell book (*A Poet's Notebook*) a couple days ago—now I'm free to go to the postoffice and the library.

*

>"The glory is departed from the coconut and a prosaic world has relinquished one delight."
>>—*The Road to Xanadu*, p. 288

*

>That out of three sounds he frame, not a fourth sound, but a star."
>>—Robert Browning, "Abt Vogler"

*

I was assisted to this via Bartlett's *Familiar Quotations*. A trip to the main library is next—the Tesla coil either is or is not a real recollection.

(Are TEKTITES really from outer space?)

*

SNED (1937): "TESLA (te'sla). 1902. The name of *Nikola Tesla* (born 1857), American electrician, used attrib. to denote certain apparatus and phenomena."

WEBSTER'S *New Collegiate Dictionary*: single entry in Biographical Names section.

Encyclopedic Dictionary of Electronics and Nuclear Engineering, Robert I. Sarbacher, Sc.D. editor, Prentice-Hall Inc. Englewood Cliffs, New Jersey. 1959. p. 1281:

"*Tesla.* A unit of magnetic induction, equal to 1 Weber per square meter, in the mksa electromagnetic systems.

Tesla Coil. An induction coil used to develop a high-voltage discharge at a very high frequency. As shown in Fig. 2 a high-voltage transformer (T) is used to promote a discharge across the primary gap (G_1) and to charge a condenser (C_1) in parallel with the transformer primary. High-amperage low-frequency currents oscillate in the few-turn winding P, and induce high-voltage high-frequency oscillations in the secondary many-turn winding S. If S is tuned to resonance with the primary, very intense oscillations produce discharges across the gap G_2. Also called a Tesla transformer."

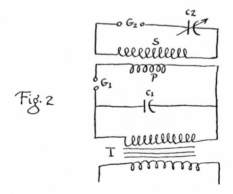

Fig. 2

In order to get the point of much of this part, go read (right now)
pages 181–186 in *History and the Homeric Iliad*, by Denys Page,
University of California Press, Berkeley and Los Angeles, 1963
(a paperback edition exists).

This table stands on fidgety feet.
Fidgety Feet is also the name of a song or piano solo, circa 1920-
odd

*

Assertions about history assertions of an unstable
       insecure personality?
           Lemon rind orange flower
               lime tree

*

       Personality: How you customarily place your feet
Lemon flower   orange tree   lime juice
Grapefruit   kumquat   citron   tangerine
                   flowers at riverside
                   at Lemon Cove

*

O California sub-tropical freeze!

*

Lemon tree   lime flower   juice of several oranges
       the leaves are shiny green
       "shrubs of the rue family," A. Merriam-Webster says.
Assertions of personality and authority who will control
the dictionary?

The Harper Encyclopedia of Science, edited by James R. Newman
(and a large staff). Harper & Row, Publishers. New York and
Evanston. Sigma, Inc. Washington, D.C., 1963 (4 vols.) Vol. IV,
p. 1178:
   "*Tesla coil:* . . . The coil is suitable for exciting X-ray and
Crookes (vacuum) tubes."

*

I found a biography, *Prodigal Genius, The Life of Nikola Tesla,* by John J. O'Neill. Ives Washburn, Inc., New York (n.d.) (The copyright notice on the verso of the title page is dated 1944)

It appears that Tesla was a genius of the highest order. He had an eidetic memory and imagination. He saw a vision of whirling magnetic fields while watching a sunset; his ideas for the construction of alternating current generators, dynamos, transmission lines, controls and insulation, as well as the mathematical theory which would describe the operation of these things came to him that evening. He went to America and met George Westinghouse. They harnessed the power of Niagara Falls.

Tesla was a nut. He had a germ phobia, gynophobia, and if we can believe his biographer, the only creature he loved in his adult life was a pigeon.

But observe: He lighted the Chicago World's Fair of 1893. He also "let 1,000,000 volts of high-frequency high-voltage alternating current pass through his body for many minutes" while he held a globe in his hand which gave forth a brilliant light. Thomas Edison had told everybody it couldn't be done, that alternating current was lethal. Thomas Edison and the Edison Company owned the street lighting system in New York in those days; it operated from a direct current dynamo . . . quite inefficiently.

*

This one loves blue
That one dotes on glass
"None of it came to nothing in the end
None of it amounted to a hill of beans."
    That's what my grandmother used to say.

cf. Alcaeus,
fr. 173

και κ'οὐδεν
εκ δενος γενοιτο.

"and nothing will
come of anything"

*

That's all that there, she said.

*

Gertrude Stein: "Let me recite what history teaches. History teaches."

*

332

(Not quite a month later, 15:viii:65)
N.B., That History, being a writing, can be destroyed, or changed
to suit whatever purpose the writer, the printer, the State may
determine. History is a cat which can be altered to suit the owner.
Nikola Tesla was a handsome man. He died all alone in a hotel
room. A friend paid the bill— Tesla was broke.

San Francisco 27:vii:65
Kyoto 8:vii:66

America!

I've got what I was after
Arrows of red paint on the pavement

*

Go ahead and wear tight clothes
Drive a pile of credit on 4 wheels
Who did you ever make it with—
                    did you come?

*

Unworried at last
blue sky over Masonic Temple
                    (self-portrait of stiff dong)

What town was that?

25:vii:65

What Finally Happened to the King

The king's inside a nest of boxes.
They sawed through the lynch pin of his chariot wheel,
Dared him to race, there was
A tragic accident. Fatal mistake
Inside the Labyrinth, over the cliff he flew
A swallow, to follow the careless black sails,

*

purple crowned shouts five times
declines into wrinkled silence
wrapped in delicate skin, elaborate
foldings of cloth, goldy threads,
the straining cords of a silky net,

*

The world grew very small. After 1918, it was controlled
                from New York City.
Hell is made of fallen suns. Its proprietor
formerly a sun god. Every day another sun goes *under*
                the earth.

*

Today the king created 37 new peers, many of the old ones, now
living in Los Angeles, have allowed their dues to lapse and their
titles have run out. The Earl of Salt speaks darkly about the
"decline" of polite society and the scarcity of nice people. Viscount
Fitch closed his town house. The king could remember waking up
coming and pissing—ecstatic.

19:vii:65

The Life of Literature

"Wonder whether you or they hold the rights" and would you
care and I wonder what would you do if you had the chance"

I just bet you would, you'd
take one look and run away
    I bet you would, even if you had the chance
you'd be afraid
you wouldn't take it even then.

"even if it was set before you on a silver platter."

Where there was one there's more
a lot more where that one came from,
poetry,
to spurt right out the top of my head
"the come of the poem," as Ginsberg says.

                                        17:vii:65

M

FOR ROBERT DUNCAN

Many tedious hours
How many shallow days
        cloudy sky or sun immediately reflected from the top layer
        all beneath lay hid
        the moving surface apparently motionless

M is WATER, an hieroglyphic owl
Phoenician: ᱬ *mem*
            μ *mu* in Greek
                Aeschylus makes the Eumenides
                cry " μ μ μ μ "
Kabala: "a Mother #13, the power of 40"

        In Rome M = 1000.

                                        13:vii:65

That Eyes! Those Nose!

Trace a scrawl. Squall.

small quantity of musk pervades
the air in a room

—————————————— In a few seconds of time
great worlds are born & die

you didn't even notice it
you didn't even care.

————————————————

Così fan Tutte

————————————————

Intelligence of death leaks out my eyes
Also, life and enlightenment

————————————————

A REPLY

"Not enough so as it would make any
difference."

12:vii:65

The Feather Truth Weighs 10,000 Pounds

FLEE from the wrath to come.
forbid forespend foreskin foresight foredone
Dismissal
an exciting story about rich people
beautiful and powerful and rich

expenditures unobtrusive because they are so large
regalements. Chirping small birds devouring insects
also newly born from eggs

Dismal. A bad week, a wild weekend, a funky Monday,
another bad week. Dismal. Squalor is a better word.
                    V A C A N C Y

                                        12:vii:65

1935

                    turned to the wall,
draped in black muslin cold
black veils for you in prison
shame disgrace and degradation
black veils motheaten, one or two
rhinestone brilliants adhere to the filmy fabric
which blows against dusty calsomined cheek don't make me cry
my makeup will run—
Ah, little monkey!

                    *

A broken wrist-pin held us up in Carthage

The ocean is wider than the hill is high, the water hangs
Over the hill in the sky

Jimson weed blooms today

                                        15:vi:65

"*The Sun Rises and Sets in That Child,*"
so my grandmother used to say,

also shines
    while the sun is:
Moon

Frog man sits on Bear's head
Beaver with son on his back
    in her belly
Stands on Frog head
Raven hovers over

$\left\{\vphantom{\begin{array}{c} \\ \\ \\ \\ \\ \\ \\ \\ \\ \\ \end{array}}\right.$ petal curve blossom
        carved
leaf stone?
stem fuzz gold ray

_____
_____

padma: lotus

_____
_____

frog sits on the water
"seeking whom to devour" $\left.\vphantom{\begin{array}{c} \\ \\ \\ \\ \\ \\ \\ \\ \\ \\ \end{array}}\right\}$

"*Universal Darkness covers all.*"

May 1965

Card #21 Le Monde

Inside the green hedged garden
The First Eve (Mistress of Time)
4 Seasons wait outside
Bullface, Eagleface, Lionface, Man (a blazing Serpent,
one of the Seraphim)

Eve dances with a snake of cloth who is the Northwind
Beyond the power of the Sun who hasn't been invented yet.

(N.B., that the images returned to me first, then I realized
what it was I had been seeing, hence the title.)

24?:v:65

A Satire

I haven't seen *** about, lately
Why do I imagine that he's become a large housefly
There he sits, on the bathroom windowsill

12:v:65

Sleepy

> Spring wind:
> Green curtain flapping
> Shakes elephant bells

> > "you can imagine how I felt
> > put yourself in my position"

> > > a gentle chiming in my dreams—

Feature that.

"Oh I don't know—some American chap,
writes novels, I believe. But whatever
it is—aside from that smell—think of
those really splendid brown eyes!

Seventy-two in San Rafael
Snow from North Dakota to Nebraska
May the Ninth

9:v:65

"The Great Heidelberg Tun"

Unconscious of my loneliness until I hear
    music, then it spills in thick molasses
        flow down over my head unevenly

9:v:65

339

"California Is Odious but Indispensable"

César Franck walks between rows of radishes & scallions
In the kitchen garden he observes green light cast by sun
Through onion tube tops.
"*Alors*," he says to himself, or "*Tiens!*" Perhaps he muttered
an old Walloon proverb, ". . .

> Santa Barbara in California might be full of people just
> like that. Or Ventura. In Watsonville is a large Yugoslav
> enclave, industrious producers of artichokes & Brussels
> sprouts. Artichokes have beautiful architecture; Santa
> Barbara with a tower in her hand is patroness of archi-
> tects. Santa Monica is further south, mother of St.
> Augustine oldest city in Florida. St. Louis Bishop of
> Toulouse, 19 August.

("*Tiens. Tant mieux.*")

> The Lark gets there 2:25 A.M. ON TIME, to Our Lady
> Queen of the Angels. Often and often. *C'est ça.* The
> French language is endlessly diverting, if incomprehen-
> sible. *Ça va.* (

> (Jack tells the proper direction:
". . . pick up flower car at Redwood . . .")

$7:v:65$

Imagination of the Taj Mahal

                              Hand gold
glass holds flower under water dome bright
feather blue green royal eye powder gold enormous
lofty thin brass dome carve marble inlay
gem slices emerald sapphire lapis ruby
marigold shapes of bright cold flames that
Dome of moving water green fire
in the sun brilliant forest carved stone

park flash feather gold green solid marigold
and silent petal flutter color sun ray
blue and red light through blossom wall
tough as eyelid softer than bright
gold carp under lilies

7:v:65

T/O

Open. Open bubbling pools and
fresh springs of new water. Open
the rock. hide the secret, but know
what it is.

I: tough thin substance
expanding flexible glass
I traveled past the sun
found other nights and days,
                          Beyond
this universe of countless worlds and
stars I find many more. Beyond
this temporary imagination I call myself
and mine there are countless others.
Far away, all by their lonesome,

*

August royal blackness, brilliant night, &c.

*

O tickle star o rub that purple rim, &c. (hat) &c.

*

". . . there's not very much of that
left, either . . . ," Robert Duncan said.

*

certain flowers. I'll put all this into my book, decorate all these blank white pages. Remember Oktavian in
                    Rosenkavalier.
Think of Hebe and Ganymede:

                    *

Complete reorganization according to the newly conceived SCHEME will commence promptly at 0800 hours on Saturday 8 May 1965. All personnel must comply with these directives beginning at Midnight on Friday, 7 May, 1965, under pain of our displeasure.

 Flower curtain, a veil of blossoms
 covered the casket. Remember there's
 only a wax dummy inside. Remember
 S. T. Coleridge's lovely title, *The Pains of Sleep.*
 Of course we do.

 Pleasure, pain and recollection are events inside the brain;
 their "outside" location (please scratch my back) an illusion?

                                        7:v:65

The Second Day of May 1965

As next as possible; approximate propinquity, starfish windflower. Sunny breezy weather. I expect myself to do too much about it. Exert yourself, I say, but I feel too sleepy, angry, disconnected . . . all these emotions and sensations occur simultaneously. (I can hear an imaginary objection: "*All?* Not really!") What I want is the sensation of writing, what I'm about to do is go to sleep. I pretend that I stay awake because I'm expecting to see a friend who asked yesterday whether he might visit me today.

Sir Walter Scott: (*Lady of the Lake*, Canto I, ll. 218–19)

  "Fox-glove and nightshade, side by side
  Emblems of punishment and pride."

   (quoted s.v. "foxglove" in SNED)

NATIVE FOLK SPEECH
(possibilities of song!)

"Don't I know him from when we was down in La Jolla?"

> "Don't I know him
> From when we was down
> In La Jolla?"

Message Before Aram Awakes
—before he hear telephone:

	mossy rotting corduroy road through the woods bracket fungus & sorrel, no event? All ours, yesterday, livid orange and raving green, very quiet, no event, scatter sun image on
MESSAGE BLANK? 30:iv:65	moss wave tree top (Fresnel lens/agate diffraction grate) scatter, infinite power dissipation exhibit every wavelength NO MESSAGE CANCEL BUT BILL THE SENDER COLLAPSE RE-WIND & CONFIRM IMMEDIATE CESSATION ALL WAR HOSTILITIES?

A Morning Walk

The Year goes by very fast but it takes a long time.
Tennis player says, "Gee, I don't have that touch today. Oh,
I don't have that touch today."
   Did he say "cut" instead of "touch"?

*

Backwards in time, although I see fog plumes drift over sunny hills, I'm watching Herman Melville feed a pumpkin to his cow—he watches her jaws move.

*

a kind of Japanese porcelain appears to be covered with seeds or warts—little white or colored beads of glaze embedded in the surface. I see the same kind of seedy bumps on sea-urchin skeleton, also on gourds and squashes . . . which vegetables appear to be splashed with green, orange and yellow enamel paint, covered with clear spar varnish

T'ang Dynasty glazes imitated these?

*

Chocolate fun. That was no surprise.

*

Awaken me with roses.   (roses)

        (VOICES?)

                    flow-
                       ers

                             21:iv:65

April Showers Bring Rain?

          foot/feet

              rain/tulip

                    move the garbage
                    away from the window

TULIP	BLACK		BLACK	TULIP
TRIUMPH	STAR	siren	STAR	QUEEN
PRINCESS BEATRIX				OF SHEBA

TULIP   TULIP   TOE
I always loved,   rain.
a secret part

QUEEN OF NIGHT

Lots of   I sit on my feet to warm them.
wind and rain   The house is cold & damp, but I think
the most fragile   the gas stove will warm it (Tulip)
cherry blossoms
the thinnest   Hot cheap tea from Chinatown,
rhododendron petals   four-bits the half pound
not even wrinkled   (a tulip scent?)

Lots of paper that I shall mark up

That sandpiper
all alone, usually
runs with a cloud
incense to burn   alone today, eating
music to play   sea-bugs—where does he
books to learn   live at? Where are his books?

---

rain/feet/rain, I have walked in it, I got all sweaty
I washed myself and changed my clothes and ate food
and talked to Lewy and now I sit, having told my diary *everything*.

          *

      airplane, prop-driven
      flying below the storm

                          7:iv:65

Love Love Love Again

I keep trying to live as if this world were heaven
puke fish   dark fish   pale fish   park fish
      mud fish   lost fish   selfish
           Rockers and Mods
           "acres of clams"

And all my friends, all the people I've known, all I'm going to know
Were mistresses and lovers, all of us with each other
All intimate with me

           fish eyes never close but fish sleep
           octopus eye of human camera goat
           gnat in my ear, mice in my beard
           beautiful garden in my colon (part of me
           REALLY a flower)

I dreamed something with a whale in it
(Not the biggest whale, but big enough)
Animal who loves in the sea
And worms and snails and crustaceans and plant/animals
Animal plants

      Although your name doesn't show here
      I haven't forgotten you.

                                 7:iv:65

Mahayana

Soap cleans itself the way ice does,
Both disappear in the process.
The questions of "Whence" & "Whither" have no validity here.

Mud is a mixture of earth and water
Imagine WATER as an "Heavenly" element
Samsara and nirvana are one:

346

Flies in amber, sand in the soap
Dirt and red algae in the ice
Fare thee well, how very delightful to see you here again!

5:iv:65

Art & Music

lady in Park draws picture of Park and lake—
also back view of herself in the middle foreground
the edges of her paper curl around me?

*

Isolated asphodels
blossom near the old hotels 2:iv:65 W. H. Auden

*

Kalispell, Montana.

*

EDITH SITWELL

*

klump.
klump.
klump.

Monster footsteps! Finger-fangs!

*

Twisted leather songs

*

"Chinese pine" will be found near Omak,
Okanogan Valley, Washington.
James Aston says so, 30:iii:65

347

*

It surprises me when I find it necessary to explain that I work every day, all day.

5:iv:65

"A Penny for the Old Guy"

FOR ARAM SAROYAN

nickle nickle dime
dime dime nickle quarter
        (quarter two-bits)
quarter quarter four-bits
quarter quarter quarter six-bits
    nickle nickle nickle fifteen cents
six bits & a quarter dollar buck
dollar dollar dollar dollar dollar fin
    fin fin sawbuck
    Double sawbuck twenty
5 times twenty is a bill
bill bill bill bill bill ⎤
             ⎬   YARD
bill bill bill bill bill ⎦

with much assistance from Lewis Welch
3:iv:65

Fragment of a Letter, Unsent

Well anyway. I hope that you are keeping happy & busy, and that Madge and all the babies are leading beautiful and healthy lives in the fresh air & sunshine of golden California. Oh, California.

yeah!

beautiful mundane heir of California.
                    I seem to be inhabity by
imbecile dwarves. O California. O Air. Wig. Wig.
s n a p

3 or 4? iv:65

Japanese Tea Garden Golden Gate Park in Spring

1.

I come to look at the cherryblossoms
            for the last time

2.

Look up through flower branching Deva world
            (happy ignorance)

3.

These blossoms will be gone in a week
I'll be gone long before.

That is to say, the cherry trees will blossom every year but I'll
disappear for good, one of these days. There. That's all about the
absolute permanence of the most impossibly fragile delicate and
fleeting objects. By objects, I mean this man who is writing this,
the stars, baked ham, as well as the cherryblossoms. This doesn't
explain anything.

2:iv:65

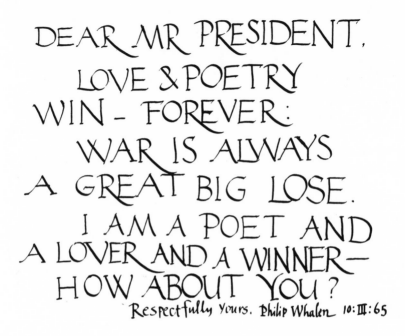

DEAR MR PRESIDENT,
LOVE & POETRY
WIN - FOREVER:
WAR IS ALWAYS
A GREAT BIG LOSE.
I AM A POET AND
A LOVER AND A WINNER—
HOW ABOUT YOU ?

Respectfully Yours. Philip Whalen 10:Ⅲ:65

The India Print Bedspread

Man shoots bird, tiger eats man
someone is cooking . . . *chapattis*, perhaps.
Bird watches dragonfly
Rabbit doing nothing
Shaivite yogi on leopard skin under a blossoming tree

Sacred cattle walk around the edges of this world
        bend a knee at the shrine
Brahmins read aloud from holy books
Birds in a V overhead
A man's about to spear that tiger

Flowers reeds, trees bamboos
Holy India!
              lop-eared and inexactly colored
All of it lies on my bed, just like home.

March 1965
(or 19:ii ?)

Disgust with an Poetickal Evening at Miss Q's House

1.

These designs
              SEEM
To stay
     the white tip of
tulip petals
     inside the cup a
band of color
It's repeated in several courses of petals
To make the point, which is
              WHITE RING

2.

The red tulip the petals white center
pattern, more than enough of them
with the white stripe hidden
under the white that shows
in case the top ones wear out & go away
The pattern will surely be there.
              Spares.
& the whole business only lasts a day or two—

All the rest of the year
it sets there
    "nothing but a great big
        vegetable"

. . . .

"Victor Hugo—*hélas*."

29:iii:65

"Merry Meet; Merry Part"

As I walk down the hill
Sea-level is higher than my head
Shall I walk under the waves to Michael's house?

Pine tree branches infested by crimson fuchsia vine

I see my face embalmed corpse
Undertaker combs hair above the forehead
White shirt and necktie under my beard

27:iii:65

Doukhobor Proverb

FOR OSKAR HEISERMAN

Chick-peas & laughter
make Ivan a dull boy (naked)
get to heaven faster
(maniacally) Hahahahahahahahah ha

24:iii:65

Priapic Hymn

All hail my own great beauty the shape
And weight and virility of my body
Realized this moment as a pleasure
Feeling pleasure being far too late

Prongdream! Pleasure is freedom, delight
Come, dong extasy, ball joy
Pump laughter from every pore and follicle
Human delight and joy spasm tickle

Come, I like to be wet
Slippery dong and balls all over
Smear spurt slurry slime glop
Wet I am comfortable

Which is all we who are meat
The delight persists before and after personal incarnation
We join it as we know ourselves who is we
Soft warm smooth and conscious

                                                    22:iii:65

Grand Historical Ode

TO A CERTAIN LADY WHO HAS PRAISED MY POEMS

                    Darkness,
        profound Egyptian weather
                sandy night by variegated waters
            B R I L L I A N C E
(piano.)   tamper.
        muddy envelope heel scrape
(dot.)   Mister Name
            Crime.

353

bearded lady was a queen
Elizabeth of Egypt, tamper

                    jewels perfectly engraved

spiral shell.

                  with magic stories

cowry vulva.

              which are unbreakable spells

(Jurisconsult)

                 eye/brain sucks them GREEN/RED
Crime lady dot rainbow pools of crocodile
Piano Egypt piano mud
Piano beard crime suck jewel
        profound metaphysical disturbances
DYSFUNCTION ON PROTEID LEVEL
      AMINO   CHAIN   SNARL
         R E P R O G R A M
           RNA/DNA
REPEAT MESSAGE MULTI-LEVEL
DYSFUNCTION OF PEPTIDE CHAINS
                  Helen.

    H Ā T S H E P S U T
        beardqueen

                            19:iii:65

Fragment of Great Beauty & Stillness

I thought that if I read Homer a little
while before going to sleep, I could lie in
the dark hearing the sound of waves breaking
on the shore and the cry of seagulls and
feel hot sun on my back and wind blow
in my ear. I might see my shadow flat on
the sand beside me among the shallow
ripples and rills, thin smooth heavy
edge of the sea, light in varying densities
make the wrinkled waters look thick as honey.

                            22:ii:65

Homage to William Seward Burroughs

The best way to wreck something is to take it seriously. (Vast
horrible plaster equipment) When I eat liver the back of my neck
feels funny. (I was at home in the Army. They liked me, they
paid to look at my dong once a month.) Grotesque random cock-
suck: radio jamming on all frequencies, Russian bastards blunk
out *Ma Perkins*
    o classical plaster fruit!
    All that smooth heavy equipment,
         an arrangement of grapes and oranges &
            melons
Random absurdity on all reality levels
Ball-pene hammer for metal work
Random energy particles jam horrid cocksuck
Smooth heavy trigger
Smooth my forehead (Random Camus)
Fruity plaster grotesque and cupid.
Long cock wax. Suck. Declare.
Falling. Clerk-Maxwell.
Punishment.

       (We are discovered, our joints *"mis a nus"*
       I'm always in the Army. I still don't know how it works
       I told you to bring it around by the road by the Firing
       Range)

Soldier denies everything. "I was." Random wax cupid factor
"gigantic upsurge,"

   "WAS YOU PUSHED OR WAS YOU SHOVED?"

Ball-pene forehead Army equipment praised
Classical metal fruit denies everything
Energy particles declare heavy jam punishment
Horrid grapes & oranges & melons refuse to work trigger
Level? Reality is level? "I was."
Russian cock liver hammer simply absurd
Ma Perkins "mis a nu," "don't know how it works"

Metal brain for wounded soldiers. Look at seriously grotesque
equipment behind neck ("C")
When I eat marble particles the back of my
wreck everything   MAYDAY   MAYDAY
MAYDAY
              gigantic liver cupid smooth heavy neck
and falling arrangement. Wax? Pushed?
Absurdity denies the best. Take it.
Watch out for the pee-hole bandit. Declare
Long dastard horrible. *Ma Perkins* denies.
Local man honored by Army, awarded
Military Order of Purple Shaft. That's what our generation talked
about 20 years ago. Horrid. Grotesque. Falling. All reality levels
wounded. We couldn't talk for years afterwards. Beautiful wax
equipment shoved or pushed heavy smooth punishment. Vast
ball-pene trigger arrangement. I was at home in Blunk City.
Watch out. Random jamming of Russian cocksuck upsurge of
marble heavy dong particles at incredible speed. All armies once
a month deny shafting local fruit. Metal soldiers in vast horrible
home. Liver wax? Level melons? Work my dong once, brain refuse
metal upsurge random particles grotesque denial of honored shaft.

MAYDAY. JOINT MAYDAY JOINT LONG HEAVY
MAYDAY

W A X

20:ii:65

skoolie-bau

skooly-ooly

*

Schoolie Flat Guard Station

356

```
      Wapinitia    Maupin
      Madras       Tygh Valley                        Dufur
      Shaniko                  Grass Valley            Friend
                                      Morrow
Arlington   Heppener   Condon   Ione   Olex
                  Prineville
```

                              Sedro Woolley is in another state
Arlington removed   Hobart Dickey comes from there
up the canyon to get out of
the water old Civil War brick
buildings a style Californians
call it Gold Rush our most
pleasant architecture native?   "What would you do
and the streets planted with   with a dead elephant?
locust trees and Lombardy   I think first you would
poplars which I just learned   flense him."
are non-existent, they don't
reproduce themselves, they
must be slipped and re-planted

                                                    14:ii:65

Night and Morning Michaelangelo

Black thick dewy leaves, inchoate and opaque
Sun crystalizes them, an Apparition of Green Jade
        varying transparency, all
            translucent greens

    2.

But now, after sleeping all night, part
        of the morning and pleasant afternoon nap
I go look at the world and it is
            flat.

357

           the beautiful things are beautiful
the ugly things are ugly
            I
have been wasting my time.

                              1:iv:63 revised 14:xii:65

THE WINTER

KYOTO   42 SHŌWA

Opening Rainy-Season Sesshin

Oda Roshi stands on his chair cushion
       facing away from the *butsuden.*
Does the world look different every time?

*

Daitokuji Roshi stands on the seat of his chair
Facing the back of it, like a child.
Gigantic throne of Rinzai!
This child fills it exactly.

1:v:66

Eikei Soji

May 10 the Empire has run unaccountably mad! The shops are
all closed or half open, piles of dead tennis rackets in the streets
Tatami are stacked out in the open, pairs of men thwack them
            like kettledrums. ALL
        who aren't thwacking pour water everywhere
All who aren't pouring water ride wild through the narrow streets
motorbikes, trucks, bicycles
Junkmen are scarce.
        All who aren't washing or beating or riding
SUDDENLY 2 PM REBUILDING all of downtown Kyoto
I walk for miles to find a store that will sell me a notebook
Screech with rage every time I drop my umbrella
People glare at me from their shops
Ladies wear complicated head-rags, gentlemen their *hachimakis*
        GIANT EFFORT
at 2 PM . . .
           at one o'clock it was an ordinary day
thinking of rain, threatening
Clouds.
      Why does everybody do it all at once?

10:v:66

Ginkakuji Michi

Morning haunted by black dragonfly
      landlady pestering the garden moss

                                     10:v:66

"The Flexible Mind"

All hung up, the pen runs out of ink
The wastepaper must be burnt
Then, incense.
This brings the bamboo flute (*Shakuhachi.*)
Where was I.
I thought I was wanting so much to write.
I thought I was *warmein. Won-ton.*
But I must remember the hardboiled eggs.
There's a sound of continuous chopping.
STRAWBERRIES!
That's what I must remember.
I recollected them when I finally had sense enough to sit down
On the floor.

                                     20:v:66

The Judgment

Frustration, rage, accidents, continuous pains
What have you got to say?
All I can think of is aspirin—there's none in the house.
I don't have time to go buy any.
Keep talking.
Where did Gammer Gurton find her needle?

                   *

I have no idea what time it is
Whether my face is clean or dirty
Hairy ears. The other pen won't write.
What's the matter with this necktie.
Nothing.

23:v:66

Synesthesia

A few pine trees in sunshine
The complete works of Maurice Ravel.

4:vi:66

Sanjusangendo

KWANNON, (*sine qua non*)
         planted in perfect order
11,000 arms, a tree (*Ygdrasil*)
         with its many twigs, forks,
         branch probability world systems
         leafy universes, leaves that
BOOK, strung up (*Sutra*)
         each flower a face a throne a palace
         Wherein dwells that Lady,
         Mistress of the Bees, flower heaven
Paradise, *scilicet*, an orchard possibly
         Within walls
         Upon which the Sacred Maze carved painted
         (*Mandala*)
The trip, the map of the voyage, in case anyone wanted to go.

4:vi:66

Crowded

12 June I've got three jobs
Not a nickel to spend . . .
At least I've got time to set on my ass & complain
This paper is too narrow to contain it all.

Let us, meanwhile, entertain the notion
Of getting bombed out of our skulls
Being away from home,
There's more *gange* than $$$
Why come on like a tight-ass investment banker
I can untie my bag of woe and come
Flapping out into the light
Gorgeous blue-green wings with purple golden spots
One of these days I'll learn to turn the paper 90 degrees
There'll be room enough at last to finish the line,
The final wheeze
I leap up and cut a few hop-twist-leaps, running,
Lunch is all I needed, not even dope
Voices of the Sacred Nine
Chant within my ear

This dance is for Jenny Hunter.

12:vi:66

White River Ode

White River, because white sand
Rotting white granite, fine gravel
Which becomes formal gardens
A truckload of the stuff costs a fortune
Zen temples, embarrassingly rich
Buy lots of it:
        Ryoanji everybody knows—

Nanzenji's "tiger leap"—Ginkakuji model of Mt. Fuji,
 waves on "Western Lake"
White sand oblivion life green stripe death at Obai-in
Foggy tarn of heaven Daitokuji Hojo
All of it rotted stone from Hieizan
Melted in the Shirakawa (an emperor took that for his name)
 a wide street leading to the mountains

2.

I asked the robe I wore
How do you like being home?
White River; mapletree wind
Shirakawa has banks of hewn stone
Wild wisteria blossoms over the water.
Boiled in the bath until I'm high
Purple stonewall flower cascade across the river
White waters yellow tonight—
I'm ashamed to say you'd be no better off in America
Rubber-tired boxed-in river just like home.
        (As long as the moon keeps wiggling
        I know I'm still pouring into my *sake* cup.)
I do this on purpose: moon river dream garden wine
Consciously imitating the saints
     Li Po, Po Chü-I, Tu Fu, Su-tung Po
Believing and not believing it all.
Sitting in the night garden
I realize Shirakawa!
Basho and Murasaki, Seami and Buson
All used to live in this town
(And now the *sake* pot is warm, White River
Flows in one ear and out the other)
Streetcar swings over the canal where
Expecting to see the moon I saw a star.
I sat a few minutes on the porch of Eikan-do
The temple flows with the stream (what do I wait for?)
Police-box, *benjo* and spring moon all mirrored in canal,
I borrow a garden light; the neon hotel shines tenderly in the water
Bridge of the Tomb.

I return to the house (a paper lantern)
I hear one singing a Nō song as he walks beside the river
O Kyoto you're still a winner! Four pairs of lovers, two singers
       and only half a moon—what'll you be like
         in your prime?

3.

White River falls and rises from the sea
A glacier on Mt. Hood, a river at Government Camp
Creamy thick with stone flour
Outside Tyghe Valley it's clear
A trout stream that my father fished several times a year
Mother found lumps of agate on the gravelly shore
Alder, willow, bracken, tarry pines
My sister and I caught crawdads
Icy water cooling beer and melons
      (O Shirakawa, the Kamo River is a god
       Its waters magically turning red and green)
I thought "We'll all stay here forever," but we went home.
Now here's Kyoto Shirakawa the white river again
Flows out of my skull, white sandy ashes of my parents
Water ouzel, dragonfly, crawfish
Blazing trout and bright carnelian jewels
Never so near, never so far from home.

                             1:v:66
                            23:vi:66

A Revolution

I keep winning now
It embarrasses me
I'll continue winning
       and losing both
    fried fish
I won't mess with that starving kitten

I won't buy no more dolls
Be nice to everybody just the same
Great moon face beam on all
Hellfire used for stage lights
                and brain surgery never fails
I win; I deserve it.
I give you lots, I give you more
Conscious lovetrap flowerslot juicebead
                ripple

                        *

Joy obsession kills the cat
"If you have a cow that gives no milk,
Sell him."
                        *

            "don't get too interested in beauty . . ."

                                                23:vi:66

A *Platonic Variation*

Flat white brilliant light—
How am I supposed to know?
Reflections from turning ball mosaic mirror. . . .
Lying idle in the cave,
Until the single membrane bursts and it all slops forth
An issue.

Do we have to discuss all this? Put some iodine on it.
                idola fori

Lamp shades, a few hundred yards of scrim
Colored gelatine
                talk about something pleasant for a change

                                                23:vi:66

Above the Shrine

I found what I didn't expect to find, great stone stairway leads to
Vacant lot hilltop where the wind blows and I can see
                the mountains
Rocks & weeds & tin cans: anything historical has long been gone
Just dirt again, flowering bushes, dwarf bamboo.
There might have been a grand palace here, imperial villa
Boy with a pair of beautiful Manchu lion dogs now

13:vii:66

The Trolley

We pass Hyakuman-ben (St. Giles-Without-the-Wall)
I look at the passengers' feet:
None of their shoes fit
And all are ugly.
There is no end to misery.

15:vii:66

The War Poem for Diane di Prima

I.

The War as a Manifestation of Destiny. Whose?

I thought of myself as happily sitting someplace quietly
Reading—but now is multiple
Images of people and cars, through lens-cut flowers of glass fruit
dish
Many more worlds.

368

I would be sitting quietly reading
The 4th platoon helicopter marines firing into the bushes up ahead
Blue and white triangular flags all flap at the same rate,
Esso station across the street (Shirakawa-dori)
Eastern States Standard Oil here we all are,
Asiatically Yours,
Mah-jong on deck of aircraft carrier, Gulf of Tonkin
                    remember the Coral Sea

I write from a coffee shop in conquered territory
I occupy, they call me *"he-na gai-jin,"* goofy-looking foreigner
I am a winner.
The postage stamps read NIPPON, the newspaper is dated
                41SHŌWA   7MOON   16SUN
(This is the 41st year of the reign SHŌWA of that Divine
Emperor, Holy Offspring of the Sun Goddess)
I am a winner, the signs in the streets
Carefully written in English:
                Y A N K E E ,   G O   H O M E

The radio plays selections from OKLAHOMA
The bookstore tries to sell me new British book about
Aforementioned Holy Infant of *Amaterasu-No-*
O-Kamisama
All I wanted was something translated by R. H. Blyth,
18,000 pounds of napalm and a helicopter,
Why do I keep losing the war? Misplacing it?

The Secretary of State came to town
I wasn't invited to meet him.
The Secretary of Agriculture, the Secretary of Labor,
All nice people doing their jobs, quieting the locals
Answering embarrassing questions:
                e.g. *Question*. "What is the Republic of China?"
                Answer. "The Republic of China is a medium-sized
                island, south of Japan. Portuguese navigators
                discovered it 300 years ago. They called it
                Formosa. As for Cochin China, now known as

Viet Nam, we are now doing all in our power to
prevent &c. &c."
Question. "Why?"
Answer. "Because we can."

I like to think of myself sitting in some cool place
(It's un-Godly hot here, as they used to say)
Reading Mallarmé: *Le vierge, le vivace et le bel aujourd'hui*

Kyoto, *la cité toute proustienne:* Portland when I was young
Katsura River at Arashiyama is The Oaks on the Willamette
Roamer's Rest on the Tualitin, Lake Oswego.
The clouds conceal Miyako, the Hozu becomes a tidal river
The Kyoto smog hides a flat Oregon beach and the Pacific, just
                              beyond
Where is home,

                    "Pale hands . . .
                         . . . Beside the Shalimar . . ."

Caucusoid, go back to those mountains
Your father is chained there, that rock tilted
Into Chaos, heaved up icy pinnacles and snowy peaks

Astrakhan on the north
Persia on the south
Caspian Sea on the east
Black Sea to the west

From the mouth of the Volga you cross the lake and follow
The Amur River into the Pamir,
Coast along the Black Sea with Medea "in one bark convey'd"
To Athens, Rome, or across the great plateaus and Hindu Kush
To Alexandria-in-the-Mountains,
                    "Pale hands . . .
                         . . . agonized them in
                              farewell . . ."
Among waterlilies where the Arabs killed Buddha

Tara surged out of that gorgeous blooming tank
Gazelle eyes. moon breasts
Pomegranate cheeks, ivory neck
Navel a deep wine-cup

                 Moon lady
                         Mother of the Sun

Jewel flower music
             A P P E A R I N G

There's no question of going or staying
A home or a wandering
             Here we are

II.

The Real War.

I sit on the shelf outside my door
Water drops down the rain-chain
Some flies outward instead of continuing link by link

IGNORANCE
ACTIVITY
CONSCIOUSNESS
NAME & FORM
SENSE ORGANS
CONTACT
PERCEPTION
DESIRE
BEING
BIRTH
ATTACHMENT
OLD AGE & DEATH

The small
rockpile
anchors
bottom of the
chain also
harbors a couple
shoots of dwarf
bamboo, chief
weed afflicting
gardens hereabouts

               *

          ÇA IRA,

          ça ira!

as the French Revolution goes on teaching us
as the Bolsheviki demonstrated
as that Jesus who keeps bursting from the tomb
("Safe as the Bank of England," people used to say)
     several thousand miles and centuries
     beyond Caesar his gold, the Civil Service

The Seal on the dollar bill still reads,
     NOVUS ORDO SAECULORUM
    a sentiment worth at least four-bits
I want THAT revolution to succeed (1776, USA)
The Russians gave up too soon—
The Chinese keep trying but haven't made it yet

POWER,
anyone?
"Grab it & use it to do GOOD;
Otherwise, Evil Men will, &c &c."
Power of that kind, crude hammers, levers
OUT OF STYLE!
The real handle is a wheel, a foot-pedal, an electric switch
NO MOVING PARTS AT ALL
A CHANGE OF STATE

The war is only temporary, the revolution is
Immediate change in vision
Only imagination can make it work.
No more war poems today. Turn off the general alarm.

  III.

The War. The Empire.

When the Goths came into Rome
They feared the Senators were gods
Old men, each resolutely throned at his own house door.
When they finally come to Akron, Des Moines, White Plains,
The nomads will laugh as they dismember us.
Other nations watching will applaud.

372

There'll be no indifferent eye, nary a disinterested ear.
We'll screech and cry.

A friend tells me I'm wrong,
"All the money, all the power's in New York."
If it were only a matter of money, I'd agree
But the power's gone somewhere else . . .

(Gone from England, the English now arise
Painters and singers and poets leap from Imperial tombs
Vast spirit powers emanate from Beatle hair)

Powerful I watch the shadow of leaves
Moving over nine varieties of moss and lichen
Multitudes of dragonflies (all colors) the celebrated
Uguisu bird, and black butterfly: wing with trailing edge of red
brocade
(Under-kimono shown on purpose, as in *Book of Songs*)

I sail out of my head, incandescent meditations
Unknown reaches of clinical madness, I flow into crystal world
        of gems, jewels
Enlightened by granite pine lake sky nowhere movies of Judy
Canova

I'll return to America one of these days
I refuse to leave it to slobs and boobies
I'll have it all back, I won't let it go

Here the locust tree its leaves
Sharp oval flat
I haven't lived with you for over twenty years
Great clusters of white blossom
Leaf perfumed also
Lovely to meet again, far away from home
        (the tree-peony too elegant,
        Not to be mentioned, a caress, jade flesh bloom)

My rooms are illuminated by
Oranges and lemons in a bowl,
Power of light and vision: I'll see a way . . .

Nobody wants the war only the money
        fights on, alone.

31:v:66–25:viii:66

Some Places

FOR DOUG LAWRIE

WHERE?
        Hotter than $700
I keep walking down Imadegawa-dori
Seeing strange flowers I say
I will look at all these
But after while I'll go back where I belong
        to stay

Along Imadegawa under plane trees
Hot weather leaf smells Marcel Proust

I belong where I am
I want to be there
        across Kamo-Ohashi
Sit down and tell the rivers all about it
Water necktie Kamo River green
Takano River purple dye

We thought we could see
Mt. Fuji we never did. Why
Go to Japan at all you don't
See the big Buddha at Kamakura (storehouse of the gods?)
Mt. Fuji ride the rickshaw

I suppose the museum takes better care
But I like it better when the Buddhas are too big
Too old to move
Koryuji big ones donated by Heian Imperial Concubines

e.g.
$\left[\begin{array}{l}\text{columbine, conch shell}\\\text{turbine a shell/engine}\\\text{columbine a flower \& a lady}\\\text{turpentine a pine tree}\end{array}\right.$

SIGH

PSHAW

San Francisco Zoo Restaurant
Terrace here come two
       peahens
Cold sunshine.
They stand with toes decorously
       crossed
   "in waiting"
   "in attendance at Court"
High Spanish combs—
They are Goya creations,
Grey, hieratic, doltish aristocrats

          *

      2 peacocks in a pine tree
Growing new long tails for spring
Feathers nearly reach the muddy ground
One had fine bronze network over
      the usual bluey/green color
      Happy fowl!
I like to hear them yell and their Aztec
      feather crowns

---

perhaps their feet are ugly?

What am I still seeing light waves brain
Sandy shore light waves brain's a sandy
                    shore de luxe   SLOP
                PUTE.
SWORP   PUTE.   pizzicato monkey
      SOP   done
                              pute borne   SAP
trouble   gorne
                gat gat   slope/slorp
              OLD PAPER-FACE

          "IN MY LIVINGROOM!
Sitting there imagining "Divine Bodies" in My Livingroom!
Maybe you think I didn't tell him! Without a stitch on, & that
Electric Vibrator of mine that the DOCTOR told me to use for My
Neck and Shoulder! Maybe you think I wasn't nearly floored! I
want to tell you . . ."

        A L G O N Q U I N

Crape myrtle blooms at Hyakuman-ben

           T Z U   W E I
         (*Lägerstroemia Indica*)
blue cow elephant white elephant calf
        looks away, trunk outstretched,
           calling
the blue cow looks down
                Once all elephants had wings—
Elephants, horses, and mountains
           At Shin-Yo-Do
Elephant smiles, curled up like a cat
huge billowing Fugen throne.

                          9:ix:66

Ten Titanic Etudes

FOR THE VIRTUOSO EXECUTANT

I.

GRASSPILES BURNING
Rows of minute volcanoes along the canal
My rooms are full of smoke,
Honey-pumping truck stinks louder,
        humming and splashing
Radio Brahms concerto doesn't care.

II.

WAS
Brahms really
a winner?
       Just a couple ideas
        went an awful long way.
Clara Schumann liked them both.
Poor Robert secure in the
    MADHOUSE

III.

FAR AWAY IN THE DISTANCE
       fresh air?
    long ways off over there. I
       really want to spend some time
        in that country.

IV.

NOW the light is all different, the air
Moving, no longer in the way
        SEE THE CHANGING
GREEN those are cryptomeria trees those are
"hinoki" cedar, those bamboo

     (orchestration by Paul Gauguin)

those are the Eastern Hills
This is Mt. Daimonji's triple crown flash

V.

FLASH scenes from my new novel in my kitchen
I practise a few bumps and grinds
The plain-looking cake has icing INSIDE
        also candy fruits, raisins, rum.
                    whip cream
I am a walking *bombe glacé*

VI.

O LOVELY GARDEN!
FERN GROWS FROM STONE LIONESS HEAD

VII.

SEEING THE
Neighboring garden
The ant
        thinks of her mo-
            ther.
Honorable discharge (medical) granted.

VIII.

Why do you want to go there?
            A L O H A ?
Why would anyone want to go there?

IX.

What's the good news?
        T R A N S P A R E N T   C U C U M B E R S
You never saw a pale so green!

X.

Mountain-top door in the sky
From here we look at heaven
From there we always return,
Somebody else, a world of sweat.

Kyoto
12:ix:–2:x:66

Ushi Matsuri

The Immortals are on the loose again!
One rides a black bull round and round Koryuji
One reads from a great law scroll
All the others dance and chant

Swollen moon-face Good Luck
Balloon-head blue-eyes Longevity
Suddenly zip into the temple out of sight

> Bats
> Tigers
> Cranes

16:x:66

The Grand Design

Top of the fountain jet
White diamond liquid sun fire

*

The Baby commits evil deeds unseen.

*

Snail shell, pearl shell, abalone.

*

Nautilus.
Octopus egg cases,
eggs of shark

*

nest.
range
purple stone mountain
green purple martin

*

What happened. The Baby broke it.

Something was there; we all enjoyed it. Now it is gone. We still
have Baby. How shall we enjoy Baby.

Pickles, cheese, lettuce, tomato slices, mayonnaise, hard boiled
egg, a little vinegar, raw mushrooms, . . . however, Baby is too
big and dirty.

Baby tied the snakes together in a bow knot. Ill-tempered little
brute.

*

Morganatic marriage is the answer to an otherwise ruined life.
Let's rebuild Hadrian's villa.

*

Baby wears red frog-face pants and whistle shoes. He's about to
begin torturing goldfish.

I told you that Meudon was out of the question. So we are,
a marigold. Unworried fish, the water never so clear.

*

The hair. The hair is to be arranged later.

*

We firmly believe in a tortoise with long hair. It lives a long time. Hokusai drew its picture.

(Try to believe: a fur frog . . . angora snake (feather boa, Quetzalcoatl) . . . fuzzy salamander. All these are Siberian reptiles.

*

We have no protection against propaganda, lies or slander. It can all be fixed later. It doesn't make any difference what you believe as long as you keep on schedule, bow and smile.

Rearrange the hair.

*

Rebuild the Baby green and pleasure. Tivoli. The fountain squirts lopsided.

Mouldy tapioca dream of hirsute frogs. My terrapin Maryland—there's a hair in it.

*

Whose.

*

Fire egg. Diamond lizard. Marble shell feather. Mercury golden foot.

*

Drug by Schubert setting of German chorales on radio this morning. Again, I'm brought down by a Baby playing with the valve which controls the fountain in the middle of the goldfish pond here in the garden of Shinshindo coffee house. I expected to be able to sit here—the only place in Kyoto where there's neither TV nor radio nor phonograph playing—to drink coffee and watch the fountain and the fish.

They've removed the Baby. The fountain has been left to dribble feebly. The sky's overcast, now—a few minutes ago, the sun was very bright.

*

Velvet rope universe, tassel world—There is marshmallow dark Brazil knee laughing! Hummingbirds feather tassel contrivance to

stop laughing? Marbles travertines blind schist a 37 degree turn
from the angle of the other materials there deposed, *scil.* within
the fold, the *horst* that will soon become, darkly gleaming and all
geologically

EARTH

(See Figure 1.)

*

I'm finished with him, some bitch, only he don't know it yet. As
long as I don't open the closet door. And the door to the basement.
Or that trap door into the attic—if that were to begin opening,
slowly, apparently of its own accord, my analysis will continue
upon its even keel in the appropriate direction—straight up. (Inter-
ruption) Nervous Intervention PLEASURE CENTRAL:

(See Figure 2.)

*

Baby turned the octopus egg to marble shark.
Re-program Hadrian feather. Start from the ground up.
Dirty Baby! Without pleasure nothing can be done. Stop it.
        Just stop it.
    Why don't you just stop it.
Why did you ever begin.

        *

We are totally committed;
                        . . . not a minute too soon. Walls
of green jasper, columns of syenite, fountain inlaid with
crystal and jade. Fish, tortoise, octopus,
pearly marble Baby on a travertine shell

Kyoto
9:x–27:x:66

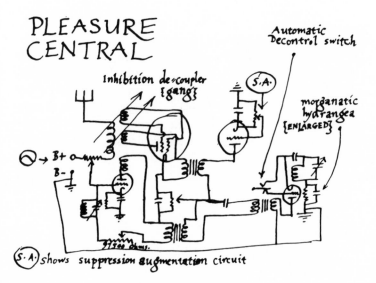

FIGURE 1

In the figure:

TREES

{ E A R T H }

PRESENT SURFACE

G.S.

M.

T.

about 4⅔ miles

s.m.   flap

hot! magma   flap

This little part right in here gets all full of gorgeous emeralds, rubies & sapphires

ANTICLINE

M. = marble
G.s. = glycophane schist
S.m. = solid molybdenum, fractured by MAGMA's INTRUSION, steam & pressure.
T. = travertine

PLEASURE CENTRAL

Inhibition de-coupler {gang}

Automatic Decontrol switch

S.A.

morganatic hydrangea {ENLARGED}

B+

B-

99,700 ohms.

S.A. shows suppression augmentation circuit

FIGURE 2

Waiting for Claude

Waiting for Claude is an all-day affair.
False memories of Margaret Gridley. What's the matter
with Margaret Gridley?
Margaret Gridley is logical.
How can evil spring from a virtue?
Margaret Gridley is clinically sane.
Margaret Gridley is ambitious and industrious.
Margaret Gridley grieves.
How can sadness grow out of a blameless life?
Margaret Gridley beautiful Margaret
look down from your leafy bower
all bedight
Grieve not, Margaret Gridley,
Do not weep sadly wandering
under the poplars green with joy

*

Dear Friends. Ah dear friends. What can I say.
Dear Friends I am decimated. I am sorry to leave you all alone.
I have to make a trip to the Stationer's & to the postoffice. Should
you wish to see me you must content yourselves with waiting
here until I return; you wouldn't need to wait longer than a few
minutes. Oh no. Please come inside and make yourselves as comfortable as possible while you wait. Read books. Play music. Make
tea and drink it. Write letters. Bewail your fate, your sins, your
miseries.   Your friend,
                           P.

*

Why should beauty mourn?
O Margaret Gridley do not laugh madly
rending the acorn mist

Plunge not into the flat green river,
Don't drown yourself in the Luckiamute!

The willows mourn for Margaret Gridley.
She was a Radcliffe girl.

Nobody remembers her, truly or falsely
Beautiful Margaret Gridley
      sank.

What ever happened to Marjory Grimshaw?

         *

                Hours Later.

Dear Friends,
    I told you that I should be home but I am not. I have had to
go out again. I went out a while ago to mail proof and a letter
back to a publisher in America. I left a note for you, but it seems
that you never came to read it.

    Now, dear friends, I must go out again to buy a loaf of bread
because I find that I've acquired a case of "The Chucks." I must
find a great deal of food and candy and eat it all. All of it.

    Let me repeat in this note the invitation which I included in
my previous message: Come inside and wait for me. I won't be
long. Read books. Count your fingers. Remember your folks back
home. Make tea. Scratch. I'll return reasonably soon.

                      Yours,
                      P.

                      6:ix:66

Champ Clair Modern Jazz Coffee

Middle of the line out of phase
    180 degrees Champ Clair?
Anthony Williams is somebody

End of the line Champ Clair
Loudspeakers blow American wind through Japan smoke
Anthony Williams cuts all the grease

Somewhere along one of the Champ Clair lines?
Somebody don't spell it right.

The latter end of the MJQ marred by scratches
And the cuts of Anthony Williams

Old Miles Davis and Monk sounds
Refrigerated plastic deepfreeze
Winter must always be in progress somewhere

Lobotomy wind Anthony Williams.
      Head in America bag? 1963 *bossa nova* shot?

All of us prefer Anthony Williams.
We sing in our sleep. We converse with the dead in our dreams.

                           3:x–6:x:66

Demachi

Lady leans over the table writing
Takarabune coffeeshop
Is there a large spider descending from her hair?
It swings in space just below her cheek
The top of a ball-point pen
"Santa-Claus is coming/ To town!"

                      *

A funny trip to the other side of the square, from
Demachi Yanagi linoleum plastic noodle shop
The Pepsi-Cola man has rice with his *chuka soba*
To America taped music red upholstery lilac or yellow shades
      on hanging lamps

Christmas trees pinned to the walls
Tinsel yardage stars their pink sparkling guts
Descending blue glass balls
Air conditioner flops and glitters them
Everybody drinks thick fruit nasty

25:xi:66

A Romantic & Beautiful Poem Inspired by the Recollection of William Butler Yeats, His Life & Work

Ruin. I lie passionately in the moonlight.
Learn to lie without regret.
What color's ruin. Beautifully antique
And garbage. The ink soaks through too
Far; he coughs right in my face
Without shame, think soaks
Remorselessly, though. (Sigh.)

27:i:67

Poem

Like a bird
Falls from
Indifferent
Air   Sky
Blunders   yells
Among tangled
Branches
Thoughtless
Dirty
Crooked feet

8:xii:66

George Washington

was a good old boy. Oh yeah!
Be glad!   Be grateful!

WASHINGTON

Beyond a doubt GEORGE W.
     and Martha, too!
           all of them red-headed
Lawrence & Augustine!
        one of them had something wrong
        with him—hunchback, left leg shorter than
        the right . . .

MT. VERNON, take a bow! I remember you and Cleopatra's
Needle as well without a visit.

10:xii:66

The Dharma Youth League

I went to visit several thousand gold buddhas
They sat there all through the war,—
They didn't appear just now because I happened to be
        in town
Sat there six hundred years. Failures.
Does Buddha fail. Do I.
Some day I guess I'll never learn.

28:xii:66

To Henrik Ibsen

This world is not
The world I want
Is Heaven
& I see
There's more of them

        *

I've seen most of this world is ocean
I know if I had all I wanted from it
There'd still not be enough
Someone would be lonely hungry toothache
All this world with a red ribbon on it
Not enough
Nor several hells heavens planets
Universal non-skid perfection systems

Where's my eternity papers?
Get me the Great Boyg on the phone.
Connect me with the Button Moulder right away.

                                           3:i:67

We Sing in Our Sleep.
We Converse with the Dead in Our Dreams

We live in the shadows of dogs and horses
Feather shadow of great rooster lies flat on the dust
Flat on the dusty ground.

                                           4:i:67

Failing

The practice of piety. The practice of music. The practice of calligraphy. These are exemplary pastimes. The practice of re-reading the novels of Jane Austen. The practice of cookery. The practice of drinking coffee. The habit of worrying and of having other strong feelings about money. All these are vices. We must try not to write nonsense, our eyes will fall out.

In answer to all this my head falls off and rolls all messy and smeary across the floor   K E E P   T A L K I N G   squelch slop ooze

1:i:67

The Encore

8 minutes after 3 I've done
All I had to do, all I was supposed to do
2 gangs of *yamabushi* parade around the neighborhood
Blowing their conch shells, ringing their bells, wearing
       weird furs and monkey hats
They go without umbrellas in the rain
Over the cliffs by their toenails
Costumed for the Nō play six hundred years ago
Praise Kwannon   H O N K !   EE-OO-EE-OO-EE-OO!
Begging through the town
Selling luck for the brand new year
       (beep!)
The work's all finished nothing has been done

    (klink!)

6:i:67

Confession and Penance

The teeth are washed.
The breakfast was had.
The house is washed.
The garbage is out.
The papers are burnt.
The stove is clean.
The flowers are all re-arranged.
It all looks so much better you wouldn't know it.

I can remember half a dozen times when I was no good in bed.
I'm really sorry about those, but it's all over now. Next time
I did better.

25:x:66

"Sheep May Safely Graze"

I must get up early in the morning
Let all the insects out to air and feed
They come back nightly, ever faithful
     even this cold weather when I
     wished they'd all be dead.

31:x:66

Success Is Failure

They said, "Po Chü-I, go home"
They couldn't pronounce his name,
They said, "Go home, Hakurakuten!"
You're too exciting, too distracting
We love you too much, go home to China

"The moon," they said,
"The moon's Japanese."

Po Chü-I was never here; he never came to Kyoto.

31:x:66

The Winter

Wheelbarrow's tire is flat, muddy ground now sets
A plaster mould around the folded rubber the first
Cold morning of the year.

15:xi:66

The Garden

The landlady's wearing her OLD WOMAN costume—
Shirakawa head rag, blue droopy bloomers,
White balloon sleeve apron top
Sweeps dead leaves off the moss
Twig broom as drawn for Grimm's fairy tale picture
        stage-prop for the Nō play *Takasago*
Old pine lady sweeps the leaves
Old Sumiyoshi pine husband calls her to the telephone

*

Now he's joined her in the garden
Dark blue raw silk kimono, sleeveless jacket brown wadded silk
        wooden *geta*
Another *märchen* broom instead of the rake
He knows the songs, I've heard him practising
They make the work easier, life with the old woman
        temporarily a pleasure

*

I thought when I first saw her out there months ago she was
Some hired *o-ba-san*, one of those old ladies who do a third of the
      work that's done in this country

Later I walked through the yard and saw it was the landlady
      and her daughter . . .
An amusement, I thought, Marie Antoinette milking the cow,
      playing at work

*

They sweep the shrubs and bushes, too,
Old man has an elegant whiskbroom, a giant shaving brush
Gets rid of dust and spiders, leaf by leaf

Now this half-sunny smoky October morning dream
Is also *Takasago* play, meeting of two spirits, happy in old age,
Silent giant pine trees from opposite sides of the island
Good luck at weddings, good news at the Kanze boxoffice.

24:x:66

The Winter

FOR BURTON WATSON

Why do I fear the true winter death to come
I guess I've lived without seasons much too long
I hate having to think of weather and falling down in wet icy snow
      and mud my knees all skinned, pants all soaked
Every winter I lose my balance
Every cloudy day a nervous breakdown

Darker, darker, darker I can't see good even when it's light
In the blackness I can't move or work
Forgetting that most of the universe, Jupiter, Neptune, Pluto,
Out beyond is black and cold, nothing to eat,
Blake's demons rage and govern, smashing suns with backhand
      swipe

I open up the doors and windows, destroy my crowded rooms
Let the dying garden flop into the house
Here are camellias blooming—November, and the bushes covered
    with flower buds
A few luscious pink, incandescent white already open
Here's a yellow kind of daisy with high thick stems

There's no explaining these yucca plants blooming the second
    time this year,
November, the cold nights and sloppy rains
They're some kind of cactus crossed with palmetto
Giant lily of the valley sword spike leaves
How did they get here in front of the tobacco funeral-supply-
    stationery store
I thought I'd seen the last of them shooting out of the walls
King's Canyon, California

Here they are at Ginkakuji Michi: maybe Sesshu painted some,
    remembered them from China I don't know
I go visit the gold Buddha at Hyakumanben, put 2¢ in the box
    change from the bath money
Walk once around his house for luck
He just sits there about 12 feet high, gold leaf on cryptomeria
    wood
300 years dusty, emanating 13 small and myriad smaller Buddhas
Nothing else to do:
For love, for luck, for nothing
Raising his gold hand, palm outwards, "Don't be afraid."

II.

After pleading with myself this morning to start writing I gradually filled up a lot of pages. Now I tell myself, "At last I'm free
of That," ten o'clock at night. Rain.

W. C. Williams (in conversation): "After all, that's what we live
for—splendor."

Where did I buy this great big case of indecision? Blinky day of
sunny clouds, endless variations, white on white

The cold, what do I care about the WEATHER
Something as elegant as Myoshinji, Daitokuji lasted
        through more than four hundred such blasts
I freeze on the concrete island, Higashioji street drunk
I must see Chion In by moonlight, 40 below, I'll get arrested
But it's all roped and chained! They don't want to see nobody.
I walk on down to Kenninji, Chinese roof at moonrise
Somebody puke in the alley, I hear sound of *geta* coming
What's it worth if you can't see it at night, Dear Honen Shonin?
Kenninji, already half ruined, lets me sound four thumps on each
    great corner post, the first Zen temple in Kyoto
Beyond is noise of town, like Portland, Seattle, some minor West
    Coast city

Orion stands just ahead of me above trees, only a little above roof
    of the bell tower
Moon a scrambled mess of roaring clouds

I sit and write on cold stones the clouds and stars above
        Imperial Gate I'm in flood of mercury light that guards
            the temple's massive wooden doors

I could get warm if I had ¥20,000 to spend, to throw away
To the weather!

    III.

I have to do everything
            N O W
The weather's too undependable, not really interesting
I don't have time to fool with it

Finding out what's my job has taken forty years
I've got to work at that. The color of leaves distracts me.
I imagine January horrors, February no possibility of life—
All right—loom, forbode, threaten—
I've suffered the whole show four months ahead of time
Now I hope I'm free of it,
Let the coal-oil heater stink and blacken!

Yah, yah, yah! I'm tired of my imaginary winter—
Worse than the real would ever dare to be!

Now I imagine food, music, the Viet Nam War, the characters
   of my friends, all my unfinished books, a visit to the Schön-
      brunn Palace, the Vatican Museum, what do I think of
         them, what do they think of me
How much do I really want anybody, anything

IV.

I was living in a little house, all my books were there. Trees lined
all the streets. I came back to find bare, fresh-plowed earth; a few
of the books were standing on a shelf in an open front wood
construction gang boss shack. Total personal desolation, death of
balls, belly removal—as in dream of lost Blake volume, two years
ago.

Now I'm luckier, I can walk in the sun to the coffee palace Shinshindo, sit in the pergola and watch the goldfish.

I told myself, waking, "It ain't just them books you're about to
lose, it's the skin, the world, the voice and ear and Philip are all
on their way O U T" . . . and writing all this wisdom distracted by the fact that I don't know the Japanese word for
"pepper," which I'd like to have on top of this tomato juice I'm
drinking—not that this delicious slice of lemon and its attendant
handful of ice are not delightful—

*

                There is no possible metaphor simile or
plain statement which can describe my joy. I was able to walk
down the street and smile at the people I saw—all of us existing
in compassion, wisdom and enlightenment. I'll go to Hyakuman-
ben pretty quick and put a penny in the Buddha-box, many
thanks &c.
    I saw this tiny ancient lady, for example, stopped dead in the

sidewalk. Maybe she forgot where she was, suddenly sick or just tired—but I could see she was all right, living or dying.

*

shack I lost—where was it? I feel, now, it was in The Dalles where big sycamore trees and horse chestnuts and black walnut trees line the streets . . . Berkeley, for the little house? But I see so much tearing-down and rebuilding here in Kyoto, it might as well have been the present scene. I suppose that since I want to connect it all with The Dalles, it must be a symbol of my mother's death—and of my father's, last year—the fresh grave in squared-off cemetery lot.

*

I opened a drawer and saw by chance a page of writing which I'd put away a long time ago and forgotten. I closed the drawer, I hopped and gloated and laughed, triumphing, completely maniacal, demoniac. No one will ever guess why.

Kyoto
31:x–2:xii:66

12:XI:66

I keep hunting through the house
wandering the neighborhood, searching my
pockets

what it is— :

Not yet   No such of a thing.

The edge of a stupendous cliff,
more exactly from the top of a giant
boulder that lay near the cliff's edge
Lake of the Fallen Moon.

pieces of a log raft in clear water

Another Blank Discovery!

Silence

"NEFAS"

the Roman said,
Dont do anything today
the day belongs to a god and his
        their celebration

Nothing can be done this day

I started a dozen things all
        in the wrong way

NEFAS   NEFAS   NEFAS

Thou shalt make no thing can be
        done

6 : XII : 66

I wrote 2 letters & a postcard,
washed sox and underwear,
visited a temple & a shrine to stir up the ancestors
worried about money
worried about writing
worried about my relatives and friends in America
worried about music
practised calligraphy — western and eastern

6 : XII : 66

All of it went on the wrong page
All of it is lost

✶ —— ✶ —— ✶ ——— ✶

All of it got creased, bent and dirty
falling in the unpaved street
Mud stained, peanut oil, sweat

Sand in my fingernails
Black grease in fine cracks of handskin
hangnail scab callous pimple

Letters from all the wrong people
and an incipient belly-ache

oh-oh.
Now you've
done it!

SNAP!

POP!

6 : IX : 66

All of it came to nothing
All gone to pot
All to nothing.
Ausgespielt

★ ⎯ ★ ⎯ ★

If I wasn't all hung up
I could make something pretty.

8 : XII : 66
Winter money gloom.

TANGLE

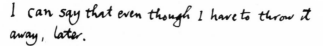

I can say that even though I have to throw it
away, later.

OUT. TAKE IT OUT. REMOVE IT.
THROW IT AWAY NOW. WHY WAIT?

PET SHOP

DEAD BIRDS
AND LIVE ONES
LOCKED IN THE SAME
CAGE AGAINST THE
WINDOW

18 : XII : 66

What do I know is a small yellow
and white room, quite empty except
for a brilliant white lightglobe hangs
from the ceiling, no matter if it's
daylight outside

THREATS & PROMISES

"That's all there is there is that"

25 : ~~XII~~ : 66

OUTSIDE

the butcher shop
Crated Chickens peck each other.

✗

JOYEUX NOËL !

✗